A SHORT ACCOUNT OF THE
AFFAIRS OF SCOTLAND

A SHORT ACCOUNT OF THE
AFFAIRS OF SCOTLAND
IN THE YEARS 1744, 1745, 1746
By DAVID, LORD ELCHO

Printed from the Original Manuscript at Gosford

WITH A MEMOIR AND ANNOTATIONS

By THE HON. EVAN CHARTERIS

WEMYSS CASTLE

JAMES THIN

1973

THE MERCAT PRESS: EDINBURGH

This is a facsimile of the 1907 edition, published in
Edinburgh by David Douglas. 500 copies of this edition
have been printed.

No.

Published by

JAMES THIN, Bookseller, South Bridge
EDINBURGH

Printed in Great Britain
By Unwin Brothers Limited
The Gresham Press, Old Woking, Surrey, England
A member of the Staples Printing Group

CONTENTS

PAGE

MEMOIR OF DAVID, LORD ELCHO, . . . 1

A SHORT ACCOUNT OF THE AFFAIRS OF
SCOTLAND IN THE YEARS 1744, 1745, 1746.
BY DAVID, LORD ELCHO, ... 225

APPENDIX :—

A. LORD GEORGE MURRAY TO THE PRINCE OF HESSE, 451

B. LETTER ABOUT LORD GEORGE MURRAY, . . 452

C. EXTRACT FROM CORDARA'S *Expedition of Charles
Edward, etc.,* 453

D. SIR JAMES GRAY TO THE DUKE OF NEWCASTLE, . 458

E. THE QUEEN OF ENGLAND TO PRINCE CHARLES
OF MECKLENBURG, ... 459

F. ORDER OF GENERAL HAWLEY, JAN. 12, 1746, . 459

G. LORD GEORGE MURRAY'S CULLODEN ORDER, . 461

INDEX, ... 463

b

LIST OF
PLANS AND ILLUSTRATIONS

DISTANT VIEW FROM THE SEA OF WEMYSS
CASTLE IN THE EIGHTEENTH CENTURY.
Adapted by WILLIAM HOLE, R.S.A., *from a Drawing by* SLEZER.

Vignette in Title-page.

DAVID, LORD ELCHO, 1741, . . . *To face page* 1
From a Painting at Gosford.

CHARLES EDWARD, 1745-6, . . . „ 227
From a Painting at Gosford.

BATTLE OF GLADSMUIR OR PRESTON-
PANS, FOUGHT ON SATURDAY, THE 21ST
SEPTEMBER 1745, ... „ 272
By the Author.

THE PRINCE'S ARMY THAT MARCHED TO
DERBY, ... „ 324
By the Author.

BATTLE OF FALKIRK, FOUGHT ON
FRIDAY, THE 17TH JANUARY 1746, . . „ 372
By the Author.

BATTLE OF CULLODEN, FOUGHT ON
WEDNESDAY, THE 16TH APRIL 1746, . „ 432
By the Author.

David, Lord Elcho.
1741.

MEMOIR

OF

DAVID, LORD ELCHO

I

Upon a page of a Bible which for generations has been in the possession of the Wemyss family at Wemyss Castle there is written, 'My son David was born at 3 A.M. Aug. 21st 1721.' This David was Lord Elcho, writer of the Narrative which follows. Born a year later than Prince Charles, with whom his destiny was to be so closely linked, he was the eldest son of James, 4th Earl of Wemyss (1699-1756), his mother being Janet Charteris, daughter of Colonel Charteris of Amisfield. Of the Charteris family, Elcho says in the pages of his *Journal* that 'it had been renowned among the nobility of Scotland since the year 1320.' Whatever degree of truth this statement may contain, certain it is that the notoriety of the family name was immensely heightened by the indecorous excesses of the colonel. The marriage of Elcho's

A

parents, effected with romantic secrecy, and in the face of much opposition, brought considerable wealth into the family, but it was destined to turn out badly, ending in separation and unseemly squabbles over the monetary dispositions of the owner of Amisfield.

But the early years were unclouded, and these were spent by young Elcho with his parents at Wemyss Castle. The family from which he was descended had given, through the storm and stress of the seventeenth century, what was on the whole a decided, although an intermittent, adherence to the House of Stuart. When the occasion demanded, they had shown that belief in divine right and kingly authority was compatible with political judgment and independent action. At one time they were to be found on the side of the Crown, at another resisting encroachments which they considered an abuse of the royal prerogative. Thus John Wemyss was one of those who carried the 'crimson pall' at the coronation of Charles 1. at Holyrood in 1633 ; in the same year he was created earl, and in 1641 he was appointed by Charles to act as Commissioner to the General Assembly. These favours, however, did not deter him from active opposition to the episcopal policy of the King in Scotland, and in the successful resistance to the imposition of the service-book there were few more uncompromising Presbyterians than the first Earl of Wemyss and his son. The second earl, David, sided openly with the Covenanters, and though 'not reputed an extraordinary soldier,' he rose to prominence among the military party. At Tippermuir he was in command of the forces opposed to Montrose and suffered a disastrous defeat, but the Covenanting committee did not abate their confidence in his capacity, and he continued to hold his place in the counsels of the Kirk.

In 1650, when the Kirk party had determined to support Charles II. on his taking the Covenant, the second earl was appointed by Parliament one of the Commissioners to welcome Charles in Scotland, and though he had taken no part either at the battle of Dunbar or in the march into England, he actively promoted the restoration of the King. Together with his wife, the Countess of Buccleuch, he was present on the occasion of Charles's entry into London, and, in a journal which he kept, this fact is noted in the following terms: 'Charles Secund King of Scotland, Ingland, France & Eirland did returne to his crownes. One 29 May 1660 he entered London and with His Majestie his two brothers James Duke of York and Hendrie Duke of Gloster. I was ther.' The third earl, David, 'a fine personage and very beautiful,'[1] 'succeeding in 1705, was in 1707 chosen as a representative peer for Scotland. Migration to London at this period was an event of the first importance in the annals of a Scots family. Lord Wemyss bore the change uneasily, and fretted for the north ; but with the thrifty mind of his race he discovered solace in his house in Soho Square, which he describes in a letter to a friend 'as one of the greatest pennyworths ever I see.' In the same letter he continues : 'As for the rattle and pleasures of London, noebody is or can be less affected with these then I am, & my wife hes as little taste of them as one could wish. . . . Playes & operas & park are places either of us are very seldom seen in & baiting vissits which we have noe fondness for, but must just keep up mannerly with the world, we live as retird as if we were in the Highlands of Scotland.'

The dull visit is a bye-product of our social

[1] *John Macky's Memoirs*, 1733, p. 250.

system common to all periods and countries, but at that time the lot of a purely Scots family can hardly have been enviable, and the earl's frugal satisfaction in his 'great pennyworth' must have ill concealed the asperities to which his family were subjected. On the accession of the House of Hanover, Lord Wemyss retired to his home. He was suspected of Jacobite leanings, but the rising of 1715 found him disinclined to take an active part, and though the tide of rebellion rose high in his native county, he maintained an outward neutrality and gave no support to the Earl of Mar and his followers.

His son, the fourth earl, and father of David, Lord Elcho, succeeded to the title and estates in 1720. He lived for several years in retirement at Wemyss, taking no share in public affairs, but proving himself so far a Jacobite in sentiment as steadfastly to decline taking the oath of allegiance. Subsequently, from letters among the Stuart papers,[1] he appears to have corresponded with James at Rome, and to have acted at least on one occasion as emissary to Paris on behalf of the Scottish Jacobites. We find his name included in 1745 by Lord George Murray in his list of those

[1] Browne's *History of the Highlands*, vol. ii. pp. 444-5.

who were or might be of the Council of Prince
Charles at Holyrood, and at the time of the
siege of the Castle of Edinburgh, reprisals were
threatened against Wemyss Castle by General
George Preston, the commander of the besieged
garrison.

If further bias towards Jacobitism were needed
to ensure the political training of Elcho, it was
only necessary to turn to the house where he first
saw the light.   Within the walls of Wemyss
Castle there lingered a crowd of memories to
recall to his mind the cause of the Stuarts.   It
was at this castle that in 1548 the Dowager
Queen Mary of Guise had stayed on her way
from St. Andrews to Edinburgh.   A sculptured
medallion existed, and indeed still exists, on the
castle wall to commemorate the visit of Mary
Queen of Scots and her first meeting with her
future husband, Henry, Lord Darnley.   There
also in 1591 James vi. had been a guest, and on
two occasions, in 1650 and 1651, Charles ii. had
sought shelter and hospitality.   Originally built
in the twelfth century, it must at this time still
have shown traces of its former strength and
importance as a fortress for repelling attack from
the sea.   For it was by virtue of its eminence in

this respect that the office of Admiral-Depute of the Firth of Forth had been conferred by James vi. on John Wemyss, and had been continued by successive monarchs to subsequent owners of the property.

Wemyss Castle stands on a rocky point of the eastern coast, and, rising high above the shore, a grey outline against the wooded hills of Fife, it is one of the first features of the mainland sighted by vessels as they skirt the May, or, rounding the Bass, beat up to Leith and the harbours of the Forth. It was here then that Elcho spent his early years, and it was among these Stuart traditions that he imbibed those principles which were to shatter his fortunes and condemn him to a death in exile. History hardly offers a case more typical than his of persistence in an outworn monarchical tradition. In the pages of Elcho's Journal we can trace, step by step, the whole process of the evolution of a Jacobite. From his earliest childhood it would seem that his father regarded espousal of the Stuart cause as an essential feature in his son's curriculum.

In these years, 1720-30, the restoration of the Stuarts might still be considered within the sphere of practical politics. The marriage of the

Chevalier de St. George had revived and the birth of his son had encouraged the hopes of his supporters. The disillusions which had followed the events of 1715 had been forgotten. Hatred of the Union, the disarming of the clans, and the imposition of the malt-tax had served to keep alive the embers of disaffection in the north. Jacobitism was an element of which the politics of Europe continued to take cognisance, while in England it was a force which, though largely veiled under intrigue, was sufficiently evident to influence statesmen and parties. It was therefore towards something tangible, and not the pursuit of a forlorn hope, that Elcho's education was directed. Before the age of nine he had been taught by a non-juring minister of the English Church that allegiance was due not to the usurper at St. James's, but to the King over the water, and that the Episcopalian ritual in no way suffered by the omission of the prayers for the House of Hanover.[1]

Thus initiated and prepared, he set out in 1734 for Winchester, in the company of his father. In those days, if all went well, such a journey occupied from twelve to sixteen days,

[1] There is at Wemyss Castle a Prayer Book wherein the names of the Stuarts are pasted over the names of the Georges.

and was performed by persons of wealth and
position in a coach drawn either by six or four
horses. North of the Border the roads were
perilous and precarious, often difficult to trace, and
dangerous to traverse. Tedious and costly, the
expedition was only undertaken upon grave provocation, and persons of thrifty habit travelled to
London either by the coach which left Edinburgh
once a month, or more commonly by riding the
entire distance. Choosing the western route,
they passed through Carlisle, Penrith, Kendal,
Lancaster, and Preston, and so, as a lad, from
the window of the great coach as it creaked and
lumbered on its way, Elcho must have caught
glimpses of the very towns which, eleven years
later, he was to enter in a brief hour of conquest
at the head of Prince Charles's life guards.

At Winchester, where he was placed under
the care of a Jacobite tutor, Elcho found that the
school, like the rest of the world, was divided into
Hanoverians (or 'Georgites,' as he calls them)
and supporters of the Stuarts. Thus the head-
master, Burton, was a Jacobite, the second master
a Georgite, and on one occasion, when Elcho
himself was in difficulty over a set of verses and
sought assistance from a fellow-pupil, he was

met by the question : 'Are you Georgite or Jacobite?' The answer proving satisfactory, the help was rendered, accompanied by the threat that if he was ever seen making friends with any of the Hanoverians, he would have to go elsewhere for his verses. Partisanship indeed seems to have played a larger part than education in the school world of that day. Learning was mainly restricted to the seventy scholars resident at the college; the wealthier boys boarded in the town with their tutors, and by gambling, cockfighting, and tavern life acquired a 'polite taste for pleasurable vice.' No wonder that Elcho became one of that mob of gentlemen who spelt with difficulty in the eighteenth century. But if books were neglected, no pains were spared to bring home to the boys a due sense of their earthly prerogatives and temporal distinctions. At church on Sundays peers and the sons of peers were conspicuous in robes of blue, red, or green, baronets and knights in black, while the 'untitled gentlemen' sat apart in the ordinary dress of the time.

The everyday life of the school was marked less by titular than by racial differences, and young Elcho, with nationality aflame in his blood, was driven to a course of boxing as the best means of combating the charge that his origin was Scottish. Here again the school was a reflection of the greater world without—a reflection multiplied by youth and the ardours of personal conflict. For the Scots were still outer barbarians, Scotland but a mean and tributary state. To hate the Scots, to despise them for their manners and speech, and to sneer at them for their poverty were the commonplaces of a well-ordered Englishman. The immigrants from the north were regarded in London with as much suspicion as if they were aliens from some remote and barbarous continent. They were ridiculed at court, satirised on the stage, and lampooned in the streets. So late as 1775 Garrick declined to wear tartan dress when acting *Macbeth* lest he should be 'hissed off the stage.' [1] In the pages of his diary Hugh, Lord Marchmont, tells how their loyalty was questioned and their offers of assistance at the time of the rebellion rejected. At Winchester the common taunt was that in Scotland they grew no wheat. Not many years later Dr. Johnson, giving point to the popular prejudices, wrote in his *Dictionary*: 'Oats, a

[1] Doran, *London in the Jacobite Times*, vol. ii. p. 350.

grain which in England is generally given to
horses, but in Scotland supports the people.'

'Pray, sir,' asked Boswell on one occasion,
'can you trace the cause of your antipathy to
the Scotch?'—'I cannot, sir,' was Johnson's
reply. This inability in the eighteenth century
may have been widely shared, but the antipathy
was there, pronounced, aggressive, and corroding.
Sir Joshua Reynolds regarded it as a duty 'for
Englishmen to oppose a party against them (the
Scots),' and it was many years before trade and the
free play of commerce were able to break down
those barriers which the Union had called into evidence. In the early years of the century the Scots
had no art with which to win sympathy, and no
literature with which to compel toleration. The
result was a bitter conflict of ideas, a prolonged
period of misunderstanding, and an atmosphere
in which an ardent temper, already opposed to
the reigning house, could speedily acquire a deep-
seated hostility to the Union. Hatred of the
Union was to supply the solitary political motive
for the rebellion of '45, and as in the case of
others, so with Elcho, contact with the southern
world consolidated all preconceived antagonism
to the Act which had made the kingdoms one.

As Ulysses said of Ithaca, so might a Scotsman have said of England, that it was 'rough,
but a good nurse for youth,' and certainly it
formed an exemplary training-ground for a future
rebel. From home and parents Elcho was as
isolated as though they had been in India, and
such must have been the case with all Scots
boys educated in the south at this period. Between 1733 and 1741 he had sight of his father
but once—on the occasion of the latter's visit to
Winchester in 1735. The holidays were passed
in the company of a tutor, during the winter in
London, during the summer in visiting towns
and viewing the 'grand country houses of the
nobility and gentry,' occasionally as guests, more
often as tourists. What a contrast he must have
discovered here with the habits of his native
land ! Ramsay [1] tells us that in Scotland it was
still customary in the early part of the eighteenth
century for the whole company in a country
house to eat broth out of one large plate ; that
guests arrived without notice on the chance of
finding accommodation, and that 'nothing was
more common than to lay two gentlemen or two
ladies that were not acquainted in the same bed.'

[1] Ramsay, *Scotland and Scotsmen in the Eighteenth Century*, vol. ii. p. 66.

In London Elcho gave himself up to enjoyment ; for him the ' rattle and pleasure ' of the
city possessed no terrors. He studied music,
frequented the opera, and witnessed gladiatorial
combats in which ' two men would inflict terrible
wounds on each other with sabres to gain a sum
of money.' He had indeed a precocious relish
for combats of all kinds, and at Winchester, when
not vindicating his accent with his fists, was a
constant spectator at cock-fights or encounters
between rustics ' for a hat presented by the lord
of the village.' In London the vigilance of his
tutor seems to have been lax, and with other
Winchester schoolfellows he would visit ' taverns
where women were called for as publicly as a
dinner or a bottle of wine.' In 1738, in accordance with the fashion of the time, ' the young
Æneas' set out for France with his tutor, exactly
in the manner which Pope was just then satirising
in the fourth book of the *Dunciad*. Like the
poet's hero, Elcho

> ' sauntered Europe round,
> And gather'd every vice on Christian ground,
> Saw every court, heard every King declare
> His royal sense of Operas or the Fair.'

In spite, however, of its obvious dangers, the

practice was justified by the elegance of manners which it encouraged. University education in Scotland was at a low ebb. Principals and professors were in receipt of salaries less in amount than the wages of a mechanic of the present day. Learning was mediæval and scholastic. Teaching and lectures were carried on in Latin, a language which the student was presumed, more often erroneously than not, to have mastered before entering the University. Religious zeal and the orthodoxy of the day were showing more care for a pious habit of mind than for sound instruction.[1] A minute and harassing system of superintendence was in vogue. By their sharp and vigilant solicitude, surreptitious censors ensured that moral backsliding should synchronise with detection, and sought by a series of fines to stimulate impoverished students in their struggles with temptation. For law, for medicine and surgery, for divinity, or for the acquisition of polite learning, those able to afford to travel were driven abroad, to Utrecht, to Leyden, to Paris, and the universities and academies with which more enlightened ideas had endowed the Continent.

[1] This subject is discussed, with interesting details, in chap. xii. of Mr. H. G. Graham's valuable *Social Life of Scotland in the Eighteenth Century.* 1899.

Elcho was taken first to Rheims, where he spent
ten months in a French family, learning the
language and taking lessons in fencing and
dancing. 'Following the usages of the French,
he attached himself,' he tells us, 'to Madame the
Baroness de Foulie, who took great pains to teach
him the language and make him understand the
manners of the French.' With the assistance of
the Baroness, he entered freely into the provincial
life of Rheims, paying visits during the morning,
at five o'clock attending the assembly, where
'mediator,' piquet, and backgammon were the
diversions, and at seven visiting the theatre, concluding with supper and games of hazard. Later
in the same year (1739), the poet Gray and
Horace Walpole spent several months at Rheims,
in the very same society, of which Gray has left a
full and picturesque account.

From Rheims Elcho was, in February 1739,
transferred to the Academy of Angers. Ten
months' residence in the animated seclusion of
Rheims had sufficed to dim his political orthodoxy,
but in Angers he found a colony of English,
Scots, and Irish ; he was quickly drawn into the
vortex of party feeling and national prejudice,
and enlisted himself with all his former vehemence

on the side of the supporters of the Stuarts. At
the head of the 'Georgites' was the Earl of
Fitzwilliam, at the head of the Jacobites the
Chevalier Cotton; and enrolled under their
standards were Lord Charles Manners, Viscount
Quarendon, eldest son of the Earl of Lichfield,
the Chevalier Newdigate, Messrs. Talbot, Stuart,
Barlow, Pitt, Castleton, Dashwood, Macormic,
etc.—all students at the Academy. The course of
study inclined to the lighter side of education.
It is not without interest to read what was then
thought necessary to round off and complete a
man of the world. Let us take a day at Angers
in the summer. At five o'clock A.M. the day's
work began with riding. This was followed by
instruction in fencing, the rest of the morning
being taken up with lessons in mathematics,
design, and music. Dinner concluded, there was
an adjournment to the dancing saloon, where
steps and figures and the intricacies of deport-
ment occupied the afternoon till it was time to
dress for the assemblies in the town. At the
assemblies, concerts and comedies were given, and
the weary student, late in the evening, returned
to supper and games of hazard. After a year of
this inspiriting substitute for an university train-

ing, he left Angers, and with three brother academicians and a tutor, all of the same political persuasion, started on the usual grand tour of eldest sons. After visiting the principal towns of southern France, mixing with French society, consorting with Jacobites, and acquiring a liking for the country and the people, which was to be of service to Elcho later when in exile, they resolved to prolong their tour by a journey to Rome— then the Mecca of the fervent Jacobite. Crossing the Mont Cenis, where their postchaises were taken to pieces and conveyed over the pass like a mountain battery on the backs of mules, they travelled to Milan by Turin and Genoa and the northern towns of Italy. Here again their progress may be illuminated by reference to the letters of Gray and Walpole, who had made precisely the same journey a month or two earlier. At Milan they were spectators of an execution, a scene which in the eighteenth century was considered an ordinary feature of an educational tour. In this instance the effect was heightened by the presence of a hundred masked noblemen, to one of whom, after drawing lots, there fell the sorry office of executioner. From Milan they passed on to Florence. In Florence he dined with Sir Horace Mann, and on another

occasion with Prince Craon, governor of the
city for the Emperor Francis 1. Prince Craon
gave as a toast the Chevalier de St. George.
Here was evidence that they were nearing the
shrine of Rome, the refuge of the Stuarts, where
the sun of Jacobitism was casting its setting rays,
and devout worshippers were swinging censers in
rivalry if not acute opposition to each other. In
Florence at length he caught up Horace Walpole.
In one of his letters written after '45, Walpole,
describing the appearance of the Prince of Hesse
to Sir Horace Mann, says of him, ' He is tall, lusty,
and handsome, extremely like Elcho in person.'
Other references in his letters are less flattering,
and we shall see later that Walpole is one of the
authorities for the accusation of cruelty brought
against Elcho after the campaign.

On October 25th, 1740, the party reached
Rome. The arrival of Elcho, a fresh recruit, was
a matter of moment; the members of the
Chevalier's Court hastened to ' call.' Edgar the
secretary, Irwin the physician, Hay the chamberlain, Fletcher and Archer, gentlemen of the
chamber, the Earls of Winton, Nithsdale, and
Dunbar, gentlemen of the Court, all vied with
each other in their attention to the newcomer

from the promised land. Lord Winton was for
the moment in disgrace ; a blow struck in the
presence of the Chevalier had condemned him to
exclusion from the Palace, and he was living no
longer under James's roof in the Piazza di Santi
Apostoli, but in a 'little boarding house' which
the Chevalier had secured for him.

Dunbar, brother of Lord Stormont, and raised
to the peerage by James, was acting as tutor
to the young Princes. Also about the Court
were Sir Thomas Sheridan, an Irishman and
a Roman Catholic, and Strickland, both of
whom were to play their part in the '45. It
was customary, in accordance alike with loyalty
and etiquette, to seek an audience with James.
Writing many years after the event, Elcho says
he was prompted to the step by his tutor. Calm
and cool-headed observer as in later life he
proved to be, it is difficult to account for his
want of enthusiasm at such a moment. His
whole education had been directed—and successfully directed—to inspiring him with Jacobite
ideas ; he had been taught not merely to sympathise with James as his lawful king in exile,
but to regard him as the sovereign by divine
right, who would sooner or later be re-established

on the throne of his ancestors.   And divine
right was not at that time the politic claim of
decadent kingship, but an active and living prin-
ciple animating those who held it with the zeal
and the tenacity of a religious doctrine.

Nor were these the only attributes of James
in the eyes of his adherents.   He represented to
them the sole channel of redress and the only
instrument by which the grievances and injustice,
that in the opinion of so many had resulted
from the Union, could be alleviated   Holding
these convictions, and believing that he would
one day be called on to maintain them with his
sword, Elcho must surely have been sensible of
the dramatic significance of the moment which
brought him for the first time into the presence
of the representative of the Stuarts.   And unless
we are to charge him with a radical lack of
imagination, in reading the restricted phrases in
which he describes the interview, allowance must
be made for the passage of years during which
bitter enmity had taken the place of enthusiastic
loyalty, during which hopes had been frustrated
and illusions had been lost.

Through the agency of John Hay a meeting
with the Chevalier was arranged.   What followed

is best described in the words of the *Journal* :
' Mr. Hay came for me, and about seven o'clock
in the evening we found ourselves in a little
street which approaches the side of the palace.
There was a cellar door at the place where we
entered. He pointed out a staircase to me, bade
me ascend it, and said farewell. I did so and
found Mr. Edgar : this ladder or secret staircase
led into his chamber. He opened a door for me,
pointed out a suite of rooms, and told me that
I would find the Chevalier in the fourth chamber.
And, indeed, I found the Chevalier St. George
standing there. I kissed his hand and he made
me sit beside him, near the fire. He was a tall
man and spare with large features, and exactly
resembled the portraits of his father, King James
II., and his uncle, King Charles II. He said
to me that he knew my father to be very loyal
to him, and that, if ever he ascended the throne
of Great Britain, he would reward him for it.
He asked me many questions about my travels
and my relations, and appeared to know well
about Scotland and Scottish families, particularly
those that had been raised to peerages since the
Revolution of 1688, whereby his father had lost
his Crown. He spoke of these last as " gentle-

men," and not by the title of " my lord."   He
rang a little bell and the two Princes, his sons,
who were in the side chamber, entered : I kissed
their hands and called them " Your Royal
Highnesses " as I had styled their father " Your
Majesty."   The Chevalier made his eldest son
and me stand back to back to see which of us
was the taller.   This Prince—Prince Edward—
was a year older than I was and was much taller.
After having overwhelmed me with politeness
he bade me adieu : and I returned to Mr.
Edgar's room, where I supped with him *tête á
tête*.   On parting from him he said to me that
the Duke of Bedford[1] was the man of all Great
Britain who had most often ascended the staircase.'

James had some excuse for holding out hopes
of reward to those who should assist him.   In
October 1740 events were assuming an aspect
favourable to the Stuart cause.   Fate, which had
been so fickle, which had doomed so many hopes
to disappointment, and had pointed along so many
vain and deluding avenues to success, was at
last offering promise of a fairer future.   As
children fling pebbles on the surface of a pond
and watch the ripples as they spread and die

[1] John Russell, fourth Duke of Bedford, 1710-1771.

away, so had the Jacobite party from time to
time cast upon the calm of Europe plots and
schemes. Again and again had they seen the
ripples fade and vanish into nothing. But
now it seemed as if Jacobitism really were
about to take its place with positive issues. Sir
Robert Walpole had been reluctantly forced into
hostilities with Spain ; Charles vi. was dead ; and
the succession to the Austrian monarchy was on
the eve of rending the countries of Europe with
war ; while in Paris had already commenced those
negotiations between James and Cardinal Fleury
which were to culminate in the attempted invasion
of England by the forces of France in 1744.

These weighty considerations, however, did
not hamper the gaiety of the hour. Life in
Rome was conducted in the spirit of Capua,
and, save for lessons in music and Italian from
an Abbé Dubois, it was wholly given over to
amusement. Daily, after dinner, Elcho would
go to the Villa Borghese, where Prince Charles
and the Duke of York sought exercise and
recreation. Charles, as became a future hero of
romance, kept apart and spoke little with those
who came to pay him court. In the gardens
of the villa he diverted himself with the killing

of blackbirds and thrushes, and in playing a
'Scotch game called goff.' The Duke of York
was friendly and a talker, and showed more
promise than his elder brother—so writes Elcho.
Charles's skill with the gun was well known.
Mr. Lang, in his charming and vivid account
of the Prince's boyhood,[1] quotes a letter from
the Duc de Liria, son of the Duke of Berwick,
written 1727, about the Prince : 'The Prince of
Wales was now six and a half, and besides his
great beauty was remarkable for dexterity, grace,
and almost supernatural address . . . he could
ride, could fire a gun, and, more surprising still,
I have seen him take a crossbow and kill birds
on the roof and split a rolling ball with a bolt
ten times in succession.'

James himself divided his time between Mass
and the opera. He was devout and musical.
State and circumstance attended his visits to the
opera, which never commenced before his arrival.
He supped during the performance, in the royal
box, and was visited every evening by the French
ambassador, the Duc de St. Aignan. Elcho says
that there were no women vocalists, the female
characters were sung by men dressed as women,

[1] Andrew Lang, *Prince Charles Edward*, p. 27.

and practically trained from their earlier youth
for the purpose.   English society was gregarious
and insular ; daily it would gather either at Lady
Pomfret's or at Lady Mary Wortley Montagu's,
and at conversazioni in the town the English
would, true to the traditions of their race, collect
in groups and remain separate from the Italians.

On one occasion Prince Charles, invited by the
Prince of Caserta to a shooting-party, chose Elcho
to accompany him.   This was better sport than
killing blackbirds and thrushes in the Borghese
gardens.   The first day they killed two hundred
and fifty woodcock, the second day twenty-five
deer, and the third six hundred wild duck.   In
the evenings there were concerts and dancing.
Ordinarily Prince Charles would lead in the minuet,
or if English country dances were given, the
leadership was confided to Mr. Roy Stewart, a
gentleman of the Prince's train.   Did Charles
look forward ?   Did he see in dreams the day of
momentary splendour when he would be leading
minuets in the palace of Holyrood, in the rooms
haunted by the sombre tragedies of his race ?

Italian society was gay and heedless.   Byron,
writing in 1820 from Ravenna, says : ' It is a
dreadfully moral place, for you must not look

at anybody's wife except your neighbour's.' The cynicism of the description would apply to the Rome of which Elcho wrote, would apply, indeed, to Italy generally; for whether at Rome, or Venice, or Ravenna, the moral code was the same. Wherever there was a coterie of rank or a concourse of fashion, there the *cicisbeo* was an accepted institution and a stereotyped feature of social life. In the morning he would call for his lady, accompany her on her round of shops or visits, share her amusements of the afternoon, and frequent her box at the opera in the evening. Italian husbands, Elcho tells us, were guided by a kind of rule-of-thumb morality. They considered it better that their wives should 'limit themselves to one lover' than that they should exercise a wider licence, 'as in Paris and other cities,' where 'cicisbeism' was not recognised.

II

DURING Elcho's residence in Rome, the Carnival took place, filling the streets with its processions and lively confusion, 'all mime and masque and Christian fools with varnished faces.' He entered into it with zest, buffooning, as the custom was, during the day, and in the evening attending balls or giving concerts. Seeing that at these concerts the first violin received ten sous and the other members of the orchestra only five sous, it was possible alike for the indigent and the thrifty to give entertainments without financial embarrassment.

I can find no certain mention of him at this time in the letters from Walpole's spies. John Walton, that indefatigable chronicler of the small-talk of espionage, writing in December 1740, says : 'Un Ecossais nommé Eicx est fort entré dans les bonnes graces du fils aîné du Prétendant.' 'Eicx' may stand for Elcho. Walton was residing himself in Florence, and had

to decipher the news sent him by his agents in
Rome ; this gave scope enough for error in the
interpretation of names, and what is here stated
of 'Eicx' would accord with the facts relating
to Elcho. Of Prince Charles a few days later
Walton wrote : 'On observe dans le fils aîné du
Prétendant une très forte inclination pour les
Femmes et la Danse. On l'élève dans une mol-
lesse extrême.' As will be seen later, this differs
from the information which Elcho has to give.

It was common knowledge in Stuart circles
in Rome that they lived under the observation of
persons in the pay of England, but singularly little
news of importance was suffered to escape from
the Palace in the Via di Santi Apostoli. Elcho
suspected, and rightly suspected, the Abbé Grant
of playing the spy. Grant insinuated himself
into their society, and was all things to all men,
a Jacobite to Jacobites, a Georgite to Georgites,
and an agreeable companion to every one ; he
may indeed at this time have been one of
Walton's agents, cardinals and lacqueys being
alike the correspondents of Walpole's informer.

Elcho was now deeply committed to the cause.
His education had borne fruit, and familiarity
with the Court in Rome had ratified and sealed

his allegiance. Thenceforward he must be regarded as an active and militant Jacobite.

Before his final departure from Rome in April 1741, he was admitted to a farewell interview with the Chevalier. In a concluding estimate of the principal figures of the little Court, he says of James that 'he appeared to be a Prince most affable, most well informed and most sensible. Bigotry was his worst fault.' Of Charles he writes, 'he appeared to have no tastes except for hunting and music, and had no conversational power'; and, emphasising his preference for the Duke of York, he adds that the Duke 'was suave, loved conversation, and pleased people more than his brother.' And yet it was by the grace of his person and the charm of his manner that Charles was to gather about him the loyalty and devotion of his followers, and gain for his memory an abiding place in the heart of a nation.

From Rome Elcho travelled to Bologna, where he again fell in with Horace Walpole. Walpole's society, the pictures, the palaces, the enchantment of the manifold arcades and the excellence of the opera, caused him to tarry here several days, and it was not till the first week in May that he reached

Venice. The fêtes of the Ascension had attracted
thither many English travellers, among them
Lady Pomfret and her two beautiful daughters,
Lady Charlotte Fermor, afterwards governess
to the children of George III., and Lady Sophia;
Lord Lincoln, subsequently second Duke of
Newcastle; Sir Francis Dashwood, a future
Chancellor of the Exchequer, and known to
fame as President of the Hell Fire Club; Mr.
Jackson, the Consul at Genoa; and others.
There were shows and pageants, the flutter of
flags and the echo of salutes, the Marriage of
the Adriatic, with its gorgeous ceremonial, excursions to Murano and the islands, the opera,
and the evening muster of the fashionable world
on the Piazza di S. Marco, in all of which the
English travellers took a delighted part. Save,
indeed, that the Venetians were masked, and
that over the sparkle and vivacity of their freedom there hung the constant menace of the
Council of Ten, the life of the eighteenth century
differed little from the life of to-day. Such
difference as existed was to be found mainly in
the palaces, where the families of the Venetian
nobility still resided. In these the father, mother,
brother, sister, with the younger branches, formed

a co-operative household under a single roof, presided over and administered by a member of the group. Each individual had his own table, his own gondola and servants, while his expenses and his monthly allowance were paid from the common fund. Marriage of a member of the nobility with one not noble involved exclusion of the children from the ranks of the caste. The members of the order, with their title of Excellence, their lines of ancestry extending into a remote past, and their high and picturesque offices of state, were haughty in the extreme, and deemed their rank to exceed that of all other men save sovereign princes. In their relations with foreigners they were subject to jealous rules of government. Under no circumstances were they permitted to address an ambassador, and in the event of an ambassador entering a café, it was the custom for all the nobles present to leave immediately. Service in the land forces of the Republic was generally considered below their dignity, and their preference inclining to the sea, the ships of the Venetian fleet were in all cases officered by nobles. As to the ways and manners of the social world, the rapacity of the gondoliers, the importunity of the beggars, and the enjoy-

ments of the populace, on these the passage of a
century and a half has left but slender traces.

In Venice Elcho mentions that he was introduced to an Earl of Wemyss. It appears that
in the sixteenth century a member of the family,
forsaking Scotland, had entered the service of
the House of Austria as a soldier of fortune,
had fought with distinction, and been raised to
the title. Subsequently he had joined the forces
of the Venetian Republic, under whose banner
his descendants had lived and served. The Earl
of Wemyss of whom Elcho writes was the aged
and sole survivor of this branch of his family.

Quitting Venice at the end of May and
travelling by Innspruck, Munich, and Strasburg,
June finds Elcho once again in Paris at the
Hôtel d'Orléans in the Rue des Petits Augustins.
Here he quickly adopted the mode of life prevalent among young Englishmen, became possessor
of a carriage, formed an attachment to a lady
at the opera, and engaged masters for music,
dancing, fencing, and mathematics. In dancing he
received instruction from one Marseille, a famous
teacher, who would arrive at the hotel in a coach,
attended by four lacqueys. The lessons were of
an abstruse and complex character, including,

besides the various dances of the epoch, such subjects as marching, saluting, presenting oneself in a
reception-room, sitting down and serving at table.

On the 13th of October, the day of his
departure, he found the gateway of his hotel
blockaded by the lady of the opera to whom
his attentions had been paid ; a crowd having
collected, whose sympathies were with the com-
plainant, he was compelled, with scant chivalry,
to escape by the back door. But at St. Denis,
where the postchaise was awaiting him, the lady
was beforehand, and Mr. Æneas Macdonald, the
Scottish banker and Jacobite, had to be called
in to adjust matters before Elcho could proceed
on his journey to England.

Thus, after an absence of three years, he found
himself once more about to revisit his native
country. He was now a finished product of
the grand tour, not merely a virtuoso

'half cur'd, and perfectly well bred,
With nothing but a solo in his head,'[1]

and, as the custom was, with a trunk full of
spurious old masters from Italy, and a lumber
of *bric-à-brac* from Paris, but a man having a
cultured acquaintance with music and languages,

[1] *The Dunciad*, Bk. iv. ll. 323-4.

and instructed in all that the Continent had to
teach of the elegances and graces. He was thus
in a very different position for dealing with the
contumely to which his Scottish tongue and his
uncouth manner had formerly exposed him. He
was in the full plumage of a 'fine gentleman.'
The fashions of France and the refinements of
Italy might be counted on to secure him respect
in the society of London, where, according to
Walpole, manners 'had dwindled to rusticity.'

With some consciousness of the change in his
worldly equipment, on an October day in 1741 he
started from Dover to ride post to London.
Wearing high boots after the French manner, his
hair arranged in a plait, with a Parisian whip and
cocked hat, the very glass of fashion, and a
macaroni to the tips of his fingers, he approached
the outskirts of Rochester. Passers-by detected
in the cavalier the figure of a Frenchman. On
the instant a hue and cry was raised,

> ' And all and each that passed that way
> Did join in the pursuit.'

Ignorant of the cause of the commotion, he
suddenly found himself assailed with angry cries
of 'Down with the French dog !' Pelted with
stones by a rapidly increasing crowd, he was

forced to fly, and putting spurs to his horse, only succeeded in reaching safety in the open country beyond. Whether he appeared as a Scotsman unadorned and plain, or transfigured by his Parisian graces, England seemed equally determined to refuse him either sympathy or welcome; and the remainder of his journey was given over to reflections on the irony of the adventure.

In London, moreover, a not less disconcerting experience awaited him. Together with Lord Strafford,[1] who had lived much in Paris, and who, after the habit of France, carried a muff and a cocked hat, Elcho paid a visit to the theatre at Drury Lane, where Garrick was just then beginning to delight the fashionable world. Hardly were Elcho and his companion seated, when pit and gallery were thrown into an uproar. On all sides shouts were raised of 'French dogs,' and 'Down with the muff,' and as the objects of the demonstration refused to withdraw, the more turbulent portion of the audience betook themselves to spitting and flinging apples and candles. As the violence showed no sign of abating, the

---

[1] William Wentworth (1722-1791), second Earl of Strafford (of that creation), married 1740 Lady Anne Campbell, second daughter of the Duke of Argyll.

only course open was to retreat. These episodes did little to reconcile Elcho to England and the English, and his former antipathies, which foreign travel had tended to obliterate, rapidly revived.

In London he found his brother, Francis Charteris. Being now in a proselytising spirit, Elcho determined to make him a Jacobite. The guardian of Charteris was the Duke of Argyll, who was opposed to any attempt to bring the lad under Jacobite influence. But Elcho gained his point, and Charteris was packed off to the Continent with a Jacobite tutor, and eventually became a supporter of the House of Stuart.

From London Elcho travelled north to rejoin his father at Wemyss Castle. Here he found Lord Leven and Lord Sinclair. Lord Sinclair had taken part in 1715, but had been pardoned while in exile. He counselled Elcho to enter the service of King George, and to turn his back on the Jacobite cause. The Stuarts, he said, were an ungrateful race, and regarded everything done for them simply as the fulfilment of a duty; and it would, he added, be madness to risk life and fortune for so weak a dynasty. These arguments of expediency caused Elcho to hesitate, and at one moment he appears to have thought of applying for a post under the Crown ; but a deciding influence in the shape of Sir James Steuart,[1] who shortly afterwards came as a guest to the Castle, determined him to adhere to the path of loyalty and adventure.

His home at this time offered little to restrain his wandering disposition. His father and mother were now finally separated, while between his father and himself a quarrel had arisen over the management of the estates. Attempts to arrange matters proving unsuccessful, Lord Wemyss took his departure for England, while Elcho, remaining in the north, spent the winter (1742-1743) visiting in Scotland. In the course of his wanderings he was a guest at Dunrobin, at Alloa, at the house of Forbes of Culloden, and enjoyed the hospitality of John Murray of Broughton and the Earl of Traquair, through whom he was made more closely acquainted with the party intrigues. In the early part of 1743, the marriage of his sister Frances with Sir James Steuart at Dunrobin Castle bound him in relationship to one of the most extreme and ardent Jacobites of the time.

The summer of 1743 found him again in London. He frequented society but little,

---

[1] Sir James Steuart Denham, 1712-1780, political economist.

spending most of his leisure at Vauxhall, or
among the noisy pleasures of the recently instituted Ranelagh Gardens, 'into which everybody
that loved eating, drinking, staring, or crowding
was admitted for twelvepence.'[1] The English,
with whom he had been friends while abroad, he
now found were less demonstrative and cordial,
and the Cocoa Tree Club, where Jacobites
resorted, and the house of the Duchess of
Hamilton,[2] where he met persons of his own
nationality, offered the only social atmosphere
congenial to his tastes.

Events of importance had meanwhile occurred
which were not without significance for the
Jacobite party. In January 1742 Sir Robert
Walpole had been driven from office. Party
vicissitudes in England were watched with un-
remitting vigilance and hope by the followers of
James, but the change of ministry had led to
disappointingly little increase of strength in their
political influence. A faint and sluggish support
was always to be found in the political world, but

[1] Walpole, *Letters*.

[2] There were two Duchesses of Hamilton living: (1) Anne,
daughter and co-heir of Edward Spencer of Rendlesham, and
widow of James, fifth Duke; (2) Elizabeth, daughter and sole
heir of Digby, Lord Gearard, widow of James, fourth Duke.

it was difficult to locate, and doubly difficult to
measure. At no time, however, after the early
part of the century, in spite of the inflated
gasconades of Sempil[1] and Bohaldie,[1] could the
movement in favour of the Stuarts claim in England either the vitality or the cohesion necessary
to bring it to a successful issue. Every month
as it passed diminished the prevailing discontent,
and every year saw the natural tendency to come
to terms with an accomplished fact, promoting a
reconciliation between the people and 'the elderly
German' who occupied the throne.

In France alone did the cause in those days
seem to be advancing. To the Court of France,
through the medium of Sempil and Bohaldie,
came accounts from first to last favourable to the
interests they were promoting. To Fleury it was
represented that the city of London, the heart of
the Empire, was on the side of James, that in
the country a numerous and powerful aristocracy
were only waiting for the moment to declare
themselves in a similar sense, and that provided
France would despatch a force to the shores of
England, a successful rising would most certainly
follow. Summarising the situation in a letter to

---

[1] The Jacobite agents in Paris.

M. Amelot,[1] dated January 28, 1744 (when it had been finally determined to send troops to England), Sempil wrote : 'Le succès est infaillible : rien ne peut s'opposer au transport des troupes, et le concours de la nation sera unanime dès qu'elles auront mis pied à terre.' But during the earlier years of negotiation the sceptical and cautious Fleury dallied and delayed, raising hopes which it is now tolerably certain he had no intention of fulfilling, and promising assistance he had very little idea of affording.

In Scotland, since 1740, John Murray of Broughton, that active and sinister figure on the Jacobite stage, had been busy as agent for the party : to him while in Edinburgh had come Bohaldie from Paris with positive assurance that the French were preparing to help, and that a landing might be looked for in the autumn of 1742. But the autumn passed without further sign of activity on the part of France. Suspicion arose among the Scottish Jacobites as to the exactitude of Bohaldie's information. John Murray was deputed to visit Paris and investigate the situation. Before his arrival in that city Cardinal Fleury was dead (January 29, 1743).

[1] Amelot de Chaillon, Foreign Minister, 1737-1744.

It was a commonly held belief that with the
Cardinal the Stuart cause lost its most willing
and powerful friend, but Captain Colin [1] has
shown conclusively that it was only after the
death of Fleury that Louis xv. and Amelot,
his Minister for Foreign Affairs, began seriously
to entertain the idea of an invasion of England.
To Fleury the Stuarts had been no more than
pawns on the political chessboard, which he
might move or not, as suited the purpose of
the moment. But with his death an alteration
took place in the uses to which the Jacobites
could be put.

The defeat of the French at Dettingen (June
27, 1743) rendered a diversion which would
have the effect of withdrawing British troops
from the battlefields of Germany a political
move of primary importance. But before com-
mitting themselves to a policy of active aggression
the Court of France desired more certain intelligence as to the position of affairs in England.
The means chosen for obtaining it were curiously
inadequate. Nothing, perhaps, is more striking
throughout these preliminaries than the worth-
lessness of the persons in whom confidence was

[1] *Louis XV. et les Jacobites.*

placed, and the insufficiency of the facts upon which policy was determined. In this case Amelot, not altogether trusting the information retailed to him by Sempil and Bohaldie, despatched one Butler, an equerry of Louis, to visit England during the summer, and report upon the strength and efficiency of the Jacobite party in that country.

Thus in 1743, while the Scots through Murray were testing the sincerity of France, France through Butler was endeavouring to inform herself of the capabilities of the English Jacobites. The mission of Butler terminated in October; towards the middle of that month he returned to Versailles with a report chiefly founded on the gossip of a few reputed Jacobite peers, with whom he had caroused in London and consorted at Lichfield races. In spite of its precarious foundation the report was considered entirely satisfactory. Murray in the meanwhile had returned with the news that France was conditionally planning a descent on the coast of England.[1] Everything, therefore, was pointing to the occurrence of events of high importance when,

---

[1] *State Papers, Domestic, George II.*, B. 86, No. 69. This, however, differs from *Memorials*, p. 42.

in September 1743, Elcho again set out for France.

Landing at Boulogne he paid a visit to Earl Marischal, then residing at his country seat, some two leagues from the town. He found Marischal in the midst of his 'menagerie of young heathens'[1]—Mademoiselle Emetté, a child of Turkish origin, whom his brother[2] had taken captive at the siege of Oczakow (1737), Stepan a Tartar, Ibrahim a Turk, and a third male attendant reputed to be a Thibetan and related to the Grand Lama. Marischal had adopted Emetté as his daughter, just as, earlier in the century, Baron d'Argental had adopted a Turkish child, Mademoiselle Aïsée;[3] but whereas Aïsée won for herself a place in the literature of France and enjoyed the friendship of Madame du Deffand and other celebrities of the day, Emetté lived unnoted save for her relationship to Marischal. Here Elcho learned that his father, Lord Wemyss, had passed through Boulogne in the spring of '43, on his way to Versailles. Lord Wemyss had been sent

---

[1] Andrew Lang, *The Companions of Pickle*, p. 31.
[2] Marshal Keith (1696-1758).
[3] See Edmund Gosse, *French Profiles*, p. 35.

by the English supporters of the Chevalier to solicit from the French Court some demonstration in favour of the House of Stuart. The English Jacobites steadily declined to put signatures to incriminating documents.[1] They remembered that owing to want of such a precaution, James II. was apprised of the names of those who were favouring the Prince of Orange in 1688. Their negotiations were conducted with the French Court by word of mouth. It was necessary, therefore, from time to time to send representatives, of whom Lord Wemyss was one, to further their cause at Versailles. This was typical of their procedure, for not only were they circumspect when plotting, but when the moment for action arrived they proved that they had neither daring nor spirit.

While engaged on this mission in Paris, Lord Wemyss received a letter from James containing a reference to Elcho. ' When you see your son,' he wrote, ' with whom I am acquainted, and whom I esteem, make him very kind compliments from me. I hope the time is not far off in which I may be able to give you and your family distinguished marks of my favour.' But owing to

---

[1] Colin, *Louis XV. et les Jacobites*, p. 13.

the breach between father and son, this message
was never delivered.

In Paris Elcho found Lord John Drummond,
who had lately received a commission from Louis
to raise the regiment of Royal Scots, the companies of which were to be commanded by Highland chiefs attached to the House of Stuart.[1]
Here also he made the acquaintance of Lord
Sempil and Bohaldie, who gave encouraging
reports of the dispositions then being made by
the French Court ; but his Stuart loyalty was for
a moment in jeopardy.   Profound dissatisfaction
with the treatment he had received from his father
suggested service under the Hanoverian Crown as
a safe and easy form of revenge.   The advice,
however, of his younger brother, then in Paris,
and already a full-fledged Jacobite, prevailed ; and
he was saved from a step so much at variance with
the habitual firmness of his character.

In the month of December 1743 was celebrated
the marriage of Louis Philippe, Duc d'Orléans
(1723-1785), and Louise Henriette de Bourbon
Conti.   On the evening of the ceremony Elcho
and his brother, in 'magnificent dresses,' which

---

[1] In the Stuart Papers may be seen the names of the various
captains of companies to whom authority was given.

had been made for the occasion, attended at Versailles. Here they enjoyed the privilege of looking on while Louis played lansquenet, and later in the evening they were permitted to stake and lose twenty-five louis d'or at the King's table.

Though but twenty-two years of age, Elcho had now seen much of the world and much of what a life of pleasure had to offer, and there is already a note of sedateness and fatigue in his references to the diversions of Paris, to its theatres, its public baths, its gaming-houses and suppers, and its parties to Versailles and the neighbourhood. On the occasion of a supper-party given by himself he had a narrow escape from an appalling disaster. He had invited a cosmopolitan gathering of ' actresses, a Hanoverian Baron, a few Swedes and Danes, and other strangers.' Illness prevented the host from being present. In the middle of the festivity an alarm of fire was raised, and before the guests had time to escape the floor gave way, precipitating the party into the room below, where all, to the number of sixteen, perished in the flames. Elcho expresses artless horror that his guests should thus have lost their lives at a moment when they were ' thinking only of pleasure.'

This winter he was a frequent visitor at the house of Æneas Macdonald, the Jacobite banker. He observed one day in December that a Mr. Buchanan, who habitually resided there, had left. He made inquiries of Macdonald, who replied in confidence that Buchanan, together with Bohaldie, had gone on a secret mission to Rome, but that Elcho would shortly learn the object of their journey. This in fact betokened the commencement of a new phase in the drama. On November 13, 1743, Amelot had definitely announced to Lord Sempil that Louis xv. had determined to despatch to England those forces which the English Jacobites had stated to be requisite for the success of the rebellion. On December 10th Louis communicated the project in a letter to his uncle the King of Spain. And it was in accordance with this policy of the French Court that Bohaldie had been sent to Rome in order to summon the Prince to France.

The weary years of waiting, of espionage, of eavesdropping and intrigue were at last to give place to action. A brighter stage of that romantic endeavour and impossible aspiration, to be brought to nought in the last tragedy of Culloden, had now been reached. At dawn on

January 9, 1744, Prince Charles Edward, after saying farewell to his father, whom he was never to see again, took his departure from Rome. As has been often stated, it was given out that Charles and Henry his brother had left the city on a hunting expedition. Outside Rome, Charles assumed the disguise of a Spanish courier, and, provided with passports by Cardinal Aquaviva, posted through the snow to Massa, while Henry, remaining at the hunting lodge, continued to send baskets of wild geese and other game, stated to have been killed by Charles, to friends in Rome.

So successful was the plot that even on January 25th Walton was writing still under the impression that Cisterna was the goal, and hunting the object of the Prince's journey, though he notes the fact that more luggage had been prepared than usually accompanied him on such expeditions. Only on January 28th did Walton despatch to Newcastle certain intelligence of what had occurred. Writing again on February 4th, he apologises for the tardiness of his information ; his principal correspondent in Rome had chosen this critical moment to die. Congratulations, he adds, had poured in upon James, and the most accomplished writers of the day were busy inditing

poems on the subject of Charles's enterprise.[1]
History and mythology were being ransacked for
parallels, and in the flight of Demetrius from
Rome to regain the kingdom of Syria pedantry
had discovered what was considered a most propitious and appropriate precedent.

Bohaldie returned to Paris. Charles pursued
his journey in the company of Buchanan and the
Maître d'hôtel of the Bailly de Tencin, a man
' fort usité à voyager par mer et par terre '[2]   At
Genoa he was joined by Sir John Graeme or
Graham, a son of Mr. James Graham, solicitor
to the late King James, and, travelling under
Bohaldie's cipher name of Mallock, he reached
Paris in the first week of February. A few days
later Elcho was taken to see Charles at the house
of Lord Sempil, where he was lodged. ' I found
the Prince,' he says, ' all alone in his chamber,
drinking tea. He opened the door for me and
shut it himself, and seemed very uneasy. He
told me that the King of France had made him
come, and had promised to send into England an
army of ten thousand men, commanded by Maréchal Saxe, who was to assemble and embark them
at Dunkirk. He delivered to me on behalf of

[1] *State Papers, Tuscany*, February 1744.   [2] *Ibid.*

his father the commission of a colonel of dragoons,
and directed me to appear at Dunkirk towards
the end of the month of February 1744.' To
Marischal Charles gave a patent to command in
Scotland.

Shortly afterwards Charles and Bohaldie started
for Gravelines, there to await the setting forth of
the army to England. Within a few days Earl
Marischal left for Dunkirk, with Lord Louis
Drummond and Macdonald of Glengarry[1] as
aides-de-camp. Elcho joined them on March 1st.
At this point the Narrative appended to this
Memoir takes up the story, and it is only
necessary briefly to supplement the facts therein
stated. The details which Elcho gives of the
measures adopted by the French Government are
substantially correct. He was, however, unaware
that even while the preparations were being
pushed forward with so much apparent energy
at Dunkirk, doubt and hesitation had already
crept into the counsels of the Ministers in Paris.
Trustworthy reports had been received at Versailles, which gave a different colour to the
promised reception of the French in England.[2]

[1] Identified by Mr. Lang with Pickle the Spy.
[2] Colin, *Louis XV. et les Jacobites.*

The regular troops quartered in that country were more numerous than was supposed, the City authorities had renewed their oaths of allegiance to the House of Hanover, a powerful fleet had assembled in the Channel, and it was now certain that none of the English ships would join the rebels ; while at Dover, Rochester, and neighbouring towns the inhabitants could be seen at their doors preparing such weapons as they possessed for use against the foreigner.[1]   As to the Jacobites themselves, report said they were few in number and of little account.   They had neither organisation nor plan.   Wintry weather prevailed in England, and they were averse to take saddle in it.   They were only venting that loyalty which their claret inspired.[2]   In fact, fear of the *fleur-de-lis* was damping enthusiasm for the White Cockade, and it was pointed out that the proposed action by the French would be more likely to strengthen than to weaken the authority of the House of Hanover.

On March 7th a tempest burst upon the shipping assembled at Dunkirk.   The havoc and

[1] The Swiss waiters in the metropolis offered to form a battalion for the defence of London.—Doran, *Jacobites in London*, vol. ii. p. 106.

[2] Fitzroy Bell, *Memorials of John Murray of Broughton*, p. 49.

destruction which followed gave a plausible excuse for abandoning a project which the French
Government had already resolved not to proceed
with.

Charles was inconsolable. On March 6th he
had written to his father, 'I hope in a few days
to date my letters from a place which will show
of itself that all is finished.' [1] But it was not to
be. The news of the abandonment had been
broken to him by Maréchal Saxe. He appealed
against the decision; he urged that Scotland
should be made the objective, and foreshadowed,
failing the aid of France, his own desperate call
to the loyalty of the Highlanders. 'Ne me
convient-il pas mieux d'aller périr, s'il le faut, à
la tête de ces braves gens, que de traîner une
vie languissante dans l'exil et la dépendance ?' [2]

Marischal went to Gravelines to see him.
Charles proposed that they should hire a boat
and proceed to Scotland. Marischal was too
practical for such visionary romance, and declined.
But this was the Prince Charles of the Highlands,
gallant and adventurous, the Charles of ballad and
song and of sentiment tender and undying.

[1] Andrew Lang, *Prince Charles Edward*, p. 65.
[2] Prince Charles to Lord Sempil, March 15, 1744.

Elcho loitered with the ships. On April 3rd he embarked at Boulogne, and on April 7th he landed on the coast of East Lothian and went to the house of his brother-in-law, Sir James Steuart of Goodtrees. But he had no idea of skulking undiscovered. He was determined to disarm suspicion by a policy of frankness. Having stayed one night at Goodtrees, he left for Edinburgh, and at once called on the Lord Justice-Clerk Milton.[1] Elcho was asked many questions about the affair at Dunkirk. He gave out that after spending the winter in Paris he had arrived on the coast and found an embargo laid on all ships, that he had been compelled to wait till the embargo was removed, and thus had been an involuntary spectator of the preparations for invasion, but that at the first opportunity he had escaped from a country which was meditating hostilities against England. The Lord Justice-Clerk was delighted with the youthful traveller, and invited him to remain for supper. They spent a convivial evening. Elcho was quite unsuspected, while the Lord Justice-Clerk was thoroughly satisfied with the information he had extracted.

[1] Andrew Fletcher, Lord Milton.

III

HAVING safely weathered the inquiries of the Lord Justice-Clerk, Elcho remained in Scotland till July, much of the time a guest at Goodtrees, where his brother-in-law, Sir James Steuart, kept open house for Jacobites, and where many conversions to the cause were effected. Here too a reconciliation was arranged between Elcho and his father. On July 18th he started for London, and riding with speed accomplished the journey in five days, reaching Berwick on the 18th, and Durham, Bawtry, Stilton, and London respectively on the 19th, 20th, 21st, and 22nd.

In London he found Murray of Broughton on the point of setting out for the Low Countries and France to concert plans with Bohaldie and Charles for future action. Elcho was athirst for adventure, and it was agreed that he should join in the expedition. On August 21, 1744, the friends landed at Ostend, which was then held by British troops. Departing thence for the purpose of visiting the army of the allies, they

reached the plains of Lille, where they found the
English, Hanoverian, Dutch, and Austrian armies
encamped, on August 24th. The combined
forces had recently crossed the Scheldt, but
jealousies and dissensions between the leaders had
led to helpless inaction, and the march south to
their then position fronting the fortresses of
France had been rendered useless by the absence
of a siege train, which the Austrians and Dutch
had undertaken to provide.[1] It was at this life-
less moment of the tangled continental war, which
since the death of Charles vi. in 1740 had kept
Europe under arms, that Murray and Elcho
joined the allied army. Here Elcho was to
form a brief acquaintance with military service.
General Campbell,[2] Colonel of the Scots Greys,
having provided him with two horses, he was
able to take part in cavalry exercises, and in a
general foraging expedition. He was thus able
to qualify himself in some degree for the commission he already held as colonel of dragoons
in Prince Charles's unrecruited army. But if
in military affairs there was observable a certain

---

[1] J. Fortescue, *History of the Army*, vol. ii. p. 107.
[2] Lieut.-General Hon. Sir James Campbell, K.B. (1667-1745),
third son of second Earl of Loudoun, killed at Fontenoy.

inertness, nothing of the kind could be charged against the hospitality of the regiments in camp. Every evening there was a banquet at which they were welcome guests, their hosts as a rule being the Scottish officers, between whom and the English they observed that there was little or no association. Ten days of feasting and inactivity were, however, sufficient, and on September 3rd they quitted the camp and travelled to Brussels.

Here Murray parted from Elcho in order to keep a secret assignation with Bohaldie. Murray's own account of what followed is given in the *Memorials*. There he narrates how, contrary to every rule of intrigue, he found Bohaldie in the taproom of the Sun Inn, the favourite resort of the British in Rotterdam, playing cards 'in a promiscuous company'; how he journeyed with him to Paris; how he there met Charles 'at the back of the great stables of the Tuileries,' and how they took counsel together upon the subject of a possible descent upon Scotland. The impression conveyed is that Murray used his best endeavour to persuade Charles of the folly of such an enterprise. But in the *Memorials*, which were written with the double purpose of vindicating the author and of

vilifying Bohaldie, it was essential that Murray
should exonerate himself from the responsibility
of having induced Charles to hazard his fortunes
in '45. He states, therefore, that on this occasion
(September, '44) when Charles said 'that at all
events he was determined to come the following
summer to Scotland, though with a single footman,' he himself pointed out to the Prince that
such a scheme could only be attended with
disaster. Elcho admits that Murray, when he
rejoined him at Rotterdam, repeated the purport
of this conversation. But how little value he
subsequently attached to the statement is shown
in the Journal and the Narrative, in both of which
Elcho consistently charges Murray with having
incited Charles to come to Scotland. 'Faithful
are the wounds of a friend.' But can it be
doubted that if Murray had been sincere in his
endeavour he could have dissuaded Charles and
arrested the undertaking?

One of the minor paradoxes of history is the
process by which dubious reputations are accidentally renovated. It is assumed that accusations
are made against an informer such as Murray, not
on the cogency of evidence, but because the
general trend of his character marks him out as

a convenient scapegoat. The instinct of every one concerned, it is said, would naturally be to lay the blame of failure on the most despicable figure of the drama, and so it comes about that the removal of extraneous mud leads to a complete process of cleansing. In course of time we are made to see, not any longer the lean and furtive figure of a traitor or informer, whose actual faults have been exaggerated, but a respectable citizen, whose innocence has been groaning beneath a burden of cruel accusation. The limit of his capacity for guilt becomes, in fact, his salvation. This to some extent has been the case with Murray —the tendency now is to acquit him of responsibility in the matter. His apologists say that Charles was headstrong, sanguine, and ambitious, that he was mortified and goaded by the failure of 1744, and that in the defeat of the English at Fontenoy (May 1745) he found the final motive for action. Moreover it is said ' that Charles himself always accepted full responsibility for the step, and never sought to screen himself at the expense of any of his followers.' [1] All this is doubtless true. But does it affect the view that Murray, who alone was completely aware of the

[1] Murray, *Memorials*, preface, p. xvii.

state of affairs in Scotland, who was the sole and trusted intermediary between Charles and the Jacobites of the north, and who, in 1745, con-ducted the correspondence which preceded the arrival of Charles, could, had he chosen to do so, have made Charles realise that his proposal was mere midsummer madness ? To hold such a power and to fail to use it, to be given such opportunity and to suffer it to pass unemployed —surely such dereliction justifies the accusations of Elcho and the censures of Maxwell.[1]

While Murray was thus gulling Charles with false advice in Paris, Elcho gratified his restless love of travel by a tour through Holland, in the course of which he visited the principal towns and gardens of that country. In Leyden he met the Comte de St. Germain, ' who passed as a maker of gold, pretended to have a secret for prolonging life, and played very well on the violin.' This gives but a feeble measure of this ' *conte pour rire*.' [2] The precursor of Cagliostro, he was famous throughout Europe. Paris, however, was the headquarters of his mystifications; and here through many years he successfully played on the

---

[1] Maxwell of Kirkconnell's *Narrative*, pp. 55-77.
[2] Frederick II., king of Prussia, to Voltaire, May 1, 1760.

credulity of the French. Louis xv. gave him
rooms in the Castle of Chambord, Madame de
Pompadour consulted him, and even in an age
when the *philosophes* were kindling doubt and
inquiry, there were not found wanting numbers
of persons to believe that he was possessed of
the elixir of life, that he could increase the size
of pearls, and remove flaws from diamonds without diminishing their weight. Although he was
then only in his thirty-seventh year, a popular
superstition credited him with having survived
through twenty centuries, in the course of which
he was said to have been acquainted with Jesus
Christ and to have been a guest at the feast of
Cana in Galilee. Neither his origin nor his name
nor the sources of his wealth were known, and it
was not till his death in 1784 that the superstitions
he had been able to inspire were finally dissolved.

On September 24th Elcho met Murray at
Rotterdam. Murray was the bearer of letters and
despatches to Charles's supporters in Scotland, and
of commissions appointing Lord Wemyss governor
of the county of Fife and the Duke of Hamilton[1]
a lieutenant-general of the forces in Scotland.
As these documents if discovered would be fatally

---

[1] James, sixth duke (1724-1758), succeeded his father 1743.

compromising, the travellers purchased pistols, intending, if searched, to place the papers on the muzzles and blow them into the air. Fortunately no occasion arose for testing the merits of this precautionary scheme, and on October 2nd Elcho arrived unmolested in London. In November he was once more in Scotland at Coltness with his brother-in-law, Steuart; together they visited the Duke of Hamilton, who declared his active partisanship for the Jacobite cause. The duke subsequently contributed fifteen hundred pounds to the fund which was being formed in Edinburgh for Charles, but he took no part in the rising itself.

Returning to Edinburgh in December, Elcho joined with Murray in founding the 'Buck Club,' to bring together such persons as were supporters of the Stuarts. The scheme of the club was to meet once a week for supper, and by social gatherings, association, and loyal toasts to promote the harmony and progress of the cause. At one of the first meetings of the club Murray told the members the purport of his interviews with Charles in Paris. According to his account, Charles intended to come to Scotland, with or without French support, in the course of the follow-

ing summer, and throw himself on the loyalty of
his friends. What, said Murray, is to be done?
The majority of the members voted for a despatch
to Charles insisting that unless he could bring
with him six thousand regular troops, arms for
ten thousand more, and thirty thousand louis
d'or, it would mean ruin to himself, to the cause,
and to his supporters. A document was accordingly drawn up by Murray embodying this view,
'and at a meeting in the tavern under the
Piazzas of the Parliament Close' it was handed,
in the presence of Lochiel, Glengarry, Elcho,
and the Duke of Perth, [1] to Lord Traquair, who
was to convey it to London and thence transmit it to Charles in Paris. Elcho gives a list
of those members of the club who stated that
they would join Charles in any event.[2] All
of these subsequently took part in the rising
except the Duke of Hamilton, Lord Traquair,
Macleod of Macleod, Macdonald of Lorn, and
Viscount Kenmure.

[1] Murray, *Memorials*, p. 117.

[2] It is as follows: 'Dukes Hamilton, Perth; Earls Nithsdale,
Traquair; Viscount Kenmure; Lord Nairne; Viscount Strathallan;
Mr. Murray, father of the Earl of Dunmore; Lochiel; Glengarry;
Clanronald; Keppoch; Macleod of Macleod; Macdonald of
Glencoe; Stuart of Ardshiel; Oliphant of Gask; Hepburn of
Keith; Hamilton; Lord Pitsligo; Carnegie; Macdonald of Lorn.'

The club, however, was divided against itself :
some said they would join though Charles came
alone, others said that they would join only if he
came with French assistance. But if the Buck
Club failed to effect much for the cause, it at any
rate served as a greatly needed social meeting-place
during the winter. Amusements and diversions
in Edinburgh were fitful and rare. Recreations
and the simplest pleasures were still frowned on
by the Church and denounced from the pulpit,
and the gloom of the Sabbath still cast its shadow
over the remaining days of the week. But in
spite of the admonitions against ' promiscuous
dancing ' and against the playhouse, which the
writings of popular divines represented as the
actual temple of the devil,[1] there were not wanting signs that the reign of austerity imposed by
the Church was drawing to a close. Formerly
everything which could promote animation or
lessen dejection on a Scottish Sabbath had been
condemned without compromise, but now the
spirit of enjoyment was beginning to assert itself.
To walk through the fields or venture into the
country, to loiter in the streets between the hours
of worship, to look idly from the window, or

[1] Arnot, *History of Edinburgh*, 4th ed., 1818, p. 281.

even to bathe in the sea or swim in rivers, on the Sabbath—these were practices no longer universally censured by public opinion.

In the matter of the playhouse and the assembly, the ministers, to their great mortification, were losing ground, and 'the most part of the ladies were turning rebels to their remonstrances, notwithstanding the frightful danger.'[1] In this case Elcho, we cannot doubt, was staunchly on the side of the rebels, and he tells us indeed that he attended regularly at the theatre and at dances. The plays were given at this time in the Tailors' Hall in the Cowgate, where pit and boxes cost 2s. 6d., gallery 1s. 6d.[2] Attempts to set up an independent playhouse had been attended with rioting ; the Edinburgh Presbytery had invoked the law to restrain the performances, and the enterprise had perforce to be abandoned. Even at the Tailors' Hall the drama was but a smuggled pleasure, carried on, contrary to the letter of the law, 'under the evasion of a concert of music with a play between the Acts.'[3] Edinburgh, in fact, had advanced exactly to the point which

1 Burt, *Letters from a Gentleman in Scotland*, vol. i. p. 193.
2 Arnot, p. 281.
3 Arnot, p. 281 ; J. Ramsay, vol. ii. 547.

London had reached ninety years before, when Sir W. Davenant introduced his first dramatic performances under the guise of musical entertainments.

The assemblies, which received more countenance than the plays, were held weekly in the old Assembly Rooms. Dancing began at five and continued till ten or eleven at night, the tickets of admission costing 2s. 6d. At the head of the room some lady of fashion would be seated as president, wearing her badge of office—a gold medal with motto and device, emblematical of charity and parental tenderness. The arrangements were primitive and uncomfortable, and before the entertainment was half over the room was often filled with smoke from the flambeaux of the footmen, who were allowed to stand in the entry.[1] On nights when there was no assembly, Elcho and other young men combined to give a dance. Edmund Burt,[2] in one of his letters, writes that ' he never saw so many pretty women of distinction together as at the Assembly.' Elcho writes to the same effect, and it was not many weeks before he proposed to and was accepted by Miss Graham of Airth. Difficulties arose over

[1] Arnot, p. 293.   [2] *Letters*, 1754, vol. i. p. 193.

the settlements, and as no further reference to Miss Graham occurs in the *Journal*, it is to be presumed that the engagement was broken off.

Having exhausted the sober gaieties of Edinburgh, and desirous of raising money for his intended marriage, in April 1745 Elcho started on his final journey to London. The necessary money was not forthcoming, but he remained in London till June. His life there was a repetition of the previous year—Ranelagh, Vauxhall, the theatre, tavern dinners with his countrymen from the north, Lords Lauderdale, Home, Traquair, Cranston, Balcarres, and the 'Chevaliers Douglas and de Stuart,' members of Parliament, and both avowedly attached to the Jacobite cause. Often, too, he attended in the mornings at the House of Commons, which was then investigating the conduct of Admirals Mathews and Lestock in the Battle of Toulon; here he was introduced to Speaker Onslow by Mr. Stewart, Provost of Edinburgh, who was subsequently tried for his remissness in the defence of Edinburgh against Prince Charles.

In June, together with his brother, Mr. Charteris, he left London. Thus closed his last visit to the city; within twelve months he was

an exile, never to be pardoned, and never to
revisit his native country.

Meanwhile, between Charles in France and
Murray in Scotland communication had been
meagre and vague.   Charles was collecting his
energies for the venture, but the prospect held
no tinge of encouragement.   France was apathetic.
Louis xv., indeed, afforded a pension, but the
Stuart cause had ceased to be a factor in the
politics of Europe.   The events of 1744 had
proved its poverty of resource, and no real help
was to be expected from Versailles.   The English
Jacobites were inert.   Charles could only centre
dim hopes on the loyalty of Scotland.   His
advisers were quarrelling among themselves ;
accusations and counter-accusations were darken-
ing counsel.   On all sides confidence seemed to
be ebbing, and the calls on Charles's self-reliance
were constant and extreme.

He must have been imperfectly informed of
what was passing in Edinburgh.   The Memorial
of the Buck Club confided to Traquair was never
despatched.   It was the ultimatum of the Stuart
supporters, the document upon which the fate of
a kingdom might depend ; yet Traquair, having
arrived in London, was unable to procure a

messenger cheap enough for his penuriousness. Twenty-five pounds, the lowest offer, was not low enough for this indifferent nobleman, and, rather than expend more money, he kept the letter in his pocket. After four months he had the effrontery to return it to Murray.

In May, Charles, prompted rather by his rising ambition and growing impatience than by any reform in his circumstances, despatched Sir Hector Maclean to Edinburgh with information of his pending arrival in Scotland. Sir Hector's papers were not to be opened till he found himself in the presence of the Duke of Perth. The Duke was absent from Edinburgh. Murray begged Sir Hector to await the Duke's return in the country; but Sir Hector had boots and shoes to be tried on and refused to leave the town. The authorities were vigilant and suspicious, and before the dilatory Baronet could deliver his despatch, he was arrested and his papers confiscated. He had, however, delivered a verbal message, and when Elcho returned to Edinburgh it was known in the inner circle of the faithful that Charles was to be expected— but when or in what manner or with what support no man could tell. The Narrative, it

will be seen, mentions a further letter to
Charles sent off in charge of young Glengarry
on receipt of Lord Traquair's belated news.
This letter, Murray says in the *Memorials*,
was to restrain Charles from setting out, but
it also carried a plan of campaign, a map of
Scotland, and a suggestion for the seizure of
Edinburgh Castle, not forgetting a request that
Murray might be made aide-de-camp. Murray
was at least ready to exploit the inevitable. But
the messenger lingered until it was too late.
When Glengarry arrived in France, the fatal
step had been taken. Charles, with his little
band of followers, was on the high seas, bound
for Scotland. His adventures after leaving
France will be found summarised in the succeeding Narrative.

On August 2nd Elcho was in Edinburgh. On
that day a brother of Mr. Buchanan of Arnprior
brought him a letter from Murray. It stated
that Charles had landed on the coast of Lochaber.
Elcho at once sought an interview with Murray,
and implored him to persuade Charles to return,
unless he was accompanied by troops from
France. Quitting Murray, Elcho set out for
Wemyss Castle. Crossing from Leith to King-

horn, he found himself a fellow-passenger with the Lord President,[1] who was on his way to the north to prevent as far as he could the clans from joining Charles. He told Elcho that Charles had landed in Scotland, and spoke with compassion of the future and of the many honourable gentlemen doomed to ruin, for the rebellion would be but a flash in the pan, a flame kindled among straws, and would bring evil days for Scotland. He stated that Cope had sufficient troops with which to repress the rising. Did he know that in his young companion he was addressing a supporter of the Stuarts and a possible rebel? It is more than probable; but the covert warning was thrown away upon his hearer.

[1] Duncan Forbes of Culloden, 1685-1747.

IV

THE last weeks that Elcho ever spent at his home
were disturbed only by uncertainty and suspense
as to what was occurring in the north. The
long August days were passed in feverishly waiting for word of victory or defeat, for news which
would decide his fate, summon him to throw in
his lot with the rebels, or leave him to possess
his future in peace with its promise of bounty
and content.

Would Charles return to France? Would he
raise the clans, or would he be crushed at the
outset by the soldiers of Cope? Rumour was
busy through the land, and amid the conflict of
reports Elcho and his father were debating on
action. It is easy to reconstruct the arguments
they must have exchanged as they sat in that rude
hall, where portraits of ancestors faithful to the
Stuarts seemed to smile their approval, or as they
paced the terrace slanting seaward and waited
impatiently for the message. Such discussions
must have been held in many a score of homes

in Scotland at this time. From Durrisdeer it
will be remembered that the Master of Ballantrae
set forth with his dozen men—'the white cockade
in every hat'—only on the toss of a coin.
Chance as blind, and reason as precarious, must
have determined many who were not unreservedly
either for adventurous loyalty to the Stuarts or
passive obedience to the Sovereign. But, Jacobite
as he was, Elcho needed some assurance that it
was no will-o'-the-wisp for which he was to
hazard all.   Accordingly, when word came in
the early days of September that Charles had
arrived at Perth, a messenger was sent from
Wemyss to inquire of Murray to what point
the forces of Charles were furnished for war.
Murray's answer was decisive : the Prince's
followers already numbered six thousand.[1]   A
like number were expected immediately to join,
while with the army were the Spanish General
Macdonald and the French General O'Sullivan.
' It was with fictions such as these,' writes Elcho
many years later, ' that the Secretary Murray
deceived everybody into embarking on this enterprise.'   But at the moment no place was left for

[1] Charles's troops at this time comprised approximately two
thousand men.

hesitation, and on September 11th Elcho said
farewell to his father and, attended by a servant,[1]
rode away from the Castle to join the Prince.
Staying one night in Edinburgh, he left on the
12th for Preston Hall, a house belonging to the
Dowager Duchess of Gordon.   Here on the
following day he was present at the marriage of
his brother, Francis Charteris, with Lady Frances
Gordon, sister to the Duke.   He informed his
brother of the step he was about to take.   Francis
thought it no moment to make so desperate a
course himself, but gave Elcho leave to take
what money he could find in his bureau.   Elcho
had already in his possession one thousand
guineas ; this additional sum, therefore, amounting to fifteen hundred guineas, which was to
give rise to so much dispute between him and
Charles in after years, made him a wealthy recruit
for the cause.

On the night of September 16th he joined the
army at Gray's Mill, in the neighbourhood of
Edinburgh.   The Prince was quartered in a small
room of the miller's house, and here he had his
first interview with Charles since the disaster of

---

[1] Tiddeman, who remained with him throughout the campaign
and accompanied him to France.

Dunkirk. They were nearly matched in age ;
they had been familiar friends in Rome ; Elcho
had already given active evidence of his loyalty
in 1744. Charles received him cordially, appointed him first aide-de-camp, and held a long
conversation with him. Nothing that Elcho has
to narrate is more surprising than what passed at
this interview. Hardly were they seated when
Charles began to speak of Lord George Murray.[1]
He told Elcho that he knew Lord George had
joined him only to betray him, and he warned
Elcho to be on his guard, and never to talk of
his (Charles's) affairs in Lord George's presence.
Elcho attributes this violent suspicion entirely to
Secretary Murray's influence ; he holds that in
Lord George the Secretary saw a rival too over-
shadowing and powerful, and that it therefore
became his policy to undermine Lord George
in the Prince's esteem. In this view he is
amply corroborated by Maxwell.[2] Unfortunately
Murray had weapons wherewith to play upon
Charles's credulity. Lord George had shortly
before this date been appointed Sheriff-
depute for Perthshire. He had been in com-

---

[1] Lord George had joined the army at Perth about September 7th.
[2] Maxwell's *Narrative*, p. 56.

munication with Cope, and his son was fighting
for King George. These facts were sufficient.
They gave Secretary Murray his opportunity, and
the distrust which marred the relations of Charles
and Lord George is one of the evils to be placed
to his dark account.

Charles and Elcho talked far into the night;
their meeting was interrupted only by the advent
of a deputation from the municipal authority of
Edinburgh, petitioning for delay pending terms
of surrender. Then occurred an incident not
recorded in the *Journal*, but noticed by Mr.
Lang, and detailed in the trial of the Lord
Provost Stewart, which strangely confirms the
statement as to the suspicion which had been
planted in Charles's mind.

It appears that one John Coutts, late Lord
Provost of Edinburgh, was one of the deputies.
He states that they met Lord George Murray,
who interviewed Charles, proffered their request,
and was refused; that they prevailed upon
Lord George to try again, and that then 'the
deponent (Coutts) could hear the Prince say
" My Lord Elcho, Lord George has not spirit to
put this order (the dismissal of the deputation)
in execution : you must go and do it for him."

Upon which the late Lord Elcho came out of
the room from the Pretender's Son, and bid the
deponent and the rest of the Deputies to get
them gone. That the said Lord George Murray
followed the Deputies out, and whispered to the
Deponent, " I know your pinch ; you want to
have the consent of your principal inhabitants.
Make haste to town : you'll have an hour or two
to obtain it." [1]

This evidence, given on oath, has the appearance of truth ; only part of it would have come
within Elcho's immediate observation, and that
part he may well have forgotten, or thought it
not worth while to mention.

Coutts and his party dismissed, and on their
road back to Edinburgh in their hackney coach,
Charles and Elcho were once more alone. Charles
thereupon confided to his companion that he was
in the greatest distress for want of money,
according to the Narrative that his funds
were reduced to fifty guineas, and added, with
prophetic insight, that he stood in dire need of
fifteen hundred guineas. Elcho made a ready
response by producing his purse and counting
out the required sum. Almost before their

[1] Trial of Archibald Stewart for neglect of Duty, p. 171.

interview was ended, in the 'sleepy grey of dawn,' Lochiel and five hundred men had taken possession of the city. The same day (September 17th) at noon, Charles made his entry into Edinburgh. On his left rode Elcho, on his right the Duke of Perth. In describing the scene, of which he was a witness, Henderson notes that as the procession passed through the King's Park, and drew near to the Palace of Holyrood, 'Charles seemed very thoughtful, notwithstanding his endeavours to disguise ; was very attentive to those about him, and so observing of Lord Elcho, that for above five minutes he fixed his left eye sideways upon him.'[1] The enthusiasm that greeted them, the huzzas of the mob, the cries for the House of Stuart, the entry into Holyrood, that moment so dramatic in its triumph and so fatal in its sequel, these are spoken of in the Narrative. Maxwell says, 'The joy seemed universal. "God save the King" was echoed back from all quarters of the town.' But making 'holiday to see Cæsar, and to rejoice in his triumph,' was one thing, unsheathing the sword another, and howsoever

[1] Andrew Henderson, *History of the Rebellion*, 1745-1746, fifth edition, p. 50.

ready the mob were to shout for King James, but a slender handful of the citizens were found to fight for Prince Charles. Edinburgh indeed played an inglorious part in '45. She breathed forth fire and slaughter, and when the enemy were at her gates she acclaimed them with re-joicing. She was neither Jacobite nor Hano-verian; she strove to get the best out of both worlds, and throughout the fluctuating fortunes of the campaign maintained an attitude of mathematical neutrality.

> 'What conquest brings he home?
> What tributaries follow him to Rome,
> To grace in captive bonds his chariot-wheels?'

might have been the inquiry addressed by the inhabitants to successive commanders as they swept through the streets of the capital.

The halt in Edinburgh was brief. Cope, having avoided battle in the north, had taken ship at Aberdeen and brought his forces round to Dunbar, disembarking them on the 17th September. News came to Edinburgh that Cope was advancing through the county of Hadding-ton. Charles at once determined to march and encounter the enemy. At the battle of Preston-pans which followed Elcho was mounted, but

whether acting as aide-de-camp to Charles, or
attached to the small body of forty cavalry commanded by Lord Strathallan, there is no mention
in contemporary accounts. But that he played
his part, whatever it may have been, with distinction, is attested by the fact that Charles
conferred upon him, on the field of battle, a
commission as colonel of his own Horse Guards.
In the autobiography of Dr. Alexander Carlyle we
get a lurid and theatrical glimpse of Elcho at the
close of the fight. Like Priam from the Scaean
Towers, the Doctor had been watching the tide
of battle from a coign of vantage in Prestonpans.
In the street of the village he was accosted
by Elcho. 'By and by,' he writes, 'a Highland
officer, whom I knew to be Lord Elcho, passed
with his train, and had an air of savage ferocity
that disgusted and alarmed. He inquired fiercely
of me where a public house was to be found : I
answered him very meekly, not doubting but
that, if I had displeased him with my tone, his
reply would have been with a pistol bullet.' But
Carlyle was new to war. His fancy and his fears
were inflamed by the spectacle he had witnessed,
and the youth of twenty-four, with the smoke of
battle still about him, asking for the nearest

public-house, may readily have figured to the worthy doctor as the living presentment of a swashbuckler menacing to all and sundry.

Elcho admits that Charles acted with courage and address at the head of the second line in the battle, and was afterwards humane and considerate in victory ; yet he entertained but a low opinion of him when it came to playing the rôle of a statesman, as sufficiently appears in the Narrative.

On the return of the victorious army to Edinburgh a further mark of confidence was bestowed upon Elcho, and he was appointed to the council which met every day in the Prince's chamber at Holyrood, and also made president of a committee for providing the army with forage. The Narrative, it will be found, gives an unusually full description of the life in Edinburgh ; and though the writer was familiar with the courts and festivities of foreign capitals, he states that the Prince lived with great splendour and magnificence. Waverley, we know, was 'dazzled at the liveliness and elegance' of the scene in the long-deserted halls of the Scottish palace. But contemporary records of what occurred are slender and untrustworthy. Carlyle and Henderson

deny that there was either gaiety or magnificence,
so much did Whig prejudice grudge even this
little day of rejoicing and success. Tradition relates
that Lady Wemyss, who was at this time living
separated from her husband in Edinburgh, gave
a ball which was attended by the Prince, who
with his hostess is said to have led the
minuet.

While the Highland army lay encamped at
Duddingston, and Charles, now master for the
moment of Scotland, was waiting at Holyrood
for reinforcements and the development of events,
Elcho was engaged in raising a troop of gentlemen over whom he could exercise the authority
of his commission. He obtained some seventy
recruits, for whom he appointed as uniform a
blue coat with a red vest and red cuffs. Murray [1]
says of them that ' they were all gentlemen of
familly and fortune, & tho they did not amount
to above a hundred yett I may say there never
was a troop of better men in any service, their
uniform blew and reed & all extreamly well
mounted.' Murray himself was made colonel
of a troop of hussars, ' most of them young men
dressed in close Plaid-Waistcoats and large Fur

[1] *Memorials,* p. 226.

Caps.'[1]   Other commanders of horse were Kilmarnock, Balmerino, and Pitsligo.   Maxwell of Kirkconnel acted as major of Elcho's troop, and in the ranks was Hamilton of Bangour, the Jacobite poet.

Before setting out for England, the Prince invited Elcho to go on a diplomatic mission to Paris to represent his interest at the Court of France.   But the arts of peace offered little enticement to a youth who had so recently assumed his command, and who seemed destined for so much distinction in the adventurous campaign about to commence, and he unhesitatingly declined.   The task was therefore confided to Sir James Steuart, to whom the Prince gave a thousand louis d'or for his expenses.

On October 31st the army in two divisions commenced their march into England.   Nothing in the campaign was more adroit and effective than the work done by the mounted portion of the force.   For the most part without experience of warfare, acting for the first time in concert and traversing an unknown country, the cavalry never failed to bring timely information of the whereabouts of the enemy, nor, when occasion

[1] James Ray, *A Compleat History of the Rebellion*, p. 119.

required, to act as an efficient screen to the manœuvres of the Highland army. Of personal exploit and individual experience, Elcho is becomingly reticent alike in the *Journal* and Narrative. But on the march into England it can be incidentally gathered that at the head of his squadron of Guards he was the first of the Prince's army to enter the towns which lay on the line of march.

The actual disposition of the troops in the advance to Derby was as follows. The first division, commanded by Lord George Murray, consisted of the low country regiments. At the head of this division marched Elcho with his Guards. The second division, also preceded by cavalry and commanded by the Prince, comprised the clan regiments ; while at the rear of the whole army marched the remainder of the horse.[1] Of the part played by individuals in the campaign, if we except those immediately surrounding the Prince, there is singularly little to be gleaned from the mass of literature relating to the period. It was only when authority had gripped rebellion by the throat, that we find in the staid pages of law reports and in the dying

[1] Maxwell of Kirkconnel, p. 81.

speeches uttered on the scaffold records which are in any sense intimate and personal. Thus at the trial of David Morgan of Monmouth for high treason we catch a glimpse of Elcho on a November night in Preston. One Tew, giving evidence for the Crown, stated that he lived in Preston next door to the Joiners' Arms, and that on the evening of the day on which the troops entered the town he assisted his neighbour to wait at dinner on some officers belonging to the Highland army. Morgan and Lord Elcho dined together. Asked by the Solicitor-General if he remembered 'any discourse that passed,' Tew deposed that he heard the prisoner ask Lord Elcho what religion the Pretender professed. 'My Lord Elcho shook his head, and said he could not very well tell ; but he believed his religion was to seek.'[1] Whether he was hoodwinking a Lord Justice-Clerk, or fencing with a Lord President, or gaining a recruit during the campaign, Elcho could certainly show an admirable discretion.

The entry into Preston must have been an episode of sunshine on that astonishing march. Here, in contrast to the cloudy disfavour manifest at other points, there were caps in the air and

[1] *A Complete Collection of State Trials*, vol. xviii. p. 371.

huzzas for Prince Charles as the Life Guards gaily clattered through the town ; and it was here that Mr. Townley, Mr. Vaughan, Mr. Morgan, and a few others were enlisted as adherents. Later, when the retreat from Derby had begun, this same Morgan rode up to Mr. Vaughan and said : ' Damn me, Vaughan, they are going to Scotland.' Mr. Vaughan replied : ' Wherever they go, I am determined, now I have joined them, to go along with them.' Upon which Mr. Morgan, who must have shared the prevailing Anglican view of Scotland, said : ' By God, I had rather be hanged than go to Scotland, to starve.' The unfortunate Morgan's preference was realised, for he was subsequently convicted, and executed on July 30, 1746.

At Derby Elcho was one of the almost unanimous council who voted against a further advance towards London. And with two hostile armies well-nigh within striking distance, with a third army forming between Prince Charles and the capital,[1] with the whole country population alienated and menacing, and scarce a man to be recruited or a proffer of aid to be come by, the argument for retiring on Scotland and there

[1] The three armies formed a total of some 30,000 men.

uniting with the forces landed from France [1] and those which were holding the country for Prince Charles, was overwhelming. Yet the chances of war are still weighed in the balance, and the possibilities of a successful march upon London still considered open to discussion.[2] For Charles it was the crowning anguish : thenceforward he must have known that the throne of Britain was not for him. Ultimate defeat might be delayed, but in the sullen defiance of the populace lay the answer to those vain ideas of prerogative, of facile conquest, and of general loyalty to his cause with which his mind had been nourished from his earliest years.

At no time was the gallant spirit of the Highland army displayed to greater advantage than on the return to Scotland. Daily confronted with the disheartening spectacle of retreat, marching through a hostile country in midwinter, and opposed to an enemy from whom no mercy was to be expected, they effected an orderly retire-

---

[1] In the Narrative Elcho says that news of the landing of Lord J. Drummond with French troops reached them at Derby.

[2] 'During the whole time of their being in England they received no application or message from any persons in England, which surprised and disappointed them extremely.'— State Papers, Domestic, George II., Examination of John Murray, August 13, 1746.

ment and crossed the Border with a total loss of
less than 100 men. Their conduct, it is true,
was less exemplary than on the occasion of the
advance; but during the retreat the inhabitants
were closing in on them like an angry tide, and
if excesses were committed, there was provocation
enough in the brutal treatment meted out to
stragglers and to the wounded and sick.

To Elcho with his cavalry was again allotted
the task of reconnoitring in advance of the army.
On crossing the Border he was despatched to
Dumfries with orders to disarm that town and
tax it to the amount of £2000 and 1000 pair of
shoes. The militia, numbering some 700 men,
retreated on his approach, and he finally succeeded
in levying the greater portion of the tax. A few
weeks later he had a narrow escape from being
captured during the operations connected with
the siege of Stirling. He was in charge of a
battery of cannon near the river Forth, designed
to protect the passage of guns and munitions for
the investment of the town. One night the
enemy slipped unobserved past the battery in
boats, and having landed, surrounded and searched
the house in which Elcho lodged; but he had
gone to the battery a few moments before the

search-party arrived, and thus escaped capture
and certain death.   Before the action of Falkirk
Elcho and his cavalry rendered valuable service,
but in the battle itself, stationed in rear of the
right of the Highland line, they were not called
on to act.   Nor do we hear of their playing a
prominent part until the eve of Culloden.

On April 14th Elcho had supper with Charles
at Culloden.   The Prince was in a sanguine and
exalted frame of mind, and said that he had no
doubts as to the issue of the approaching conflict
with the Duke of Cumberland ; he believed that
the English soldiers would with difficulty be got to
attack him.   He refused to listen to any suggestion of retreating and awaiting reinforcements,
and when a rendezvous in the event of defeat
was spoken of, he replied that only those who
were afraid could doubt his coming victory.[1]   ' In
short,' says Elcho, ' he indulged that evening in
boastings unworthy of a prince.   As he had consulted only his favourites, everything was in the
greatest disorder.   The persons capable of serving him were suspected or neglected, and those in

---

[1] O'Neil in his Journal says that the Prince, previous to the
battle, ordered the chieftains in case of defeat to assemble near Fort
Augustus.—*Lyon in Mourning*, vol. i. p. 103.

whom he had placed his trust had not the ability
to be useful to him.' About ten o'clock on the
morning of April 15th Elcho was despatched with
a body of cavalry to reconnoitre the forces of
Cumberland, then stationed at Nairn, about eight
miles from the army of the Prince. He remained
for three hours in a position whence he could
observe what was taking place, and failing to
detect any signs of movement in the camp, he
returned and reported accordingly. Thereupon
was held the council at which it was agreed, upon
the proposal of Lord George Murray, to march at
nightfall and attack Cumberland's position. How
the march miscarried, and how the column found
itself at the approach of dawn in baffled confusion,
is detailed in the Narrative. The *Journal* says
that when the Prince in the early twilight recognised that Lord George, who was in command
of the leading column, was falling back, he at
once believed himself to be betrayed, and it was
later the same morning that he gave instructions
to two Irish officers to watch Lord George, and,
if they perceived any treasonable design on his
part, to assassinate him. Elcho says that this
was told him by one of the Irish officers, 'a
very honourable man in other respects, but one

that believed that the Prince's charge against
Lord George was true.' Elcho alone is responsible for this story. On the other hand, there
is not wanting evidence to show that Charles
believed that he was betrayed.[1] From such a
belief to the order referred to by Elcho was no
great step. The Prince's suspicions, moreover,
had recently received a fresh impetus. Two
charges had been trumped up by the enemies of
Lord George. They had represented to Charles
that his commander had deliberately neglected an
opportunity of capturing Blair Castle when held
by the enemy, and they had asserted that a letter[2]
sent to the Prince of Hesse by Lord George was
of a character treasonable to the cause.

At the battle of Culloden, aided by Fitzjames's
horse and Avuchies' battalion, Elcho successfully
repelled an attempt to envelop the right wing of
the Prince's army. When the left flank of the
Highlanders had been finally driven back and
the day was lost, Elcho quitted the field of battle
with Lord Balmerino. Balmerino said he intended to surrender, though he well knew the

[1] Hay of Restalrig, v. Home's *History of the Rebellion*, App. No. 43,
p. 371 ; Chevalier Johnstone, pp. 104, 105; Maxwell of Kirkconnel,
p. 140 ; *Lyon in Mourning*, vol. ii. p. 276.

[2] See Appendices A and B.

fate which awaited him. He was too old to survive the disgrace which had fallen upon him, whether he remained in hiding in Scotland or sought refuge in France. Death had no terror for him ; he knew he could meet it with forti-tude. It was in vain that Elcho endeavoured to dissuade him. The following day he surrendered, and to the hour of his death on Tower Hill (Aug. 5, 1746) Balmerino bore himself with dauntless and unaffected courage. It is indeed the existence of such a spirit among the followers of the Prince that has raised his venture to the realm of enduring romance.

Charles himself, so soon as the left wing of his army had been forced back, retired with some cavalry of the piquet of Fitzjames. No question connected with the campaign has been so much debated, and none has been left so in-completely answered, as that which concerns the conduct of Charles on this occasion. The origin of much of the discussion is to be found in an anecdote recorded by Sir Walter Scott. Writing in his *Journal* on February 10, 1826, he makes the following entry :—

'After the left wing of the Highlanders was repulsed and broken at Culloden, Elcho rode up

to the Chevalier and told him all was lost, and
that nothing remained except to charge at the
head of two thousand men, who were still un-
broken, and either turn the fate of the day or die
sword in hand, as became his pretensions. The
Chevalier gave him some evasive answer, and,
turning his horse's head, rode off the field. Lord
Elcho called after him (I write the very words),
"There you go for a damned, cowardly Italian,"
and never would see him again, though he lost
his property and remained an exile in the cause.'

That no word of this appears in Elcho's Narrative does not by itself negative the truth of the
story. It is abundantly clear that the writer
intended his Narrative as a sober and considered
contribution to the history of the time. He has
avoided the mention of any exploit or event
personal to himself, and in such a category would
undoubtedly fall the occurrence narrated by Scott.
But in the *Journal* he has exercised no such
restraint, and here we find the germ of the anecdote—a germ which hearsay and tradition, ever
mindful of the picturesque, would readily develop
into the story we are dealing with. His description of what took place is as follows :—

'The Prince, so soon as he saw the left of his

army yielding and in retreat, lost his head, fled
with the utmost speed, and without even trying to
rally any of his scattered host. . . . The Prince
made a halt 4 miles from the field of battle, and
I found him in a deplorable state. As he had
ever been flattered with false hopes that the
army of the Duke would fly before him like
those of Cope and Hawley, he believed that all
his disaster was caused by treason, and appeared
to be afraid of the Scotch as a whole, thinking
that they would be capable of giving him up to
the Duke to obtain peace, and the 30,000£
sterling that the King had offered for his
head. . . . He appeared to be concerned only
about the lot of the Irish and not at all about
that of the Scots, and seeing the number of
Scotch officers around him increase, he ordered
them to go away to a village a mile's distance
from where he was, and he would send his orders
thither. I remained after their departure and
asked if he had any orders for me. He told me
that I might go anywhere I liked; as for himself,
he was about to leave for France. I told him
that I was surprised at a resolution so little
worthy a Prince of his birth, that it was unworthy
to have engaged all this people to sacrifice itself

for him, and to abandon it because he had possibly lost a thousand men in battle ; that he ought
to remain and put himself at the head of the 9000
men that remained to him, and live and die with
them. . . . But all these reasons made no impression upon him. He told me that he was
determined to seek safety in France : whereupon
I left him, thoroughly resolved never to have any
more to do with him.' Here surely is foundation
enough for Scott's anecdote. It is not within the
scope of this memoir to array the authorities who
may be quoted as being for or against the general
truth of the suggestions contained in the above-
cited passage. No independent witness was
present when the conversation so circumstantially
and so convincingly described by Elcho took
place, and if his account is to be discredited, one
may well despair of coming at the truth. Scott
believed the story when he heard it ; this is
evidence at least of the temper of a time some
eighty years after the event ; it is evidence also
of the direction in which the credulity and the
best opinion of the day were then trending.
Further, it can be shown that Scott adhered to
his belief in some such story. The entry in his
Journal, as we have seen, was dated February

10, 1826. In the year 1830 he published *The Tales of a Grandfather*.[1] Now the *Tales* were largely based on Lord Elcho's Narrative, in which, as already pointed out, there is no mention of what we have been discussing. It might have been expected that Scott, finding no further confirmation of the story, would have discarded it when writing his history ; but far from doing this, he merely modifies it as follows : ' Lord Elcho rode up to the Prince and eagerly exhorted him to put himself at the head of those troops who yet remained, make a last exertion to recover the day, and at least die like one worthy of having contended for a Crown. Receiving a doubtful or hesitating answer, Lord Elcho turned from him with a bitter execration, and declared he would never see his face again.'[2]

After parting from Charles, Elcho, accompanied by his servant, who had attended him throughout the campaign, and by Maxwell of Kirkconnel, continued his flight westward. Passing by Fort

---

[1] 3rd series.

[2] Mr. Blaikie has called my attention to an Italian book which confirms Elcho's story. The book, written in 1751, was no doubt largely founded on the narratives of refugees who succeeded in escaping to Italy. In Appendix C will be found the writer's version of the altercation between Charles and Elcho.—*La Spedizione di Carlo Odoardo Stuart Dal Gesuita Giulio Cordara.*

Augustus and Loch Arkaig, the fugitives eventually arrived at Kinlochmoidart, the house of
Macdonald.

Cumberland meanwhile remained in the vicinity
of Culloden, busy with fire and sword, and the
brutalities of a pitiless revenge. Charles himself,
with O'Sullivan, Allan Macdonald, and Edward
Burke, pursuing almost the same route as Elcho and
his companions, finally reached Borrodale, a village
on the shore of Loch-na-Nuagh, where on April
26th he embarked for the islands. The rebellion
was at an end ; with the smoke that arose from
the battlefield of ' pale red ' Culloden had vanished
the last hope of the Stuart cause. Before Charles,
now a hunted fugitive, there lay months of
wandering, hiding, and bitter privation. But in
the extreme decline of his fortunes he was to
show the qualities which, far more than any
moment of triumph or success, have made him
a figure of romance in the traditions of Scotland.
The ' bright face of danger,' the storm and sunshine on the mountain, the sheltering loyalty of
those he was at last driven to trust—these roused
in him a courage and excelling constancy ; and it
is to the period of his wanderings that sentiment
reverts when contemplating the stricken years

which followed. 'What has your family done, Sir, thus to draw down the vengeance of Heaven on every branch of it through so many ages?'[1] That poignant question, addressed to Charles in exile, recurs inevitably to the mind when considering the vicissitudes of his career. At one time the central figure of the armaments pledged by France to secure the Stuart restoration—then a mere suppliant soliciting aid from the Court of Versailles—later, in defiance of probability, master of Scotland, acclaimed at Holyrood, marching at the head of an undefeated force into the heart of England ; at Derby, debating the time and the mode of his entry into London ; then the sudden retreat, the gleam of victory at Falkirk, followed by the waning of hope and the last day of tragedy at Culloden.

Elcho's own estimate of the Prince is singularly unfavourable. That Charles had uncommon powers of endurance and 'a body made for war,' and that at Prestonpans he showed courage and humanity, exhausts all that Elcho has to say in his favour. On the other hand his comments

---

[1] King, *Anecdotes*, 2nd ed., p. 207, quoted by Lord Rosebery in his admirable review of the rebellion written as an Introduction to *A List of Persons concerned in the Rebellion*, Scottish History Society.

show that Charles was unfitted to govern or command, was obstinate where he should have been pliant, suspicious where he should have trusted, and he continues to maintain that Charles displayed neither gratitude for the sacrifices, nor sorrow for the sufferings of his followers. Such failings as these had been aggravated by his education, which had served to narrow his sympathies and restrict his outlook. Taught to regard despotism, not necessarily of the enlightened class, as the form of government best adapted to the kingdom of his predecessors, and passive obedience as the natural duty of the people he believed himself destined to rule, he had formed arrogant expectations of what awaited him in England. Thwarted in these hopes, he conceived himself betrayed ; he withdrew his confidence from those upon whose support he had depended, and he secluded himself within a circle of subservient and incompetent advisers. Furthermore, according to Elcho, the failing which disfigured his years of exile had already begun to manifest itself during the march to Derby. 'The Prince,' he writes, ' had marched from Edinburgh to Derby on foot, dressed as a Highlander, at the head of his infantry. He was very strong, supped liberally,

was often drunk, would throw himself on a couch
at eleven o'clock at night without undressing, and
was up again at three o'clock in the morning.'
It has been generally believed that this 'fondness
for wine,' though observable when he was a youth
in Italy, did not develop till after the campaign.
But if Charles showed sympathy with the habit
of the time, if he occasionally availed himself of
the congenial company of the quartermaster of his
army, Sullivan, who would sit at night over his
'favourite mountain malaga' instead of issuing
the order of the next day's march,[1] it is still
possible to accept the prevailing belief without
discrediting the allegation of Elcho. But the
gravest accusation to be brought against Charles
is that which relates to the letter written to his
principal followers after Culloden.

Elcho himself received one of these letters,
which named a rendezvous for the scattered
Highland army. According to Æneas Macdonald,
who had been to visit Charles on April 20th
at Glenbeasdale, the design was to create an objective for Cumberland's pursuit, and thereby
facilitate the escape of Charles. This view Elcho
accepts.

[1] *Jacobite Memoirs*, p. 61.

While in concealment at Kinlochmoidart, news
came that search parties of 'red-coats' were pursuing the rebels westward. Elcho and Maxwell
were therefore forced to take to the mountain
and heather. On the morning of April 28th,
when spying through their telescopes, they saw
two ships of war approaching the Bay of Loch-
na-Nuagh. Slowly the vessels bore up to their
anchorage. For the fugitives it was a period of
anxiety and suspense. No flag indicated the
nationality of the ships, and it was only when
communication had been established with the
shore, and the crews could be seen fraternising
with the Highlanders, that the watchers could
determine that they were French. Then with all
speed they struck across the hills to Borrodale, off
which the vessels were riding to anchor. Here
they found many survivors of Culloden: the
Duke of Perth, Lord John Drummond, Secretary
Murray, Hay of Restalrig, Sheridan, Lockhart of
Carnwath, and some Highland officers. All, says
Elcho, were loud in their condemnation of Charles,
who it was now known had abandoned his followers
and sought an invidious safety. The vessels
proved to be the *Bellona*, 34 guns, and the *Mars*,
32 guns, despatched by Louis to the assistance of

Charles with arms and 36,000 louis d'or. It was
another illustration of the dilatory and undecided
policy of Louis. Throughout the autumn and
winter of '45 divided counsels had prevailed in
the French Ministry. Tencin and D'Argenson
had favoured, Noailles had opposed, active inter-
vention.[1] In October, however, it had been
decided to despatch to the shores of England an
expedition commanded by the Duc de Richelieu
and accompanied by Henry, Duke of York.
Troops and stores were assembled at Dunkirk,
but, as in the case of the ill-fated scheme of 1744,
when it became known that a British fleet had
been formed for the defence of the Channel, the
idea of invasion was abandoned.[2] 'France,' writes
Elcho in his *Journal*, 'will never risk sending an
army to England without having a fleet at sea
superior to that of England, and,' he continues,
'in all cases where troops and boats have been
collected on the coast, this has been done with
the knowledge that these preparations alone would
suffice to restrain the English from sending their
troops out of the kingdom, and would compel
them to keep them at home for the defence of

[1] Luynes, *Mémoires*, vol. vii. p. 127.
[2] *Mémoires du Marquis D'Argenson*, vol. iv. p. 319.

the island, while all the time a squadron in the Channel would have been sufficient to prevent the French from thinking of such an expedition.' From the moment that the expedition was relinquished, the succour afforded by Louis was insufficient to affect the fortunes of the campaign. A force of 900 men under the command of Lord John Drummond, and occasional gifts of money, alone bore witness to the specious promises of France. No discouragement, however, deterred the Jacobite agents from pleading their cause and soliciting the fulfilment of the pledges which had been given by Louis and his ministers. In the *Mars* and *Bellona* with their treasure there came a tardy response to the appeals. But it is now clear that the Court of Versailles cared little for the House of Stuart. The rebellion embarrassed England and hampered the movement of British troops, therefore it was politic to keep the rebellion alive, but to its ultimate issue, to the fate of the throne, France was discreetly indifferent.

The money, stowed in six casks, was in charge of an Irishman, Brown, under orders to hand it over only on the sign-manual of Charles. Lord John Drummond and Elcho determined that

Charles or no Charles, the money should remain in Scotland. Brown, who had incautiously landed, was accordingly threatened with arrest unless he gave an order for the surrender of the casks. Fear prevailed, and the treasure was brought to shore.

Thus on this wild coast, fit scene for the business of buccaneers, there was added a master-touch of melodrama to the 'affair of '45.' Mr. Lang has depicted the deplorable circumstances which marked the subsequent history of the treasure.[1] Buried, dug up, transported by many hands to many places, it eventually 'set clan against clan and brother against brother,'[2] and became the familiar quarry of informers and spies. For Murray, says Elcho, the sight of this money, the proximity to so much wealth, proved too strong a temptation, and yielding to the 'opum furiosa cupido,' he decided to linger on in Scotland, to his utter undoing and the ruin of his fame.

Acting on instructions from the commander of

---

[1] The *Journal* states that Cameron received 6000 louis, Macdonald 6000, Kennedy 6000, Murray 3000, while the remainder was intrusted to Macpherson of Cluny. See, however, Andrew Lang, *Companions of Pickle*, p. 129, and Murray, *Memorials*, p. 273. Both authorities differ from Elcho.

[2] *Companions of Pickle*, p. 129.

the French vessels, the little band of refugees
assembled on the seashore at midnight, on May 2.
But their dangers were not yet at an end. The
first glimmer of dawn revealed three English
frigates, cleared for action, entering the Bay in
which the French ships were at anchor. In the
engagement which followed the issue was long in
doubt. To those on shore every chance and change
of the battle was clearly defined, and at times the
vessels would draw so near to land, that the eager
watchers could hear the cries of the wounded, the
shrill piping of the whistles, and the words of
command. But at midday victory declared itself for
the French, and the English were finally driven off.
The French had suffered severely, losing one
hundred killed ; but the same evening their ships
were sufficiently refitted to set sail for France
with the fugitives[1] on board.

So ended Elcho's share in the rebellion, and so
closed his last association with his country. The
drama which, for so many months, had agitated
the attention of Europe, and engrossed the military
power of England, had now run its fated course

---

[1] Sheridan and Hay on the *Bellona* ; Perth, Drummond, Maxwell,
Lockhart, and Elcho on the *Mars*. The gallant Perth died during
the voyage, and was buried at sea.

to irreparable disaster. No wonder if—contemplating in his own troubled mind the riotous
procession of events, the vain alarms, the scatter-
ing of disbanded energies—the greatest lyrical
poet of the age was fain to see at work mysterious,
and even supernatural agencies, and to attribute
the result to spirits of Gaelic malignity,

> ' that brew the stormful day
> And, heartless, oft like moody madness, stare
> To see the phantom train their secret work prepare.'[1]

---

[1] W. Collins, *Ode on the Popular Superstitions of the Highlands.*

V

On June 6th the *Mars* and *Bellona* arrived off
the mouth of the Loire : on June 10th Elcho was
once again in Paris. There he freely expressed
his contempt for Charles, and being now alienated
from his attachment to the House of Stuart, wrote
letters in July to Lord Lincoln, and to the Lord
Justice-Clerk, Lord Milton, asking for a pardon,
and that his name might be removed from the
Bill of Attainder.

The petition was unfavourably received. Horace
Walpole, in a letter to Mann (June 20, 1740)
says : ' Lord Elcho has written from Paris to Lord
Lincoln, to solicit his pardon : but as he has
distinguished himself beyond all the rebel commanders by brutality and insults, and cruelty to
our prisoners, I think he is likely to remain where
he is.' The charge of cruelty is reiterated in some
manuscript notes,[1] probably written by Alexander
Henderson, wherein it is alleged that Elcho proposed to cut off the right arm of every officer who

---

[1] In the possession of Mr. David Douglas.

was a prisoner. And again, in *A List of Persons concerned in the Rebellion, 1745-1746*, among the facts stated as 'engrossing the present conversation : May 1746,' is the threat made by Lord Elcho to hang Mr. Maitland, and 'his proposal to maim the officers' prisoners.' I have been unable to find any evidence to support the charge. Such accusations were lightly made. Walpole alleges it equally against Cromartie and Kilmarnock, and in his letters he transcribes every flying rumour. For instance, writing of Culloden,[1] he says : 'Lord Elcho was in a salivation, and not there.' Probably the story was one of those circulated in order to justify harsh measures and excesses. Elcho himself attributes it to Cumberland. But true or not, the story answered its purpose. Elcho was never pardoned. On the other hand, those who served with him had formed a very different judgment. Murray says :[2] 'I am persuaded he is as void of that fickleness of temper in matters of moment, of which he is accused by some of his party, as he is of the cruelty and brutality laid to his charge by the other. He has very good natural parts, and is far from deficient in acquired knowledge ; has a very quick, lively apprehension,

[1] April 25, 1746.   [2] *Memorials*, p. 122.

and not ready to be led away by any airy, superficial scheme.' And Johnstone, who was not given
to lavishing praise, says : 'He was a nobleman,
equally distinguished by his birth as by his rare
merits.'

In the month of October Charles arrived at
Roscoff in a French vessel named *L'Heureux*,[1] and
posted straight to Fontainebleau, where he was
received by Louis, entertained by the Ministers,
and supped with Madame de Pompadour.[2] Elcho
was averse from having further dealings with him,
but he was persuaded later by John Drummond,
then Duke of Perth, to call on the Prince in his
country house at Clichy. Charles refused to see
him. Elcho's plea for pardon had appeared in the
Gazette of Utrecht, his open comments on the
campaign had been repeated, there were threats
of the Bastille, and on December 7, 1746, with
Hunter of Burnside, he quitted Paris.

In 1749 was published *An Account of what
befel the Prince in France.* The description there
given of Charles's state entry into Versailles has
been often quoted.[3] Elcho is said to have been of

---

[1] Luynes, *Mémoires*, vol. vii. p. 460.

[2] *Ibid.*, p. 462.

[3] See Jesse, *The Pretenders*, ed. 1890, p. 348 ; Ewald, *Life of Prince
Charles Edward*, ed. 1904, p. 308 ; Lord Mahon, *The Forty-Five*,

the party with Glenbucket, Ogilvie, and Kelly :
the Young Chevalier is said 'to have glittered all
over like the star which they tell you appeared at
his Nativity' ; but he must have glittered unseen
by Elcho. Elcho was never in the company of
Charles after the day of Culloden.

Personal relations with the Stuarts were now
at an end. Henceforward in the Jacobite world
Elcho figures rather as a suitor for services
rendered than as a volunteer for further adventure. The divine right of kings yields in his
imagination to the ordinary right of a citizen
to obtain repayment of his debts. We shall
see him not, indeed, altogether as Mr. Lang
depicts him—'an infuriated and persistent dun'
—but from time to time urging his claim for
the restitution of the 1500 guineas advanced to
Charles in '45, and repeatedly soliciting a commission in the French service. For the moment,
however, his only anxiety was to be quit of
Charles. Elcho was too impetuous to remain
the pottering adherent of a lost cause, and for
the squabbles and intrigues which boiled and

p. 121; Lang, *Prince Charles Edward*, p. 325; Pichot, *Histoire de
Charles Edouard*, ed. 1833, vol. ii. p. 352. It should also be noted that
the Court was at Fontainebleau and not at Versailles during November. See Luynes, *Mémoires*, vol. vii. p. 460 *et seq.*

bubbled in the Jacobite ranks he had neither sympathy nor aptitude. Disgust, too, at the accusations which he says Charles was flinging against Lord George Murray for betraying him, and against Æneas Macdonald for aiding the Duke of Argyll to discover his places of retreat, was driving him further from the Jacobite fold.

In the *Journal*, in order to justify his apostasy, he dwells on every fault which resentment can discover in his former chief. Thus we find him indignantly recording that on the day on which the French *Gazette* announced that many of those concerned in the rebellion had perished on the scaffold, Charles visited the Opera. Nor does the favouritism shown to the Irish, nor the ingratitude shown to the Scots, escape his angry censure. It is indeed a respite from weariness to follow him in his travels once more to Italy, the country to which his affections seem always to have turned. Leaving Paris on December 7th, the travellers alighted at the Écu de France, on the Grand Canal, on December 26th. In Venice they found Earl Marischal. A friendship at once began between the young outlaw and the 'sagacious veteran,' which every year was to become more intimate.

To earn the friendship of Earl Marischal was a sign-manual of sound qualities. For forty years he stood for integrity, and, what was even rarer among the partisans of the Stuarts, common sense. He had fought for them in 1715 and 1719. He had been the hope of every plan subsequently contrived. In 1744, as we have seen, he was appointed to command the forces to be sent to Scotland. In '45 he had spent the winter vainly urging forward the succours of France, none recognising so clearly as he the futility of an unaided attempt. At this time he had withdrawn from active counsels, but for many years his advice was to be sought and his authority invoked by the Jacobites. Rousseau described him as republican in sentiment; and it is probable that, like Lord Pitsligo, he looked on a change of dynasty as a means of repealing the Union and regaining the former liberties of Scotland.

He was no enthusiast for the Stuarts. He regarded Charles with disfavour, and in his correspondence with him never scrupled to use plain words and wholesome admonition. He mistrusted Sempil, and despised the mediocrity by which Charles was surrounded, and he had 'suckt in such Notions of liberty and inde-

pendence, and of ye meaness of Servile submission and flattery,'[1] that the service of
Frederick II., in which he was shortly to be
enrolled, made a more congruous world for his
honesty than the vapid formalities of an exiled
Court.

From the whirl of intrigue, treachery, and
recrimination which followed in the wake of
the rebellion Earl Marischal stands forth serene,
humorous, and admirable in his wisdom. A
courtier of 'his good friend the Sun,'[2] a ' Knight
Errant sin' Amor,'[3] in his long exile he consoled
himself with the discourse of companions and
the study of books ; and if his thoughts reverted to his home, to the scenes of his youth,
to 'the hoarse sea winds and caverns of
Dunottar,' it was without bitterness or an
utterance of regret. 'A man of sense and
honour is always at home everywhere,' he said.
Driven from Paris by threats of the Bastille for
impugning the sincerity of France in her intentions towards Charles, forbidden by the Empress
Elizabeth to remain in Russia by reason of the

[1] Earl Marischal to Hamilton (1737), *Hist. MSS. Commission,*
x. i. 473.
[2] *Memoir of Marshal Keith* (Spalding Club), p. xi.
[3] Earl Marischal to Hamilton, *Hist. MSS. Commission,* x. i. 473.

urgent requests of the English Ambassador, he had
settled, a true citizen of all countries, contentedly
in Venice, dividing his time between the city and
Treviso, where he had purchased an estate.

So soon as the arrival of the fugitives was
known, the British Resident (Sir James Gray)[1]
requested the Republic to expel them from its
borders, citing as precedent the compliance of
Elizabeth ; but the Government, with a haughtiness worthy of its greater days, replied that
the hospitality of the State was open to all who
did not meditate evil against its security.   Gray
then endeavoured to deter the English inhabitants from consorting with the 'rebels,' and
partially succeeded.   But they were well received
by the Venetians, among whom their political
disabilities were ignored.

Venice was at the height of the Carnival.   The
Ridotto, as was usual during the continuance of
the festival, was opening its doors to all who
wished to try their fortune at the 'tables.'   It
was natural that those who had been gambling
for a throne, staking their lives and losing their
estates, should be allured across the threshold.
Elcho enjoyed a dazzling hour, during which his

[1] See Appendix D.

slender capital rose, fell, rose again, and finally
dwindled to a sequin. A last fortunate effort
converted the one sequin into six hundred. But
when Earl Marischal heard of the proceeding he
obliged Elcho to surrender his purse, and during
the remainder of the Carnival he doled out the
bare sufficiency for the needs of the day. He
had known the seamy side of exile himself, and
was determined to save his young companion
from the risk of a self-incurred poverty.

But another experience of a more romantic
kind was to give Earl Marischal further opportunity for exercising his wise and kindly guardian-
ship. The attention of Elcho had been arrested
and his curiosity excited by the beauty of a young
Venetian lady, the daughter of a patrician, whose
palace was not far from the residence of the Earl.
In the early eighteenth century the prosecution
of a romance was a dangerous pursuit. There
were daggers and dark canals and methods
sudden and mysterious for dealing with undesirable
suitors. Like Haidée, Mademoiselle Canale, for
that was the lady's name, had a father, and

'violent things will sooner bear assuaging
.   .   .   .   .
Than the stern, single, deep and wordless ire
Of a strong human heart, and in a sire.'

It was necessary to act with caution. During the absence of the Earl at Treviso, Elcho hit upon the stratagem of disguising the German maid, who was a member of his host's household, as the wife of a patrician, and sending her to call on Mademoiselle Canale, in the hope that the visit would be returned. Whether the disguise defied detection or whether Mademoiselle Canale was willingly blind, Elcho does not say. But the ruse was successful and the visit duly returned at Earl Marischal's house. In the meanwhile, another servant, less compliant than Elcho's accomplice, despatched to Treviso information of the intrigue which was in progress. The Earl posted back hot speed, held an inquiry, dismissed the German maid, which was scant justice, but forebore with something more than paternal delicacy from referring to the subject with Elcho. The reproof seems to have made a deep and lasting impression on the young adventurer, while his solicitude for youth throws a pleasing light on Earl Marischal.

The Continent at this time was every day seeing the arrival of fresh fugitives from Scotland. One evening, in the pit of the theatre of St. John Chrysostom, among the motley and eager audience gathered to watch a Commedia dell' Arte, a masked figure turned and addressed Elcho by name. In a moment he realised that there stood before him the soldier who had fought for James by the side of Earl Marischal in the Fifteen and at Glenshiel, the commander of Charles's army to whom he had last spoken on the fatal morning of Culloden. Little is known of Lord George Murray's escape, and there is nothing to be gathered from the *Journal*. He had paused in Venice on his way to see the Chevalier at Rome, and after a few days spent with his friends he set out for the goal of his journey. In Rome James received him with the distinction to which his services had entitled him. But Charles in Paris was still nursing his dark hatred and suspicion. From there he wrote to his father a letter which must for ever remain a blot upon his name. Speaking of Lord George, he said: 'It wou'd be of ye most Dangerous Consequences iff such a Divill was not secured immediately in sum Castle where he might be at his ease, but without being able to escape, or have ye Liberty of Pen or papers.'[1]

A few days later Charles wrote again, alleging that Lord George was in league with Secretary

---

[1] April 3, 1747. Printed by Mr. Blaikie from the *Stuart Papers* (*Itinerary*, p. 81).

Murray the informer.[1]   Be it remembered that
Lord George had done as much for the cause as
any man then living.   He had led the Highland
army to its victories ; he had organised its forces,
evolved its strategy, provided for its administration, and he it was who had supplied the mind
and energy which brought it within sight of its
goal.   Nothing can justify or excuse the letter.
But the poison instilled into the mind of Charles
by evil counsellors had suffused his whole nature.
Obstinacy had blinded him to the truth.

It was in vain that James, with the gentle
wisdom that hovers through the pages of his
letters, counselled a more generous frame of mind
and dwelt on the services which Lord George
had rendered.   Charles was obdurate, and designed himself to have the person of Lord George
secured on his return from Rome.   ' I hope to
God you will not think of getting Lord George
secured after all I have writ to you about him,
but that you will receive him at least civilly,'
wrote the distracted King in June 1747.[2]   In July
Lord George returned.   On the 11th of that

[1] ' I have good reason to suspect by circumstances together that
Murray he was in a click with L George, tho' he pretended and
appeared to be otherwise ' (*Stuart Papers*, April 10, 1747).

[2] *Stuart Papers*, Browne, iv. 5.

month he received a message from Charles declining to see him, at the same time informing him that he would do well to leave Paris at once.[1]

This show of base ingratitude may be regarded as a misleading expression of character, a break in continuity, or it may be held to conform with what is known of Charles, with his temperament, with the tendencies which in later years made him a prey to the powers of darkness. Faith must determine. But, in either case, it surely enables us to sympathise with the vehemence of Elcho's criticisms. Elcho remained in Venice till June 1747 much in the company of Earl Marischal and Lord George Murray, who revisited them on his way back from Rome.

Venice appears no more than other towns to have been free of social tedium, and the dulness of the nobles' houses drove the younger refugees towards a Bohemian world in which there figures a Mademoiselle Vigano, who eventually became Elcho's companion in his wanderings over Europe. From Venice they moved to Padua for the feast of St. Antonio. Here 'singing, fiddling, and piping,' so abhorred by

---

[1] *Stuart Papers*, Browne, iv. 13.

Lord Chesterfield,[1] claimed a large measure of
their time. The morning began with music in
the Church of St. Antonio, where the famous
Tartini was first violin ; later in the day the
ladies drove out, arrayed in a splendour fashioned
for the particular festival ; in the evening there
was the opera or a musical party at one of the
noble's palaces ; while in the intervals they interpolated games of chance or excursions, each lady
with her cicisbeo, to the surrounding country. It
is not a picture to exhilarate the imagination, but
the actors faced their pleasures gaily and made
the best of a frivolous world.

Marischal meanwhile was ill at Treviso. In
August of this year, 1747, he received from
Charles a request that he would once more become
a militant leader in the Cause. The fortunes of
the party were at a low ebb. In January James
had written to Charles : 'I have also really
seen some odd things amongst our people of late
. . . and if you dont care I am afraid their
politics and passions will soon put your affairs
in a desperate situation.'[2] The prediction had
been realised. Affairs were indeed desperate.

---

[1] *Letters to his Son*, xcv.
[2] *Stuart Papers*, Browne, iii. 476.

Through the winter of 1746-1747 there had been talk of another expedition. The English Jacobites were again brought to the front. But they were kites that had been flown too often, and there was the usual absence of definite assurance. Charles had cast loose from the recognised Jacobite agents in Paris. He had his own party, his own plans. In March he was trying the Court of Spain:[1] at Guadalaxara he was granted a midnight interview with the Royal Family, presented with 3000 pistoles for the expenses of his journey, a diamond ring, and a sword, but requested to leave. There were projects of marriage: James talked of a daughter of the Duke of Modena ; Charles, more ambitious, idly aspired to the Czarina.

Before the end of March he was back in Paris. At the beginning of April his brother Henry, ' toujours porté à la Piété dès son enfance,'[2] had slipped stealthily away from Paris to James, and a cardinal's hat, in Rome. A second Culloden to the cause,[3] and a grievous wound to the pride and affection of Charles. France was delaying

---

[1] *Stuart Papers*: also *S. P.*, Venice, April 19, 1747.
[2] James to Louis xv., *Stuart Papers*, Browne, iv. 6.
[3] T. Hay to Edgar, *ibid.* iv. 15.

'the gratifications of his distressed countrymen.'
'Happy would I be to have happier orders and
chierfull spirits which to my misfortune my friends
hinder as well as my enemys,' wrote Charles.[1]
Every courier from Rome was carrying evidence
of the deepening difference with his father. They
no longer saw eye to eye. James had got back
his Henry, a son to sympathise with him in his
piety and devotions. To Charles he was writing:
'All I have left to do is to pray for you.' The
breach was wide enough.

Earl Marischal declined to play a part in this
gloomy confusion. ' I did not retire from all
affairs without a certainty how useless I was, and
allways must be, and that my broken health
required quiet for the rest of my days,'[2] he wrote
from Treviso ; and receiving an invitation from
his brother, Marshal Keith, who had recently
entered the service of the Prussian monarch, to
join him in Berlin, he set out during the course
of the winter for the Court of Frederick.

On September 17th Elcho, together with
Mademoiselle Vigano and Hunter of Burnside,
left Padua in a *vetturino*, which they had hired

[1] Charles to Edgar, *Stuart Papers*, Browne, iv. 14.
[2] Earl Marischal to Charles, *ibid.* iv. 17.

at the cost of three sequins[1] a day, to saunter across Europe northwards to Cleves. Arriving there on October 31st, they found Gordon of Cowbairdie, Cumming of Pitully, Lord George Murray, and other Jacobites. Later, Lady Wemyss, who had not seen her son for sixteen years, and who, as we shall see, was to meet with stormy experiences on the Continent, passed through the town on her way to Basle. In February (1748) Lord George left for Cracow. He desired to secure the descent of the family estates to his son, and to prevent forfeiture he proposed to assume a false name, spread a report of his death, and live retired in Poland. But the plan was not carried out.[2]

From Cleves Elcho wrote to Charles under flying seal to Kelly, now acting as secretary, asking for a commission in the French service. No notice was taken of his application. Favours were scarcely to be looked for by a follower who had applied for pardon, and the explanation which follows, that Kelly was Irish, and therefore opposed to the Scots, scarcely carries conviction. Next

[1] A sequin was approximately 9s. 2d. The bargain included meals for the three travellers.

[2] Lord George died 1760: his eldest son John became third Duke of Atholl, January 8, 1764.

we hear of him at Liége with officers of the Scots
regiments, at Lisle with Lord Clancarty, at Sedan,
at Brussels, at country houses, or at wayside inns
where robbers in league with landlords dispose of
unwary guests, or at the grim sequel—the finding
of victims buried in the courtyard, the putting to
death of the culprits by breaking on the wheel.
Through such scenes he drifts, without purpose,
during the winter and summer of 1748, denied
every outlet to his activity. The zest of battle
and the valour of the days when the white cockades were glancing in the sun was now a 'dim-
remembered story.' His heart was possessed by
an exile's longing for home, by a restless wish to
see again the distant hills and broken headlands
of the Firth, and hear once more the cry of sea-
birds round the Castle walls. But it was not for
him that summer was bringing beauty to those
northern shores, and weary at length of wandering, he settled in November at Florentun, a
country house which he had taken in the neighbourhood of Boulogne.

Meanwhile the Treaty of Aix-la-Chapelle had
been signed, and hostilities between France and
England had ceased. In breach of previous
undertakings, Louis had bound himself to expel

Charles from his territory. Charles had published a high-sounding protest, and had forwarded it to Montesquieu, claiming that he himself was now an author. 'Were you not so great a Prince, Madame la Duchesse d'Aiguillon and I would procure your election to the French Academy,'[1] was Montesquieu's flattering rejoinder. But the protest was unavailing. In spite of warning, Charles refused to depart. Louis therefore sent his Minister, de Puisieux,[2] who, through the influence of Madame de Pompadour, had been appointed Minister for Foreign Affairs in succession to D'Argenson, to beg Charles to leave, and at the same time to offer him as inducements to do so a mansion in the canton of Fribourg, a pension, a miniature army, and not a few of the minor emblems of royalty. But Charles was bidding for popular applause. Already acclaimed by the mob in Paris, he believed that a rebuff to the Ministers of France would echo his fame through England. He declined to be lured out of France by pacific means. He seized the Minister by the arm and for answer turned him from the room. On being

---

[1] *Stuart Papers*, Browne, iv. 38.

[2] Other contemporary memoirs say De Gesvres, Governor of Paris, was sent.

told what had occurred, Louis said : ' Since the
Prince plays the madman, he must be treated
like a madman.' There followed the famous
scene of December 10th.   Charles, on arriving as
usual at the opera in the evening, was arrested by
the sergeants of the guard : after being searched,
he was bound like ' a roll of tobacco ' with silk
cords, thrust into a carriage, and driven through
the night to the fortress of Vincennes.   He sub-
mitted with dignity to these insults.   ' Vous faites
là un vilain métier,' he said to Vaudreuil, who had
been intrusted with the execution of the order,
' est-ce là ce pays si poli !   Je n'éprouverais pas ceci
au Maroc ; j'avais meilleure opinion de la nation
française.'   From Vincennes, where he was detained
for several days, he was escorted to Avignon.

No treaty obligation could have been more
scrupulously observed.   Three of his followers
were confined in the Bastille ; his house was ransacked ; even the lacquey of his mistress, the
Princesse de Talmond,[1] was arrested, while the
Princess herself was banished to Lorraine.   Deep
was the resentment shown when this breach of
hospitality became known.   The Dauphin, it was

---

[1] A Polish lady, related to the queen.   She was forty years of
age when Charles met her.

reported, shed tears on hearing the news ; in Paris there appeared scurrilous lampoons and satires against Louis, his ministers[1] and his mistress.[2] The Princesse de Talmond wrote to Maurepas : 'Now indeed is the fame of the King at its zenith, but as the imprisonment of my footman can in no way add to it, I beg he may be released.'[3] In every rank of society there were murmurs and menacing discontent. But it is no part of this Memoir to trace the fortunes of Charles. By the light of the *Stuart Papers* chinks have been revealed in the masterly incognito which he assumed after his expulsion from Paris. But the disguises, the false noses, the corked eyebrows, the stage properties by means of which he mystified Europe,[4] baffled the diplomatists and agents of England, and veiled his movements during a number of years, effectually screened him from Elcho's view.

The *Journal* states that after visiting Venice and Spain Charles settled in the Low Countries. We know that he visited Venice ; it is not

---

[1] 'Them vermin ministers,' Charles calls them in a letter to Waters (*Stuart Papers*, August 12, 1753).

[2] D'Argenson, vol. v. pp. 339, 343.

[3] *Ibid.*, p. 320.

[4] See Information of Pickle : Lang, *Pickle the Spy*, p. 288.

unlikely that he travelled to Spain. But he never settled ; he was perpetually on the wing : now in Paris hiding in the Convent of St. Joseph, Rue St. Dominique, where the Princesse de Talmond had rooms, and quarrels and reconciliations enlivened his retreat ; now in Lorraine with his Princess, or in the Low Countries, moving from place to place as evasion required ; or in September 1750 drinking tea with Dr. King in London,[1] conferring with the Duke of Beaufort and the Earl of Westmoreland in a lodging in Pall Mall, sauntering, a curious sightseer, through the streets, visiting the Tower of London, gazing at the palaces he still hoped to occupy ;[2] then as mysteriously disappearing again from view. Walpole relates that the Duchess of Aiguillon wore a picture of Charles in a bracelet, with Jesus Christ for the reverse.[3] ' Mon royaume n'est pas de ce monde,' was the motto, said Madame Rochefort, which explained the conjunction. But if Charles was to reign in no temporal

[1] King, *Anecdotes*, p. 199. The present knowledge of Charles's movements is due to the researches of Mr. Lang, set forth in *Pickle the Spy* and his *Life of Charles Edward*.

[2] See letter of Horace Mann to Charles James Fox, Foreign Office, Tuscany, December 6, 1783.

[3] Walpole, *Letters*, August 12, 1765.

kingdom, he was at least supreme in that world of mystification which he had set himself to occupy, and in which the *Journal* for the present leaves him.

Elcho was now established at Florentun. Boulogne itself had become a Jacobite centre, and here Lords Clancarty, Barrymore, Strathallan, Lewis Gordon, Messrs. Gordon of Glenbucket, Gordon of Halhead, Gordon of Cowbairdie, Hunter of Burnside, Hepburn of Keith, all names familiar to readers of later Stuart history, were visitors or residents. We know from the *Stuart Papers* that Elcho had written several letters to Charles at this time asking for his 1500 guineas, also to James, who replied through Edgar : 'H.M. thinks that the money which you say you advanced . . . having been on account of the then public service, that it can never be claimed as a personal debt either from the Prince or himself.' The letters to Charles remained unanswered. Shortly after, he caused an appeal to be sent to Lord Holland, begging that he would agitate for a pardon. Lord Holland merely replied that the moment was not propitious.

Early in the year Mademoiselle Vigano bore Elcho a daughter. Later, in December 1749, squabbles over a rival friendship of Elcho's led to Mademoiselle Vigano's departure for London, while Elcho himself left for Paris. Here, during the month of February 1750, he lodged at the house of Briel, a bagnio keeper, in the Rue Richelieu, at the rate of half a crown a day, dining every evening at the Hôtel de Notre Dame, Rue du Jardinet, with Lord Nairne, the Chevalier Maclean, young Glengarry, and Lochgarry.

In 1749 the two Macdonalds had revisited Scotland. Glengarry had soiled his hands with the buried treasure of Arkaig, then in the keeping of Cluny Macpherson, and with Lochgarry had returned to France, bringing, Elcho writes, 1200 louis d'or. Elcho also states that Dr. Cameron, after a similar expedition to Scotland, was in possession of 1000 louis. The part played by those two loyal Jacobites, Lochgarry and Archibald Cameron, is obscure. Cameron, we know, received 6000 pounds out of the treasure 'for the behoof of the Lochiel family,'[1] and the 1000 louis here referred to by Elcho may have been the residue of that amount not yet disbursed.

[1] Home Office, Scotland, Bundle 44, No. 28. Cameron of Glennevis to General Churchill, May 1753. See also *ante*, p. 104.

Nothing is to be ascertained as to Lochgarry's connection with the treasure. Glengarry, on the other hand, is said to have obtained his share of the spoil by an order bearing a forged signature of James.[1] Later, Glengarry writes (January 16, 1750) to James accusing Cameron of having received 6000 louis d'or and converted it to his own use. But the accusation carried little weight, and Cameron, the last to perish on the scaffold for the Stuart cause, was afterwards trusted by Charles at the time of the Elibank Plot. Glengarry himself at this time may already have been in receipt of English pay, though the correspondence of Pickle, whom those who have read Mr. Lang's volume will identify with Glengarry, does not begin till 1752. Thus while the chief actor is masquerading in obscurity, we see Jacobitism 'paling its ineffectual fires' in an atmosphere heavy with sordid quarrel, low intrigue, and squalid accusation.

Many of the Scots at this time were receiving pensions from the Court of France, but Elcho's claim to be included among his more fortunate compatriots had hitherto been ignored.

---

[1] *Stuart Papers*, Browne, iv. 92 ; Home Office, Scotland, 1753, Bundle 42, No. 47.

Introduced this year to Tencin, he took the
opportunity of renewing his demands. The
Cardinal sympathised with Elcho, expressed
agreement with his adverse views of Charles,
and subsequently induced M. Puisieux to grant
him an annual allowance of 1200 livres. This
raised Elcho's income to a total of 16,600 livres.

The summer and winter of 1750 were spent at
the country seat of his brother-in-law, Sir James
Steuart, in the county of Angoulême. Sir James
kept open house, and there was much interchange
of hospitality with the nobility of the town.
Living was cheap and luxurious. No district
provided such abundance of game and of truffles.
None was so famous for its sport. Nowhere in
the provinces was society so brilliant and distinguished. The great houses of the Prince of
Chalais, of the Dukes of Rochefoucauld and St.
Simon, and of the Comte de Jarnac, were lavish
in their welcome. The mornings spent in visiting were succeeded by a banquet at one of the
town houses ; games of hazard occupied the
evenings, while the nights were given to dancing,
to concerts, and to suppers. But Elcho was
appalled by the poverty of the peasantry. Miserably clothed, subsisting on black bread, sleeping

on straw thrown loosely on the floor of rude and ill-roofed hovels, they presented an ominous contrast to the life of the château, with its rustle of silk and brocade, and its heedless air of profusion.

It was in conditions such as these that the clouds were already gathering, and the forces of the whirlwind collecting their strength, and it was, in fact, of these very *seigneurs* of Angoulême that Arthur Young wrote in 1787 : 'Oh, if I were legislator of France, I would make such great lords skip again.'[1]

[1] Ed. 1890, p. 71.

VI

I⊤ can hardly cause astonishment that after a
year at Angoulême, Elcho should have found
it necessary to visit Aix-la-Chapelle. In the
eighteenth century the excesses which seem
to have led inevitably to a health resort were
treated by a cure of exceptional rigour and
duration. Thus we find him, after three weeks
at Aix, spending a corresponding period at Spa,
and finishing up with a fortnight at the baths of
Chaudefontaine. On the Continent the tyranny
of the English visitor was already making itself
felt. At the assemblies of Aix-la-Chapelle all
the dances were English,[1] and in the local pas-
times and diversions, fashions of the same origin
prevailed. At each of the resorts there was the
usual watering-place gaiety, but at Spa Elcho
found himself the victim of a Hanoverian demonstration, the English guests at the inn declining
to take part in the *table d'hôte* with so notorious
a Jacobite. An alderman, Alsop, alone placed

[1] Marmontel, *Mémoires.*

common-sense and the pleasures of the table above the exigencies of dynastic politics, and proved himself staunch enough to consort with the outlaw. Doubtless it was this experience which provoked a letter to James in October 1751. 'I was last summer at Aix-la-Chapelle and Spa for my health,' writes Elcho, 'and in those places, and wherever any of the present Government of England's Ministers or Agents are, I find their spite and malice so great against me . . . that it might be of very bad consequences least an accident should happen to me where they are, and have influence. As I have nobody to apply to for protection and looked upon as belonging to no country, it is therefore I most earnestly entreat your Majesty to procure for me a Spanish or a Neapolitan Colonel's commission,'[1] signing himself 'Your Majesty's most faithful subject.'

In response to this appeal Elcho was at last (May 3, 1752) appointed to the French service as a captain without salary in the cavalry of Fitzjames.

From a letter among the *Stuart Papers*, full of dark innuendo, and written by Æneas Macdonald,

[1] *Stuart Papers*, October 18, 1751.

we know that Elcho was back again in Boulogne in August. ' He has just left this place after being here with me two months,' writes Macdonald in October (1751). ' Nothing can excuse his conduct ; but still most of the wrong steps he took were ambuscades dressed for him by his enemies. He wants much, and I think with reason, to have a Colonel's brevet without pay in the service of France.' What were the wrong steps ? Who were the enemies ? It can only be surmised that reference is intended to the relations of Elcho with Charles. James, at any rate, paid little heed to the evil-speaking of Macdonald, and did all in his power to support the claim to a commission in the French army.

At this time a Miss Mynshull, a lady of great beauty and reputed to be an heiress, was exciting the admiration of Boulogne society. Elcho aspired to her hand, but the aspiration was not uncontested, and in the progress of his courtship Miss Mynshull was indiscreet enough to show him a letter she had received from his rival, a Mr. Turner, in which there was a threat to make short work of the Jacobite exile. Mr. Turner, however, was less warlike than his letter, and being called on by Elcho at their first meeting to draw and defend himself, declined to cross swords with a rebel. A Welsh gentleman named Gwyn, fearful that an opportunity for fighting was to be allowed to slip, stepped in and took up the challenge. In the duel which followed the Scotsman was victorious, and Mr. Gwyn was left wounded on the field. Mr. Turner took his departure for London the same evening, but not before, as was afterwards discovered, he had been clandestinely married to Miss Mynshull.

Notwithstanding these embarrassments a tour through France was arranged, and Mrs. Mynshull and her daughter, together with Elcho and a party of friends, left Boulogne to proceed to Paris. Breaking their journey at Chantilly, they found Lord and Lady Ogilvy and Alexander Murray. Murray had recently (December 1750) been electioneering in England. Summoned before the House of Commons to receive admonition on his knees for his riotous conduct on behalf of the anti-ministerial candidate at the Westminster election, he had haughtily replied to the Speaker, ' Sir, I beg to be excused. I never kneel but to God.' This attitude of defiance had been followed by six months' imprisonment in Newgate, and he had now come over to France to instil a new spirit of activity into the ranks of the Jacobite party. He had already seen Charles, who was living in Flanders (1751-1752) with Miss Walkinshaw.

Five years had elapsed since Charles and Clementina had met at Bannockburn, in the house of her uncle, Sir Hugh Paterson. There she had yielded to the grace and charm of the young Prince, and vowed to follow him wheresoever fate might lead him. These dark years of Charles's life are suddenly flashed upon by the revival of this passion. The long separation, the silence, the carrying out of her vow in the shadow of evil days seemed to give some promise of stability. But the romance was not to endure. It was to perish miserably in the ruin to come. For a few years she remained the devoted companion of his wanderings. In October 1753 at Liége she bore him a daughter, Charlotte, the future Duchess of Albany. Then in 1760, as we shall hear from Elcho, her ill-treatment by Charles forced her to find refuge with her child in a convent in Paris.

With the arrival of Murray on the scene there commenced preparations for what is known as the Elibank Plot. The project, as it came to the knowledge of Elcho, was briefly as follows : Lochgarry and the ill-fated Dr. Cameron, having gone to Scotland to organise the Jacobite forces in that country—Murray, with some officers of the regiment of Ogilvy, was to proceed to London, where he professed he would find friends enough to form a company of a hundred persons. Charles himself was to follow and remain in concealment in the house of Lady Primrose. On a given day Murray and his company were to present themselves, armed with pistols and swords, at the palace of St. James : the royal family were to be struck down ; Charles was to show himself to the people; the Restoration was to be an accomplished fact. Murray asserted that amongst others supporting the plot were Earl Marischal,[1] now Ambassador to Frederick at the Court of Louis, and the Earls of Westmoreland and Denbigh. The scheme ended as might have been expected. Murray ventured as far as London : there his courage ebbing or his perspicacity prevailing, he returned to France : the officers rejoined their regiment : Charles, after hovering on the coast, retired to

---

[1] See Lang, *Pickle the Spy*, p. 173. Walpole, *Letters*, April 27, 1753, alleges the plot was supported by Frederick.

Paris, while Cameron was arrested and executed in the following year.

In Pickle's information[1] it is stated that other persons concerned were Hepburn of Keith and Elcho's brother, Mr. Charteris. Charteris, however, is not mentioned in the *Journal*. Elcho himself considered the plot a travesty of sense, and it is unlikely that he would have countenanced the adhesion of his brother. Murray came in for much opprobrious mockery on his return, and Earl Marischal, whom he claimed as a co-conspirator, refused him admission to his house.

In December Elcho was again at Angoulême staying with his mother and two sisters, Lady Helen and Lady Walpole. Lady Walpole became engaged to, and the following year married in Scotland, a captain in the French cavalry, M. de Chastel de la Barthe. Mademoiselle Vigano had meanwhile reappeared, and a second daughter had been born to Elcho in 1751. On the return of his sisters to Scotland in the spring of 1753 they took charge of his two daughters, and seem to have relieved him of further responsibility with regard to them. *Autres temps autres mœurs,*

[1] Cited Lang, *Pickle the Spy,* p. 178.

and allowance has to be made for the freedom
of an age which could produce a situation so
singular.

In April (1753) Elcho was once more in Paris,
a constant guest at the house of Earl Marischal.
Here he met the various diplomatists accredited
to the Court of France, and notes that the
representatives most frequently entertained by
Frederick's ambassador were those of Spain,
Venice, and Würtemburg. Every Tuesday the
Corps Diplomatique, headed by the Papal
Nuncio, attended at Versailles, and on these
occasions Earl Marischal selected Elcho to
accompany him. In the Salle des Ambassadeurs
they would wait till the moment arrived for them
to be summoned to witness the concluding offices
of the King's toilet. From the presence of
Louis they would pass to the apartments of the
Queen, and subsequently visit those of all the
Princes of the Royal House. Nor were the
formalities of the day at an end until the same
ceremonious courtesy had been paid in the salon
of Madame de Pompadour, but here the diplomatists were without the leadership of the Papal
Nuncio, his instructions compelling him to withdraw on the threshold of this prohibited territory.

At the audience with the King the questions asked by Louis gave Elcho the impression that he possessed a consummate knowledge of geography and history, while in the region of genealogy he showed himself familiar with the names of all the titled persons in every Court of Europe, a department of knowledge which appears to have been largely drawn on at these diplomatic audiences. But in spite of the gracious manner and distinguished air of the King, *ennui* and disenchantment were becoming more and more apparent. The boredom of the monarch brooded continually over the gaiety of Versailles. The expedients of Madame de Pompadour and her followers were sorely tried. It was to combat the insidious foe that the favourite had prescribed a change of scene and organised an expedition to Havre, which had cost the nation one million francs.[1] It was to the same end that operas and plays were given at her theatre ; that buildings and gardens were planned ; that the service of the arts was requisitioned ; and that constant journeys were made between the familiar residences which her

[1] D'Argenson, vol. vi. p. 418 ; *Cumberland Papers*, Colonel Yorke to the Duke of Cumberland.

genius had devised in the neighbourhood of Paris.

At the same time the interest of Louis in public affairs was visibly waning. At Councils of State, while ministers were debating the destinies of the nation, the scratching of the King's pen only meant that he was busy writing the names of the hounds to be hunted next day in the forest.[1] In all branches of government it was the same, and authority and the direction of recognised policy were passing from his hands into those of the favourite. Such was the situation at Versailles.[2]

In Paris no such cares prevailed. There the natural levity and cheerfulness of society had not yet been supplanted by free-thinking, metaphysics, and the sentimentalism inspired by Rousseau. Laughter had not grown unfashionable.[3] Gambling had not made way for the irresponsible chatter of subversive criticism, nor had the volumes of the Encyclopædists as yet found a place on the shelves of the Trianon. Religion

[1] *Cumberland Papers*, ibid.

[2] It must, however, be remembered that Louis had recently inaugurated his famous secret policy, unknown both to his ministers and Madame de Pompadour. See Broglie, *Le Secret du Roi*.

[3] See Walpole, *Letters* (from Paris), 1765.

and royal authority were assailed, but their
supremacy was intact, and only in February of
this year had the banishment of the Parliament
shown that the *main levée* remained an effective
instrument of government.   But on listening
ears there already fell

> '. . . through the silence of the cold, dull night
> The hum of armies gathering rank on rank,'

and to observers such as D'Argenson there was
not wanting abundant evidence that the forces of
change were gaining irresistible strength.   The
accommodation, however, between the spectacle
of poverty and the enjoyment of wealth was
lightly adjusted, and the splendour of the entertainments which Elcho attended surpassed expectation.   The most brilliant were those of the
Spanish Ambassador.   At one of these, a ball,
Elcho notes that the dancing was postponed till
the arrival of Madame de Pompadour.   Received
by the Ambassador as she stepped from her
carriage, she was conducted to the ball-room,
and when the music commenced she took her
place in the first minuet with her host as partner.
She was at the zenith of her power.   She had just
emerged victorious from one of those struggles
by which alone she maintained the supremacy

of her position. A rival crushed,[1] a minister
defeated,[2] a fresh access of the King's favour,
were triumphs which had recently enhanced her
prestige, and evoked an outburst of judicious
homage from the followers of the Court.

Other houses which he frequented were those
of the Marquises de Grammont and Berville, the
Comtesses de Voguë, d'Estillac, and Monastrole.
At all of these the normal course of amusement
was a supper-party, followed by faro, biribi or
cavagnol. Guests were at liberty to arrive and
to leave at what hour they pleased, and neither
fashion nor constraint was exercised as to the
amount which they staked at the games of
hazard. But the contrast between wealth and
poverty in Paris was sharper even than that
observed in the country. Side by side with social
displays costing five hundred louis a night,
misery and starvation clamoured shrilly for relief.
The year 1753 had been a year of acute distress,
and it was calculated that in one quarter of Paris
alone eight hundred persons perished of want in
the space of a single month. Society, passing to
its round of brilliant gaiety, threaded its way
through narrow streets, noisome with refuse and

[1] Madame de Choiseul-Romanet.   [2] Comte d'Argenson.

filth.   But the dirt and poverty were ignored,
and the fine world lulled its senses by the use
of abundance of musk.   To such an extent was
this device carried that we find James, in thank-
ing Charles for the portrait of himself sent from
Paris, writing (1747), 'it smells so strong of
musk that I believe I must get it put in another
frame when I return to Rome.'   'At Paris
everything smells of musk, down to the very
trees in the Tuilleries gardens, against which
ladies may have leant for a moment,'[1] was the
information given twenty years later to Carlo
Gozzi by the actress Ricci on her return to
Venice, and the complaint is reiterated in the
Journal.   To Elcho the prevalence of the distress was brought directly home by the ruin of
his banker, M. Wolff; but his own losses were
partially met by a successful speculation in the
shares of the Compagnie des Indes.

This year (1754) Charles was a visitor to Paris.
The fact was made known to Earl Marischal by
a 'certain gentleman' whose name is not divulged
in the *Journal.*   The Earl's informant happened
to be in a low tavern when a man and woman
drove up in a cab, and engaged a table by his

[1] J. A. Symonds, *Memoirs of Carlo Gozzi*, vol. ii. p. 257.

side. Before they had been long seated a quarrel
broke out, and high words ensued. The man
addressed his companion as ' *coquine*.' The lady
replied : 'Although a prince, you are unworthy
to be called a gentleman.' Blows were struck,
nor had this scene of degradation terminated
when the witness left. The Earl, when told the
story, surmised that the actors were Charles and
Miss Walkinshaw. A few days later, Goring,
the near friend of Charles, who had accompanied
him in his wanderings, confirmed the surmise of
Earl Marischal. Not often may adversity have
brought a character of so much promise to a pass
so pitiable in shame. The legendary Charles, the
Charles of Holyrood, the idol of loyal hearts, the
comely youth whose name had been 'one with
knightliness,' for him, at any rate, there was no
' coming back.' The song might be sung in vain.
He was irrevocably lost. Even the faithful
Goring, he too, at last, had been driven to break
with Charles. On parting, he writes a long
review of all that had occurred, and concludes
in despairing words : 'For God's sake, sir, have
compassion on yourself.'[1] In 1746 Goring had

[1] Stouf (Goring) to Charles, *Stuart Papers*, printed Lang,
Pickle the Spy, p. 261.

reproached Elcho with speaking ill of the fallen prince. 'I knew the Prince well at that time,' says Elcho, 'and Mr. Goring came to know him too, and spoke more evil about him than ever I had done.' Earl Marischal at this time (May 1754) writes a bitter rebuke to Charles for his conduct to Goring. 'My heart is broke enough without that you should finish it,' replied Charles, and to a fine spirit so broken and 'discovered' by adversity the world cannot easily deny its sympathy.

The final stroke to his fortunes fell this same year, and is thus described in the *Journal* : 'The partisans of the Prince in England at that time granted him a pension of 5000 pounds sterling a year. One gentleman, Dawkins by name, gave a thousand of the five. All of this money was this year taken away from him for ever, and all these gentlemen became his enemies and particularly this same Dawkins. They had sent one of their friends [1] to persuade the Prince to part with his mistress, because her sister had a place in the service of the Princess of Wales at the Court in London, and they feared a corre-

---

[1] Daniel Macnamara. See King, *Anecdotes*, p. 205, for an account of this episode.

spondence between the two sisters. The Prince replied that he would not put away one of his dogs to please them, and ended by demanding more money, stating that what they gave him was not sufficient. The messenger said to him that these gentlemen were not his bankers, that what they gave him was given out of pure generosity, and that he ought to be more than content. The Prince retorted that he knew the names of all those that had sent him the money, and that if they would not continue to do so, he would send a list of their names to the King of England. All these gentlemen were so indignant at these threats that from that time the Prince never received a halfpenny from England.'

In July 1754 Earl Marischal, at his own request, was recalled by Frederick, and appointed Governor of the Principality of Neufchâtel in Switzerland. Before his departure he caused Elcho to be made a naturalised subject of Frederick in his suzerainty of Neufchâtel, and requested for his young friend that he might be made Chamberlain in the Prussian kingdom; but the fact that Elcho was in the service of France proved a bar to this preferment. The

friends parted with many protestations of affection and an undertaking by Elcho that he would
soon visit the retiring ambassador in his new
kingdom.

Elcho remained in Paris, continuing his social
life, and lightly fulfilling his unpaid military
duties. He was joined by his sister, Lady
Steuart, and they occupied rooms together in
the Rue Grenelle, Faubourg St. Germain, at a
rental of six hundred livres a year. In the
course of the winter he made the acquaintance
of Montesquieu and Maupertuis, who, he
patronisingly writes, were 'savants who did
honour to France,' and was presented to the
Comte D'Argenson, Minister of War. The
Minister laughingly inquired of Elcho if he
remembered how nearly he had been interned
in the Bastille for speaking ill of Prince Charles
in 1746. 'In those days,' he continued, 'we
would not allow any one to speak ill of him,
but now that we know him to be an obstinate
fool, you may say of him whatever you please.'
He concluded by asking Elcho his age, and on
being told, remarked that it was time that he
had made his fortune. The exile may well have
reflected that the ministers of Louis were in a

more favourable position for making fortunes than a homeless outlaw.

Slight as his military duties were, he was obliged to obtain permission from D'Argenson at the beginning of the year 1755, in order that he might visit Earl Marischal and absent himself from France for a year. In April, then, he is travelling to Switzerland ; on the frontier he finds King's troops concentrated in pursuit of Mandrin, the famous smuggler. At the head of some hundreds of mounted men Mandrin, during the winter 1754-55, had overrun Auvergne and Burgundy. Report said he was supported by the nobility, whose hospitality he had from time to time enjoyed.[1] The ordinary authorities were powerless to deal with him. In March he had withdrawn to Switzerland, and at the head of his irregular cavalry was now carrying on a huge contraband trade across the frontier ; but a force of regular troops was closing in on him, and before long held him prisoner, conveying him to Valence, where he and several of his followers were broken alive on the wheel.[2] Such in France

[1] D'Argenson, vol. viii. p. 353.
[2] For an account of this remarkable man, see *ibid.* vols. viii. and ix. ; Luynes, xiv. p. 154 ; also Saint-Edmé, *Répertoire des causes célèbres*, vol. iv. p. 311.

was the fate reserved for all high crime, and the
continental smuggler had reason to regard with
envy the treatment accorded to his kindred contemporary, the 'gentleman highwayman' in
England. In Newgate, the famous Maclean, a
few years earlier, had been visited by thousands ;
in the fashionable world tears had been shed for
his fate ; in the streets every one had been
buying his portrait and reading leaflets on his
exploits. But horsemanship has a peculiar
tendency to make crime picturesque, if not
respectable, and Mandrin, too, seems to have
enjoyed a measure of this poor popularity before
meeting his fate.

In May Elcho is once more with Earl Marischal
at Neufchâtel, living in the Governor's castle
overlooking the town and the beautiful lake.
Here he makes the acquaintance of the principal
personages of the district, and studies the constitution with its quaint forms and liberal ideas,
and admires the traditions of freedom and toler-
ance which made it the refuge of the persecuted.
The office of Governor he finds is no sinecure,
and he observes that the Earl's skill as a diplo-
matist was already requisitioned to control the
contending factions of Protestantism. Here, too,

he hears news of Charles. At Basle there were living a Doctor and Mrs. Thompson, reputed to be on bad terms, and often attracting public attention by their disagreements. One day a printseller exposes in his window a portrait of Prince Charles; gossip is at once busy; the rumour flies about that Dr. Thompson and Prince Charles are one and the same: soon there is no room for doubt. The English physician is revealed as the Stuart Prince, the wife with whom he quarrels is proved to be Miss Walkinshaw. It was at this juncture, we learn from the *Journal*, that Charles suggested a visit to Lord Marischal; but the Earl declined, and from the *State Papers* it is to be gathered that he was now entirely alienated from Charles, and 'never mentioned him but with the utmost horror and detestation, and in the most opprobrious terms.'[1]

It is to the period of this residence at Basle that Elcho assigns the formal admission of Charles to the Anglican Communion,[2] but we

[1] *State Papers, Switzerland*, May 28, 1756, letter from English envoy at Berne. Printed by Mr. Ewald.

[2] See D'Argenson, vol. ix. p. 60. ' Le Prince Édouard s'est déclaré hautement protestant et anglican là où il est réfugié,' August 1755: on information supplied by the agent of Charles.

have Charles's own declaration [1] that he became
a member of the Church of England in 1750
on his visit to London.   Hume, in his well-
known letter to Sir John Pringle, says that it
was in the New Church in the Strand in 1753.
Thus there is question of a second visit to
London, but it is unsupported by trustworthy
evidence.

Great activity was visible at this time in the
dockyards and arsenals of France.   Colonial
expansion   and   the   struggle   for   territorial
supremacy outside the theatre of Europe were
leading to constant collision between the English
and French in India and North America.   Both
nations were now preparing for the war which was
imminent.   It seemed again to be an occasion for
the renewal of Jacobite hopes.   In May 1755
Charles appealed to the Duc de Richelieu ; [2]
but the Ministers of France in their present
schemes had no place for a Stuart Restoration.
In the dissolute wanderer they no longer recognised an instrument serviceable for their policy.
None the less do we find D'Argenson recording,
with apparent approval, a conversation with 'one

----

[1] Cited Lang, *Charles Edward*, p. 451.
[2] Browne, *Stuart Papers*, vol. iv. p. 124.

of the principal agents of Prince Edward,' in which it was pointed out, ' que la nation anglaise n'est plus militaire, qu'elle est amollie par le commerce, l'avarice et le luxe,' and that the landing of eight thousand troops would cause a revolution, of which advantage favourable to France could be taken by James or Charles. But the scheme received no support, and ' our dear wild man,' as Edgar calls Charles, slipped back again into his strange and wine-solaced obscurity.

On June 10th Elcho set out from Neufchâtel to post to Venice : in his desultory travels he had acquired the habit of leisurely progress, and it was not till July the 28th that he reached Padua. On the borders of the Venetian State he was warned by the host of the inn where he dined that on the previous day a traveller and his servant had been murdered by robbers in the neighbouring forest. The bandits, he was told, who were five in number, were roaming the country disguised as hunters. Here was promise of congenial adventure. Arms were distributed to the two servants and the party set forth. The heat was intense. The travellers were proceeding slowly through the forest when Elcho, who had fallen asleep in his *vetturino*, was roused by one of the servants crying out that he could see five horsemen hard by among the trees. Elcho sprang to the ground, and ordering his followers to do the same, he covered the marauders with his musket, calling out that he would fire if they advanced. Alarmed at their reception, they retreated, and the travellers had the satisfaction of seeing the so-called hunters flit swiftly into the distant shadow of the forest.

At Padua he was among familiar surroundings, living at the Stella D'Oro, paying six paoli[1] for his board, six for his lodging, and three for each of his servants. The principal entertainers were Madame Morosini, Count Algarotti,[2] and the patrician Priuli, who later gave offence to the Republican Government and was confined for ten years in the Sotto Piombi. Elcho saw him after his release, when he told him that in the summer he had often been in danger of being roasted by the heat of the sun, and that during his imprisonment he had lost the use of his limbs, his cell being of a size barely sufficient to hold the ' uneasy pallet ' which did duty for a bed.

[1] The paolo was approximately of the value of fivepence.
[2] The friend of Frederick the Great.

The English resident at Venice, now John
Murray, soon hears that there is a Jacobite at
Padua; on August 6th he is writing to the
Foreign Minister in London, 'I have just had
intelligence that the late Lord Elcho has been at
Padua for some days. . . . If he should come to
this Town, I shall certainly make an application to
have him sent away ; but if he stays at Padua,
to be out of the way of Bustle, and means no
mischief I dont think he can possibly be in a
more inoffensive place.' Two days later he writes
that his spy has returned from Padua and states
that 'the late Lord Elcho takes the name of
D'Arcourt, and tells his particular friends at
Padua that he is *Sopra Intendente del Campo del Rè
Giacomo.* He has cloathed his servants in expen-
sive new Liveries.' Such is the unaccountable
gossip of the spy.[1] But the 'late Lord Elcho'
was far from wishing to be 'out of the way of
Bustle '; and he plunges with all his former zest
into the social life of Padua, the ceremonious
visits, the picnics and supper-parties in the
gardens of country-inns, the drives back through
the vineyards in the fragrant starlit night, the
dances, the theatres, or the comedies played in

[1] *State Papers, Venice,* August 8, 1755.

some patrician palace, the nocturnal assignations,
that whole world of exquisite manner and refine-
ment which the delicate realism of Guardi and
Longhi has so minutely recorded.

It was a life that differed widely from that of
France. Far more was sacrificed to form, to an
outward sense of observance. Nobles would
starve their tables and deny themselves all costly
amusements for the sake of their equipages, the
liveries of their servants, or the quality of the
flowered silks in which they themselves were
clothed. Much, too, was surrendered in order
that the ladies of the 'bel monde,' when visiting
in their carriages might be accompanied by four
lacqueys on foot, resplendent in livery with
swords at their side. So much indeed did sense
of the appropriate insist on this courtly ritual,
that sometimes a lad from the tailor or shoe-
maker would be hired and dressed up for the
function, yielding up his sword and his livery
and retiring to his needle or last when the visit
had been paid. Moreover the attendance of the
lacqueys was not an altogether obsolete survival.
Elcho observes that it was still dangerous to move
unarmed through the streets, that attacks were
frequent, and that it was customary at night,

when secrecy did not require other methods, to
be accompanied by an armed retainer.

In December he moved on to Venice and took
up his quarters at Lo Scudo di Francia on the
Grand Canal, where the charges made were the
same as at Padua. From his friend Doctor Rigolini he learned that the ' English resident often
had the goodness to ask news about him ' ; but we
may judge from the letters of Murray that this
solicitude was less amiable than Elcho supposed.
He made many new friends, but he laments the
jealousy of Italian husbands, which in many cases
prevented a stranger from even seeing the lady of
the house. For instance, the noble Priuli, who
had been much in France, inquired if Elcho saw
anything of the Italian left in him. ' Yes,' was
the reply, ' I still observe in you a good deal of
the jealousy of that nation.' ' My friend,' said
Priuli, ' you have rightly judged ; but it arises
from the intimate knowledge that I have of the
women of this country : they are incapable of
resisting the advances of a suitor, and as I love
my wife, it is my care to guard her from
danger.' And though Elcho was a constant
guest at Priuli's house, he was never permitted
to see the lady. It was not only in the archi-

tecture of Venice that the influence of the Crescent was visible.

Summarising his impressions of Venice, Elcho writes : ' It is an excellent place for a man that can content himself with amusements and public spectacles. Everything is cheap, and one finds here all the commodities necessary for good living, fish, game, fowl, and fruit in great abundance ; excellent wine from Cyprus and the isles of Greece ; and Maraschino, the finest liqueur in the world, from Corfu and from Zara.' The nobles, he complains, are unsociable, while the unfailing presence of the *cicisbeo* renders the society of the ladies formal and constrained. In the casini [1] alone was ceremony permitted to abate its rigour. In these, which were small apartments surrounding the Square of St. Mark and owned by the wealthier ladies of Venice, suppers were given after the opera or an evening of gambling at the Ridotto. Here were centres of freedom and intrigue, here assignations were fulfilled, and here it was possible to escape from the jostling multitude without, from the mountebanks, the musicians, the quack doctors, the

[1] John Moore, *View of Society and Manners in Italy*, vol. ii. p. 99 ; *Voyage d'un François en Italie*, 1769, vol. viii. p. 278.

vendors of provisions, the fortune-tellers, the courtesans, from that crowd so various in texture and form which made up the seething life of the Piazza. But it was a mere oasis in a wilderness of formality, where Venetian and foreigner could meet for a moment with ease. For the rest the visitor was a stranger within the gates, and the barriers between himself and Venetian society remained insurmountable.

VII

In March 1756 Elcho was again on the move, journeying back to Neufchâtel to rejoin Earl Marischal. At Fuessen in the Tyrol he is seized with fever. The local physician is summoned. Elcho observes that he is intoxicated and resists a proposal to be bled by him. But he is over-persuaded by the innkeeper, who assures him that the doctor works better in that condition than when sober. The operation then is performed with a hammer and lancet, as 'if the patient had been a horse,' and after fifteen days Elcho was able to resume his journey. On arriving at Neufchâtel the news was broken to him by Earl Marischal that his father, whom he had not seen since the September day in 1745 when he rode away from Wemyss Castle to join Prince Charles at Gray's Mill, had died this winter in Scotland.

By his will Lord Wemyss bequeathed all his property to his third son, James Wemyss: [1] the

[1] Owing to the debts contracted by Lord Wemyss, the inheritance did not exceed £2000 per annum.

second son, Francis Charteris, who in due course
became Earl of Wemyss, having already inherited
the wealth of his maternal grandfather, Colonel
Charteris. Under his father's will Elcho received
no addition to his fortunes, but he adopted the
designation of Earl of Wemyss—a title to which
his legal right was barred by the attainder.
Hitherto he had been in receipt of an allowance
of £500 paid by Francis Charteris. It was now
arranged that this allowance should be paid half
by Francis and half by James. At the same time
Elcho persuaded his mother to resign in his
favour her dowry of £500 a year.[1] Lady Wemyss
had an independent fortune of her own ; it seemed
reasonable, therefore, that her claim on the
Wemyss estate should pass to Elcho.

These transactions, which he considered were
devoid of generosity towards himself, gave him
at this time an income of 25,500 livres. By this
slight improvement in his financial position he was
enabled to live in a manner more congenial to his
tastes. On his return to Paris in 1756 he in-
creased his establishment, taking into his service
a valet, a lacquey, a coachman, and a cook, with

---

[1] In 1776 Lady Wemyss endeavoured unsuccessfully to obtain in
the Scottish Courts a revocation of this gift.

two carriage horses and one saddle horse. At
the same time he continued to reside in the Rue
Grenelle, Faubourg St. Germain. His intimate
friends were the Comte de Lubersac, commandant
of the recently instituted military school of the
' chevaux-légers de la garde,' [1] Peglioni, a general
in the Bavarian service, the Abbé Perdigou, the
Abbé Colbert, and Mr. Macdonald. At the
house of the Comte d'Argenson Elcho was a
frequent guest, and during the course of the
winter he was formally presented to Louis by the
Duc de Fleury.

His attention, however, was much occupied
with a personal matter relating to his mother.
The faculties of Lady Wemyss had for some
time past shown signs of weakening, and in her
own interests Elcho had persuaded her in the
early part of 1756 to take up her residence in the
Convent of St. Denis. While here, Elcho discovered that her riches had excited the cupidity
of Mr. Alexander Murray, the hero of the
Elibank plot. Murray, it was soon ascertained,
in conjunction with a Doctor Cantwell and a
Mr. Fitzgerald, was conspiring to abduct Lady
Wemyss and possess himself of her wealth.

[1] Luynes, *Mémoires*, xv.

Elcho considered that more drastic measures for
Lady Wemyss's security were desirable, and
believing that there was no other way to protect her, he obtained an order from the Secretary
of State for her transfer to a convent at Chartres.
In this new residence she enjoyed the spiritual
ministrations of the Bishop, but far greater
vigilance appears to have been exercised in
curtailing her freedom.   Here she resided unmolested till 1758.   In that year Charles Leslie,
brother of the Earl of Rothes, appeared on the
scene.   Mr. Leslie, a colonel in the army of
Holland and a needy adventurer, had fallen into
the debt of Mr. Crawford, the banker at Rotterdam.   With the aid of Mr. Crawford, who saw in
a union, legal or otherwise, between Leslie and
Lady Wemyss a prospect of the repayment of his
debts, a permit was obtained for Lady Wemyss
to quit the convent at Chartres and leave France.
She appears to have been fully aware of what was
passing, and lent herself readily to the scheme.
By means of the permit she was given her liberty.
Shaking the dust of Chartres from her feet, she
posted to the frontier and thence proceeded to
Brussels, the rendezvous agreed on.   Here, however, her plans and those of Mr. Leslie diverged.

She had no idea of abetting his nefarious project, and to his infinite discomfiture Lady Wemyss immediately placed herself under the protection of Mr. Murray, with whom she left for London.

Later in 1766, to finish this discreditable story, she returned with Mr. Murray to France. Information was brought to Elcho, then at Paris, that she was being kept under restraint in Mr. Murray's hotel. Elcho appealed to M. de Sartine, Chief of the Paris Police. A *lettre de cachet* was obtained, and the unfortunate Lady Wemyss was removed from the care of Mr. Murray and placed in a convent at Charenton. Here to all intents and purposes she was as strictly a prisoner as though she had been transferred to the Bastille. Murray was indignant at being thus baffled in his schemes. He appealed to Lord George Lennox, then Chargé d'Affaires. To Lord George it was merely a case of a British subject incarcerated without any charge having been established against her.[1] He therefore applied to the Duc de Choiseul, and an order was at once obtained for the release of Lady

[1] There is a despatch from Lord George Lennox setting out the facts as above stated. *State Papers, France*, vol. cclxx., Aug. 2, 1766.

Wemyss, it being stipulated that she should immediately leave France.

On the day fixed for the order to take effect Elcho and Murray met outside the walls of the convent. Elcho, who appears to have been at all times ready with his sword, there and then invited Murray to fight. Murray declined the combat, and as they waited for the convent doors to open Elcho was forced to content himself with addressing Murray in opprobrious terms. Lady Wemyss chose her own moment for departure, and when some days later she emerged from her residence, it was only to rejoin Murray and set forth to England in his company. Whether Elcho was moved by filial forethought or some more sordid motive in thus attempting to coerce his mother, it is impossible to say. He was, however, supported by his nephew, Captain Steuart, a man of the highest honour, while Lady Wemyss, in trusting herself to Murray, had certainly shown that her conduct needed some measure of supervision.

On Wednesday, January 5, 1757, while Elcho was in Paris, Damiens inflicted a slight wound on the King as he was stepping into his carriage at Versailles on his return to the

Trianon. On Thursday it was known in Paris that no cause whatever existed for anxiety. Rejoicings throughout the city were prescribed. The Church, that Church which Louis had recently been supporting in her conflict with the Parliament, was foremost in thanksgiving. Special prayers and services were ordained, and in Notre Dame the majestic echoes of the *Fac salvum regem* were stifled in the sobs of the officiating clergy.[1] In the streets the inhabitants shook one another by the hand with tears of rejoicing in their eyes ;[2] while among the poor of Paris gratitude for this singular manifestation of Divine mercy was stimulated by the distribution of 300,000 francs in charity. But it was at the Palace of Versailles that interest was focused. There consternation reigned, and the fate of Madame de Pompadour hung from hour to hour in the balance. Was it, every one was asking, to be a repetition of the fate of Madame de Châteauroux in 1744 ? Would this second reminder to the King that he was mortal lead again to the dismissal of a mistress ? The King's confessor, the Père Desmarets, was summoned ;

---

[1] Barbier, *Journal du règne de Louis XV.*, vol. iv. p. 173.
[2] *Ibid.*

the hopes of the enemies of the Marquise rose high. Machault, the Keeper of the Seals, visited Madame de Pompadour. When he left she was bathed in tears. Orders were given for her trunks to be packed : the end of her reign was surely at hand. But the Maréchale de Mirepoix arrives. The scene changes. 'Qui quitte la partie la perd, madame,' she says, and, clinging to a forlorn hope, Madame de Pompadour remains. As the recollection of the danger fades, Louis resumes his visits to the favourite ; the confessor is dismissed, Madame de Pompadour is once more supreme in power. Early in February Machault is deprived of his office, and the Comte d'Argenson, the most powerful member of the Government, the minister intrusted with the conduct of the war, receives a letter banishing him to the provinces. Such was the penalty for unsuccessful opposition to the *de facto* Queen of France.

Of the atrocious manner in which Damiens was put to death the *Journal* contains every detail. On March 28th all Paris assembled in and about the Place de la Grève. The watching of torture was a form of vice for which the opportunities were limited. This was no occasion to be lost.

'In reading the journals of the day,' says a Catholic writer, 'we are amazed at the place taken in popular life by the scenes of the Grève. It was the theatre of Paris.'[1]   Madame du Hausset relates[2] that the wife of a farmer-general, a woman of great beauty, hired two places at a window for twelve louis, and beguiled the period of waiting for the execution by playing at cards.   Nor was the instance cited exceptional. When the moment arrived, Damiens, who had been put to the question ordinary and extraordinary, was conveyed to the scaffold in a sheet.   The hideous narrative has often been told, and is only repeated here because Elcho was a veritable eyewitness, and supplies one detail at least not found elsewhere. The wretched man was fastened with ligatures of steel to a table around which were gathered executioners summoned from the provinces, and the surgeons whose scientific knowledge had been invoked to make the torments more prolonged. At four o'clock his right hand was burnt; then his flesh was torn with red-hot pincers ; molten lead, boiling oil and fat were poured into the

---

[1] Carné, *Monarchie française au 18ième Siècle* : cited J. Morley, *Diderot*, vol. i. p. 62.

[2] *Mémoires.*

wounds. In his agony the miserable man grappled hold of the nearest executioner, and only by means of a lever was it possible to relax the grip of Damiens's fingers. Towards six o'clock a horse was fastened to each of his limbs. The horses were young ; they were unable to overcome the resistance of the victim. A message was despatched to the Parliament that unless the sinews of Damiens were cut the sentence could not be carried out. The answer came back that the torture was not to be curtailed. Thereupon two more horses were harnessed. Still the strength of the unhappy man held out, and it was not till evening was closing in that the necessary order arrived. Then the sinews were severed and one by one the limbs of Damiens were torn from his body. Thus was the sanctity of the King's person vindicated, and thus, in this scene of unparalleled horror, was consummated the most infamous act of an ignoble reign.

Perhaps the most repulsive feature of the loathsome scene is the fact stated from observation by Elcho and confirmed by Barbier, that while from the vast multitude that thronged the streets, filled the windows, and swarmed over the roofs, many men withdrew, unable to endure the spectacle, every woman remained at her post till the last. Indeed the part played by women at executions in France was not always limited to that of mere spectators. Philip Thicknesse [1] relates in his memoirs the extraordinary circumstance that at Dijon, where he witnessed the execution of a youth by breaking on the wheel, the executioner was assisted in every detail of his ghastly office by his aged mother, who appeared to take a tremulous pleasure in tying the cords and arranging the posture of the wretched culprit. Nor did the incongruity in the scene inspire the least protest or surprise among the onlookers. That such repulsive exhibitions should have been tolerated in these years may go far to explain the worst barbarities of the French Revolution.

In order to appreciate Elcho's military employment at this period it is necessary to take a brief glance at the political situation in Europe. In May 1756 war had been formally declared between England and France. The first blow of the struggle had been struck in April, when the French despatched an expedition for the

[1] Philip Thicknesse, *A Year's Journey through France*, vol. i. p. 40.

capture of Minorca.   In June, Minorca had
succumbed to the victorious arms of the Duc
de Richelieu.   This catastrophe was rapidly followed by reverses in North America and India.
But a new era was dawning for the fortunes of
England.   'The wide weltering chaos of plati-
tudes regulating the country' was passing away,
and in November 1756 the destinies of the nation
were transferred to the guidance of William Pitt.
France meanwhile, breaking loose from her
traditional policy and guided by the hand of
Madame de Pompadour, had formed an alliance
with Maria Theresa.   To crush Frederick the
Great was now the motive of French statesman-
ship.   France, Austria, Saxony, and Russia were
united for the purpose.   In March 1757 a French
army of 100,000 men crossed the Rhine.   The
Duke of Cumberland at the head of the Hanoverian and Hessian troops was defeated at
Hastenbeck and forced to evacuate the Elector-
ate.   France for the moment was successful,
and rejoicings in the capital acclaimed the policy
of Madame de Pompadour.   But retribution was
swift.   At Rossbach in November 1757 Frederick
defeated Marshal Belle-Isle and compelled the
French to retire once more behind the Rhine.

They were pursued by Prince Ferdinand of Bruns-
wick, and at Crefeld, on June 23, 1758, they were
completely routed. England in the meantime
was contenting herself with a more vigorous
pursuit of the campaign in North America, with
the payment of subsidies to Frederick,[1] and
desultory raids on the French coast at Cherbourg,
St. Malo, and Dunkirk (1757-1758).

Before his downfall D'Argenson had nominated Elcho as Colonel of the Royal Scots. In
June 1757 the corps was in garrison at Gravelines with the regiment of Ogilvy, and here Elcho
was received as commander of the battalion. He
remained with them till September, superintending their manœuvres and commanding them on
two minor expeditions to Dunkirk and Bourg-
Bourg. But he was still without reward for
his services, and on his return to Paris he
renewed his application for pay to the Duc de
Belle-Isle, who had succeeded D'Argenson. Receiving no reply, and considering himself grossly
ill-used, he addressed a letter to William Pitt,
now minister in England, begging again for a
pardon, and stating that if employment were given
to him in the English service he would accept

[1] The total paid was £2,680,000.

it rather than remain attached to a country
where he was expected to serve without salary.
This naïve declaration of mercenary patriotism
received no answer. Elcho indeed had reason
later to suspect that the letter fell into the hands
of the French ministers.

The following year he was again serving with
his regiment at Dunkirk, resisting the descents
of English troops on the French coast, when
Colonel de Roth, Lieutenant-General, came as
Inspector to review the garrison. The Marquis
du Barail, Commandant of Dunkirk, entertained
the General to dinner, and pointedly omitted an
invitation to the Colonel of the Royal Scots.
On other occasions also, when Elcho and de Roth
were thrown together, the official representative
of the military authorities ignored Elcho's presence. But Elcho was not a person to be easily
rebuffed. At the first opportunity he approached
de Roth and demanded why, after serving in two
campaigns, he should still be without a salary.
De Roth drily replied, 'The King is master of
his own gifts.' It was this conduct of de Roth
which led Elcho to believe that his letter to Pitt
had been intercepted.

Thus we have seen the exile bartering his

sword and his services alternately to France and
to England, and seeking a post under Frederick
of Prussia, while from a letter of the English
Resident at Venice we know that at one time he
proposed joining the forces of the Republic.[1]   As
a soldier of fortune, thus frowned on by the
goddess whose service he was continually seeking,
he must have experienced no common degree of
bitterness at the enforced neutrality of his career.
It is easy to conceive with what pleasure he must
have heard from Earl Marischal that he had found
for him a country place, La Prise, in the vicinity
of his own château at Colombier in the canton of
Neufchâtel.   To his new property at the conclusion of his military duties in 1758 he set out.
On the way he was the victim of an adventure
which illustrates the manners of the day.   The
postillion whom he had hired for the journey was
of an indolent disposition and absolutely refused
to move at a smarter pace than was convenient to
himself.   Exasperated at the continual delay,
Elcho dismounted from the chaise to give the
offender, as he says, a few strokes with his cane.
No sooner had he alighted than the postillion,
realising what was in prospect, struck spurs into

[1] John Murray to Newcastle, *State Papers, Tuscany*, August 1755.

his horse and in a moment was bowling down the
road, leaving Elcho a mere impotent cypher in the
landscape. The carriage and luggage were finally
recovered, but the postillion, as his promptitude
deserved, succeeded in effecting his escape.

Shortly after Elcho's arrival at Colombier Lord
Marischal received the news that his brother, the
celebrated marshal of Frederick, had been killed
at the battle of Hochkirchen (October 14, 1758).
'Quelle triste nouvelle et pour vous et pour moi!'
wrote Frederick. There could be no sadder news
for Lord Marischal. The brothers had been
comrades from boyhood and loyal friends throughout a chequered life of wandering and exile. It
was the end of a faithful devotion, and left the
survivor lonely and bereaved. But Lord Marischal allowed no place for vain lamentation. He
displayed, Elcho says, the philosophy and fine
courage habitual to his character. 'Probus vixit,
fortis obiit,' he said of his brother, and in a well-
known letter to Madame Geoffrin he wrote of
him in a strain of no less homage : 'My brother
leaves me a noble legacy: last year he had Bohemia
under ransom; and his personal estate is seventy
ducats.' The body of the Marshal was transferred
to Dresden. There it was interred in the Garni-

son-Kirche, while a notable inscription [1] was en-
graved on the monument erected to his memory.

In January of the following year Earl Marischal
was 'called out of his Neufchâtel stagnancy and
launched into the diplomatic field again.' Frederick was anxious for peace ; he believed that Spain
might act as mediator,[2] and it was in order that
he might watch the development of events at the
Court of Madrid that Lord Marischal in response
to Frederick's request set out in the early part
of the year for Spain. Carlyle states that Earl
Marischal passed through London on his way to
Madrid. But from the *Journal* we learn for the
first time that he travelled by Sardinia, where he
held several conferences with the King, afterwards
embarking at Genoa for Barcelona. It was not,
in fact, till his pardon was obtained from the King
of England at the earnest solicitation of Frederick[3]
that the Earl in 1761 visited London. In Spain
there was small scope for his diplomacy, but he
was able to render service to the country which

---

[1] 'An inscription not easily surpassable in the lapidary way:
" Dum in proelio non Procul hinc | Inclinatam suorum Aciem | Mente
Manu Voce et Exemplo | Restituebat | Pugnans ut Heroas Decet |
Occubuit | D XIV Octobris." These words go through you like
the clang of steel.'—Carlyle, *Friedrich II.*, ed. 1865, vol. v. p. 273.

[2] *Œuvres de Frédéric le Grand*, vol. xx. p. 273.

[3] *Ibid.*, Frédéric au Roi d'Angleterre, vol. xx. p. 278.

had at last condoned his espousal of the Jacobite cause. And in the warning transmitted to Pitt of the family compact made between King Carlos of Spain and Louis xv., he paid tribute to the generosity with which George ii. had admitted him once more as a citizen of his native country.[1]

What, if anything, Lord Marischal effected on behalf of Frederick at the Court of Madrid is not clear. But that the mission was of importance may be gathered from the fact that Lord Marischal returned to Spain after his visit to London in April 1761.[2] The published correspondence between the King and his minister is chiefly concerned with melon seeds and tobacco. Frederick was much taken up with the cultivation of melons at Potsdam, and the seeds were a common offering from friends travelling in the south.[3] In two feet of snow, with the Austrians facing him in Silesia, the King could turn aside to discuss the matter with Lord Marischal, and dwell on the excellence of the tobacco.

[1] It has been commonly suggested that the pardon was granted in recognition of this information. See KEITH, *Dictionary of National Biography*. But the King's patent was granted May 29, 1759. The compact was not signed till August 15, 1761.

[2] *Œuvres de Frédéric le Grand*, vol. xx. p. 282.

[3] *Ibid.*, Frédéric au Comte Algarotti, vol. xviii. p. 94.

March 1762 [1] found Lord Marischal once more in his Principality endeavouring to compose the differences between the Protestant factions of the Canton, and soothe the seared sensibilities of the fugitive Rousseau.

In the meanwhile, pending a final adjustment of accounts between Elcho and his family, Mr. Wemyss had ceased paying his share of Elcho's allowance ; at the same time there had occurred a fall in the value of the dividends which Elcho received from his French investments. This narrowing of his circumstances compelled him to pass many uneventful months in Switzerland and turned his thoughts to the quest of an heiress. In this he was so far successful that negotiations were entered into with a widow, Madame de May, the only daughter of M. Herivart, a wealthy landed proprietor in Switzerland. The courtship proceeded with such briskness that four days after his introduction to the widow Elcho wrote inviting her hand in marriage. The lady returned an ambiguous answer 'asking time for reflection.' Thereupon ensued a correspondence in which Elcho pressed his claims while Madame de May maintained an attitude of hesitation. In one of

1 *Œuvres de Frédéric le Grand*, vol. xx. p. 285.

her letters—the last, it may be presumed, that she wrote—she stated that she had difficulty in resolving to marry a rebel. This was a point of honour upon which the suitor was sensitive. He despatched his valet to demand back his letters, at the same time writing that, 'rebel as he was, he had done her too much honour in dreaming of her, and that the affair must end.' A week or two later Madame de May sought consolation in a marriage with the Chevalier Wynn, and a suspicious commentator may possibly detect the influence of the Chevalier in the final letter of the widow.

The year 1759 had been an eventful year for the arms of England. The fall of Quebec had concluded the first stage of the conquest of Canada; in India the siege of Madras had been raised, and the victorious advance of the British troops in other portions of the peninsula had unerringly progressed. In Europe British and German troops, under the command of Prince Ferdinand, had defeated the French at Minden; while on sea the victories achieved by Boscawen and Hawke had shattered the fleets of France, commanded respectively by M. de la Clue off the Portuguese coast and by the Maréchal de Conflans

in Quiberon Bay. In the operations of the French
we once more become aware of the faint and fitful
political survival of Charles. From the *Journal*
we learn that from time to time he had been
residing at Bouillon, the castle of his relative, with
Miss Walkinshaw, whom rumour asserted he continued to maltreat. It was from Bouillon that he
paid visits to Paris, where he passed much time
in the society of Alexander Murray. Nor, as we
learn from his correspondence with Antony Walsh,[1]
had he ever ceased to entertain a belief in his
ultimate support by France. It is at this time,
also, that his bemused and clouded thoughts turn
once more to the disasters of '45-'46, and that in
a letter to his father we find him breaking forth
again into a savage attack on Lord George
Murray.[2]

In 1759 he was in negotiation with the French
Government, sending messages to Louis and his
ministers, and even approaching Madame de
Pompadour, whom he formerly ignored, and
whose cypher name in the *Stuart Papers* is now
La Brillante Étoile. France was meditating a

[1] Printed by the Duc de la Trémoïlle, *Une Famille Royaliste
Irlandaise et Écossaise.*

[2] See Appendix B.

descent upon Ireland. Her fleets were being
gathered for the convoy of the Duc d'Aiguillon
with 18,000 troops. It was suggested that Charles
should accompany them. But in the time of
Tencin Charles had declared 'Point de partage :
tout ou rien.' In September 1758 he had written
to Walsh : 'There cannot and never will be a
question of Mr. Burton [Charles himself] ceding
or entering into any accommodation about the
little lands of Vernon [Scotland] and Stanley
[Ireland].'[1] His sentiment was still the same.
He would be no party to retrieving a portion
only of the kingdom. St. James's remained his
goal ; he refused to embark unless the descent
was made upon the English coast. Thereupon,
writes Elcho, a Mr. O'Dun was convened to act
the part of Prince Charles. Mr. O'Dun was an
Irishman, and in feature appears to have borne a
close resemblance to Charles. It was proposed
that upon the moment of the landing of the troops
in Ireland Mr. O'Dun should be proclaimed as
the representative of the Stuarts. Mr. Lang has
published a letter[2] of Alexander Murray to Charles,

---

[1] Printed by the Duc de la Trémoïlle in *Une Famille Royaliste
Irlandaise et Écossaise.*

[2] *Pickle the Spy,* p. 409.

which fits in with this statement of Elcho's.
Murray writes (December 10, 1759) of an interview with the Duc de Choiseul. 'He [Choiseul]
then told me that in case you did not chuse to go
with Mr. de Guillon [d'Aiguillon] that it would
be necessary to send one with a declaration in
your name.' Here we have confirmation that the
rôle of Mr. O'Dun was contemplated, if nothing
more. Hawke's victory, however, rendered this
imposition on the credulity of the Irish unneces-
sary, and defeated for the third time in sixteen
years the design of a French landing in England.
Mr. O'Dun was later appointed French Minister
to the Elector Palatine.

In 1761 Elcho was still at La Prise, awaiting
with anxiety the return of Earl Marischal. The
presence of the Governor was urgently needed.
During his absence the quiet of Neufchâtel had
been rudely broken by doctrinal differences in the
Protestant congregation. In 1760 the Pastor
Petitpierre had been deprived of his cure by the
ecclesiastical authority on account of the views
he entertained on the non-eternity of punishment.
The friends of Petitpierre rallied to his support;
they persuaded the President of the Council to
reject the nomination of a new minister appointed

to the living ; a deadlock was created, and it was in the heat of the crisis which followed that Earl Marischal returned to his Principality (March 1762). The Earl, a philosopher himself and a friend of the Encyclopædists, had no difficulty in determining to uphold the deposed Petitpierre.[1] His decision raised a storm in the Principality and evoked all the intolerant spirit of the followers of Calvin. Elcho, with more insight or from a more intimate acquaintance with the feeling in the country, advised the Earl to accept the new minister. ' I informed him,' he writes in the *Journal*, ' that if he would not take this course, the Council of State would do it in spite of him. He replied that they would not dare to do so, was irritated with me, and asked why I meddled in the matter. I answered that my interest led me to do so, that I had come to reside in the country from love of him, and that my happiness, my interest, and my pleasure made me wish that he would pass the remainder of his days there. But knowing him as I did,

---

[1] Lord Marischal appointed the brother of the pastor to act as spiritual adviser to Mademoiselle Emettée, who desired to adopt the Christian faith. Ch. Berthoud, *Les Quatre Petitpierre*. Neufchâtel, 1875.

I knew well that if the Council of State received the Minister without his consent, he would take it to heart and quit the country.'

The crisis dragged on, but the Council acted as Elcho predicted,[1] and in 1763 Earl Marischal tendered his resignation to Frederick, and left Neufchâtel to visit Scotland. Before this controversy had brought his rule to an end Lord Marischal had come into unlooked-for association with Rousseau. Fleeing from persecution, that wayward philosopher had sought refuge under the aegis of Frederick and his Governor in Neufchâtel. With theatrical brusqueness he had announced to the King his arrival in a letter beginning, ' I have spoken much evil of you ; I shall probably speak more.' For answer Frederick directed Lord Marischal to provide

[1] The following account is from the pen of Voltaire : ' Il n'y a pas longtemps qu'un théologien calviniste, nommé Petitpierre, prêcha et écrivit que les damnés auraient un jour leur grâce. Les autres ministres lui dirent qu'ils n'en voulaient point. La dispute s'échauffa ; on prétend que le roi leur souverain leur manda que puisqu'ils voulaient être damnés sans retour, il le trouvait très bon qu'il y donnait les mains. Les damnés de l'Eglise de Neufchâtel déposèrent le pauvre Petitpierre qui avait pris l'enfer pour le purgatoire. On a écrit que l'un d'eux lui dit : mon ami, je ne crois pas plus à l'enfer éternel que vous, mais sachez qu'il est bon que votre servante, votre tailleur, et surtout votre procureur y croient.'—See *Dictionnaire Philosophique* (*Enfer*).

the refugee with one hundred crowns, afford him
protection, and deter him if possible from writing, or 'he will turn the heads of your subjects.'
Utterly opposed as Frederick, the student of
Locke, of Marcus Aurelius, and of Lucretius,
might be to the theories of Rousseau, he was
too enlightened to tolerate the persecution of
eccentric opinions. 'Il ne me persuaderait jamais
à brouter l'herbe et à marcher à quatres pattes,'
he wrote to Lord Marischal. 'La véritable
philosophie, ce me semble, est celle qui, sans inter-
dire l'usage, se contente à condamner l'abus : il
faut savoir se passer de tout, mais ne renoncer,
de rien.' 'But,' he continues, '. . . si nous
n'avions pas la guerre, si nous n'étions pas ruinés,
je lui ferais bâtir un ermitage avec un jardin.'[1]
Lord Marischal received the philosopher at Colombier. On seeing the venerable old man, Rousseau
says his first instinct was to weep at the sight of
that attenuated frame, so wasted by old age, but,
lifting his eyes, he beheld a countenance so open,
so noble, so animated, that his affliction gave
way to respect mingled with confidence. In
his *Confessions* he sheds abundance of tears over
the virtues of Lord Marischal, over his hospi-

[1] *Œuvres de Frédéric le Grand*, vol. xx. p. 289.

tality, his fatherly kindness, and concludes in a mawkish rhapsody which would have diverted the Earl—'O bon mylord! o mon digne père! que mon cœur s'émeut encore en pensant à vous!'

With the conclusion of Lord Marischal's reign in Neufchâtel there ended at the same time the long and faithful friendship which he had extended to Elcho. Whether their relations were embittered by the warmth with which Elcho had advocated a particular course of conduct in the Petitpierre controversy does not appear, but I have been unable to discover any trace of the friends meeting or corresponding after this date. It is preferable, however, to presume that only circumstances compelled them into diverging channels of life, and that the affection and esteem which had played a controlling part through so many years survived the change.

Forty years had passed since Earl Marischal had set foot in Scotland. He found that the ties with his country were no longer binding : his brother lay in his soldier's grave in the Garnison-Kirche, his home had passed into other hands, the aspect of many things seemed strange, and King George's pardon may well have cooled the welcome extended to the old Jacobite leader in the north. Frederick, too, was writing ardent reasons for his return to Prussia. 'While yet alive,' he wrote, 'you are enjoying the lot of Homer after his death : towns disputed the honour of being his birthplace : I would dispute with Edinburgh the honour of claiming you. If I had a fleet I should contemplate sending it to carry off my dear Lord Marischal and bring him here.' Such affectionate importunity was not to be resisted. In 1764 he retired to Prussia. He was welcomed by Frederick. Within a mile of the Palace of Potsdam a cottage was built for him by the King. There with his garden, his favourite authors, his still vital touch with the thought and movement of the day, and his correspondence with the celebrated men of the time, he passed his declining years. 'Sa douce philosophie ne l'occupe que du bien,' wrote Frederick to Voltaire.[1] 'Il loge vis à vis de Sans Souci, aimé et estimé de tout le monde. Voilà une heureuse vieillesse.' On May 25, 1778, Lord Marischal died in the home which Frederick had created for him.

[1] Œuvres de Voltaire, vol. xliv. p. 353.

VIII

It cannot be said that at this juncture the Wemyss family acted with munificence towards Elcho. The ties of relationship had never been strong, and the brothers in Scotland seem in their own interests to have made the most of the attainder which had broken the natural course of the inheritance. In the beginning of 1760 it really looked as if further supplies were to be cut off altogether : the regular allowance was being dribbled through to the Continent in diminishing quantities at irregular intervals. Elcho realised that he could no longer rely on the punctual payment of his income. Anxious therefore to forestall a complete breakdown of his resources, he proposed in 1760 that he should be paid off with a lump sum of ten thousand pounds. The brothers acceded to the proposition. James Wemyss handed over six, and Francis Charteris four thousand pounds. Thenceforward Elcho was independent of his relatives.

November 1762 saw the close of the Seven

Years' War ; saw, too, England in possession of
Canada, Cape Breton, French America, India
(except Pondicherry and Chandernagore), the
islands of Tobago, Dominica, and St. Vincent ;
while Havanna, which England had wrested from
Spain, was exchanged for Florida. In every
quarter of the globe the genius of Pitt and the
prowess of British arms had altered the balance
of power. On the Continent the renown and
authority of Prussia were assured by the retention
by Frederick of the territory he had conquered
in Silesia. Peace was once more established
among the nations of Europe. Elcho, who was
never slow to ask for what he conceived to be his
proper reward, thought this a fitting moment to
petition the Duc de Choiseul for the Cross of
Military Merit. The answer was that Elcho's
service had not been of sufficient length, and
that he must await his turn in the ordinary
course of seniority.

Elcho's regiment, the Royal Scots, also the
regiments of Ogilvy, Lally, and Fitzjames, had
been disbanded at the close of the war. Many
officers were thus cast adrift without prospect of
further service in the armies of France. Elcho,
finding himself in Paris in 1763 together with

General Groeme, the commander-in-chief of the land forces of Venice, formed a plan for constructing two battalions from the disbanded regiments, and tendering their services to the Republic. The Venetian Ambassador in Paris, Tiepolo, cordially welcomed the scheme. Officers were nominated, recruits obtained, and a memorial forwarded to the Republic containing details of the proposal. There, however, the matter ended. No notice was taken of the memorial, and nothing more was heard of the scheme. Never, surely, was an exile so hampered in his attempts to mark out a career for himself. Events frustrated him at every point. Active service abroad, pardon at home, seemed equally beyond his compass, nor, as we have seen, had his schemes for improving his financial position been attended with any greater degree of success. On the other hand he appears never to have relaxed his efforts or abandoned hope. If he was bewildered, he concealed it under an imperturbable mask of resolution ; if he was discouraged, he took refuge in a fresh pursuit of his purpose. He recognised no defeat ; he accepted no rebuff ; and in one at least of his objects, as we shall see, he finally succeeded.

The years immediately preceding and following

the peace were without personal incident. We
hear of him immersed in the parochial politics of
Neufchâtel, admitted as a burgess, entertained by
the magistrates at a civic banquet, taking part in
the provincial pleasures of the town, its suppers
and dances, and acquiring a local status of some
celebrity. If he sighed for the greater glories of
Paris, he must have remembered that in Switzerland he was at any rate a landed proprietor in the
country of his adoption, enjoying the honour and
appreciation of his neighbours. At other times
he is travelling in Germany, or staying at the
Court of Baden, flying falcons among the hills
with the Margrave, receiving from his host his
Order 'de la Fidélité' (for what particular fidelity
is not stated), or paying brief visits to Paris,
meeting his brother Francis Charteris, whom he
had not seen for nineteen years, and who it is
satisfactory to learn supplemented the halting
stipend he had doled out in past years by the
gift of a thousand pounds. Or again, we hear of
him careering over France, staying with Jacobite
friends in provincial towns; or back in Paris,
wrestling with Alexander Murray for the safe
custody of Lady Wemyss—delighting with all
his old fervour in the gaieties and dissipations

of the city, and the hospitality of the financiers, those accessories of power, who during the sway of Madame de Pompadour had acquired such a dominant social position. But never in this life of feverish haste, so full of the infinitely unimportant, is there absent from his mind the desire to return to his own land. Every change at the British Embassy in Paris, every alteration in the Cabinet in London is the occasion of a fresh appeal. But the Government was relentless. The death of George ii. brought his pardon no nearer. He was the marked man of the Jacobite rising, and was not to expect mercy or mitigation.

In 1765 he is again negotiating for the hand in marriage of a French heiress. The trenches are opened; Captain Steuart, his nephew, arranges that Elcho and Mademoiselle Truité shall have sight of each other 'without speaking, in a box at a sacred concert': they are mutually gratified. The siege advances; the lady proves a willing accomplice; nothing is needed but the sanction of the father. But there is 'reflection in their delirium,' and Elcho is warned by the young lady to ask for an allowance of 16,000 livres. The father, a wealthy proprietor from St. Domingo, proves a hard bargainer, and stands firm on an offer of 12,000 livres. Both parties seem to have imported into their discussion the methods of the slave-market of St. Domingo. The negotiations collapse and Elcho takes his departure. A little while and his commercial instincts are overpowered by his affections, and he returns with more humble views as to income. As usual he is too late. The Comte de Boulainvilliers has in the meanwhile carried off the lady at the lower figure of 12,000 livres a year. The transaction is typical of the period, and from the principal actor it receives neither comment nor apology.

On the morning of January 1, 1766, James died in Rome. For long he had been imploring Charles to visit him. But Charles was determined to keep clear of Rome and things Romish : it was part of a puerile policy, the motive of which, so far as it had any motive at all, was his desire to appear to the world as a sound Protestant, divorced from sympathy alike with his father's relations with the Vatican, and the position of his brother in the Roman Catholic Church.

When the news reached Paris that James was sinking, Charles did at last set forth. Leaving Paris on December 30, 1765, he travelled by

Strasburg and the Tyrol to Rome. What were
the thoughts in his mind on that journey? What
were the memories awakened as he looked out
once more on the Eternal City? Twenty-two
years had passed since at the bidding of France
he had said farewell to his father and quitted the
palace in the Via di Santi Apostoli. The dreams
of youth had been brought to nothing. The
hopes which gathered about him as he went had
been scattered into outer darkness. He had
passed through dazzling scenes: had reigned as
a Regent in Edinburgh, had known victory and
triumph, and then had been overwhelmed. Later
there came to him the memorable experience of
a long concealment amid a race of impregnable
devotion, an experience which might well have
raised his character to the sublime. Finally, he
had been hustled out of France like a pick-
pocket. And all—adventure, splendour, and
disaster—had ended in obliteration. Now he was
returning, a lonely and discredited exile, un-
welcomed and unrecognised, to reign only in
a kingdom of hollow tradition and desolate echoes.
But even now the grace which had once prevailed
could make itself felt. Lumisden,[1] who became

[1] Cited Lang, *Charles Edward*, p. 401.

his secretary at Rome, writes (January 23) that Charles 'charms every one that approaches him,' and there were still to be found some who would not forsake him.

Charles at once assumed the pomp and title of kingship. But it was a game which could not be profitably played without accomplices. English diplomacy was busy in the courts of Europe, in Austria, in France, in Spain, and above all at the Vatican, representing that the recognition of Charles as king would not be considered as consistent with friendly intentions towards George III. Diplomacy was successful. The powers consulted acceded to the representations. Pope Clement XIII., it is true, continued the allowance of 12,000 Roman crowns which had been made to James ; but even in the sacred city Charles was denied all claim to the title of king.

Elcho considered that Charles was now in a position to repay the famous 1500 guineas. With this idea he drew a bill for that amount, payable to the order of M. Barrazi, banker at Rome. As might have been expected, M. Barrazi shortly wrote back that he had presented the bill, but that Charles refused to accept it. This put the creditor on his mettle. He determined to make a pilgrimage in person to Rome and obtain a decree of the courts, or, if need be, invoke the authority of the Pope. Like the celebrated animal in the romance of Apuleius, who wandered over the world in search of the rose-leaves which were to restore to him his former shape and glory, the exile seems to have set his heart on the recovery of this much-debated sum. But from what is known of his character it may be assumed that his determination proceeded quite as much from a sense of fair-play and a natural repugnance to acknowledging defeat as from a hankering after the immediate fruits of success.

Leaving Paris on September 7, 1766, he entered Rome on November 7. The cost of the journey, which was performed in a carriage drawn by three horses, it is interesting to note, amounted to 2600 livres. Everywhere, he says, he was taken for a French officer. By this mistake he was able to profit, paying four paoli for a meal, for which an Englishman would have had to pay twelve. 'The Italians,' he adds, 'always charge much, but there is no nation so reasonable when they see that they have not to deal with fools.' On his arrival he took apartments in the Trinita di Monti. Here he had eight rooms, a kitchen, a stable and coach-house for six sequins a month. Like all strangers, he was driven to provide himself with meals at a restaurant at the rate of six paoli a head. It was rarely that guests were invited to partake of dinner or supper in the private houses of Rome. An Italian nobleman who had money to spend preferred to lay it out on the construction of a palace, the designing of a garden, or the purchase of works of art. It had, in fact, become the ambition of the members of the wealthier classes to have their names identified with the lasting records of art.[1] Building galleries, founding collections, promoting excavations in search of antiques, these were the serious diversions of the day. At the same time, numbers of the nobility spent large sums on their establishments, their horses and carriages, the liveries of their servants, the personnel of their retinue, and economised by giving no costly entertainments, and by even dispensing with the services of a cook. In such a case the needs of the house would be supplied from a neighbouring inn. A few of the nobles entertained, but it was the exception, and that open hospitality which prevailed in Paris was practically unknown in Italy. Concerts there were and parties for cards, and

[1] *Voyage en Italie*, vol. v. p. 137.

conversazioni, but music was cheap, and the other forms of sociability involved no expenditure at all.

Elcho at once directed his attention to attaining the object of his journey. Charles was living in the palace of his late father. In attendance, and forming an exceedingly modest Court, were Mr. Urquhart, a captain in the French army, Stafford, an Irishman who had been in his service so early as 1740, the secretary Mr. Lumisden, and Mr. Hay of Restalrig. Later, Charles's old devotion to sport revived, and he would make expeditions into the country in pursuit of game. But for the moment, as he writes to his brother, his 'situation' could not 'be amused with quels [quails] or any diversion whatsoever.' [1] He was living in melancholy isolation, parading a pomp which every one affected to ignore, and claiming a position which no one was permitted to acknowledge. Daily he showed himself, accompanied by Mr. Hay, in a coach drawn by six horses, with Messrs. Urquhart, Lumisden, and Stafford following in another carriage. Every afternoon a dismal progress was described through the streets of the city; every evening it terminated with the same spectral formalities at the palace in the Via di Santi

[1] *Stuart Papers*, February 1766.

Apostoli. Nowhere was he greeted by the populace, and as if this mute denial of his title was not
sufficient, the royal arms above the doorway of
his palace, which had hitherto reminded the passer-
by that there was still a 'king across the water,'
were secretly removed by order of the Pope.

Mr. Urquhart, who came to visit Elcho, told
him that Charles was now sunk in the last stages
of degradation, that not a day passed without some
scene of quarrelsome drunkenness, and it was a
common occurrence for Charles on these occasions
to become violent, and even beat Mr. Hay. 'I
have at last seen . . . in his own house,' wrote
William Hamilton,[1] in May 1767. 'As for his
person, it is rather handsome, his face ruddy and
full of pimples . . . . I cannot answer for his
cleverness, for he appeared to me to be sunk in
melancholy thoughts, a good deal of distraction
in his conversation and frequent brown studies.
. . . He has all the reason in the world to be
melancholy, for there is not a soul goes near him,
not knowing what to call him. He told me time
lay heavy upon him. I said I supposed he read
a good deal. He made no answer.' To such a

[1] The English Envoy at Naples. Lansdowne MSS., cited by Mr.
Ewald, p. 376.

point had dwindled he whose medal had once been struck with the motto, ' Spes Britanniae.'

The first step towards the recovery of the money was the preparation of a memorial. The document completed, Elcho placed it in the hands of the Secretary of State, Cardinal Torrigiani. The Secretary said that he would ascertain from Cardinal York whether Charles admitted the debt. The *Journal* gives the following account of what then occurred. ' I returned on the appointed day to the house of Cardinal Torrigiani, who informed me that the Prince had admitted the receipt of the sum of 1500 guineas from me in Scotland on September 16, 1745, but that he would not repay me till he was seated on the throne of Great Britain. I remarked to the Cardinal that I considered that event to be very far off, and that I wished to be paid now. The Cardinal asked why I had not raised the question sooner. I answered that the Prince had always been living incognito, that he had not had any fixed residence, and that so soon as he had taken up his abode in Rome I had come thither to reclaim my money. The Cardinal asked if I wished to raise an action against my sovereign. I replied that I did not recognise him as such, and that I would sue him if I were not prevented from doing so. The Cardinal answered that I must not be surprised to find that the Prince was protected in their country, as being zealous for their religion. I said that he had not been a zealot long, for he had abjured their religion in Switzerland. " I know it," replied the Cardinal, " but he is a good Catholic now." Seeing that I could make nothing of his Eminence, I said farewell to him.' The prospects of the creditor were little improved by a promise to pay on the Restoration. He now plunged into the thick of the ecclesiastical world : he made the round of the Cardinals. He called on the Bishops. He left no stone unturned to gain his point. From Cardinal Negroni alone did he receive practical advice. ' Do not talk of levying a distress or arresting the debtor,' said the Cardinal, ' but obtain an audience of the Pope, and invite His Holiness to detain, until your debt is paid, a portion of the 12,000 crowns which he gives to the Prince.' In due course Elcho was admitted to an audience with the Pope. Wearing his sword and hat, which he was allowed to do in consideration of his position as a titular Scottish peer, he was introduced to the presence of His Holiness by Cardinal Borghese. The Pope asked many questions about Elcho's travels, and patiently read the memorial, in which he was asked to withhold two thousand crowns a year until Charles had discharged his debt to the memorialist. If we are to believe the suitor, the Pope was moved to tears by the recital of the wrongs which Elcho had suffered, but he said that in refusing to recognise Charles by the title of King he had already given him grievous offence, and he was not prepared to interfere further in his affairs. The interview with the Pope gave the *coup de grâce* to Elcho's present aspirations after his £1500.

Nothing but his invincible optimism could have led Elcho to seriously expect repayment of this money. Unsuccessful claimants to thrones, if they have enjoyed no other prerogative, have usually exercised the privilege of ignoring their debts. Charles was the last man in the world to forgo this licence. And in his refusal he did not even think it necessary to propound the plea put forward by his father, that the money was advanced to the cause and not lent to the individual. That was a contention for lawyers and casuists. Charles more warily took refuge in mortifying silence. But the story gives point to the view of Dr. King. 'The most odious part of his (Charles's) character,' wrote the Doctor in his *Anecdotes*, 'is his love of money . . . the certain index of a base and little mind. . . . His most faithful servants, who had closely attended him in all his difficulties, were ill rewarded.' Nor was Elcho the only person at this time who was seeking recognition of his services or repayment of his debts. Sempil, the brother of the late lord, craves in straitened circumstances for repayment of the disbursements made by his brother on behalf of the cause ;[1] while in a letter of Robert Shee, formerly colonel in Fitzjames's Horse, we find a case analogous to that of Elcho. Shee writes from Metz, November 9, 1766 :[2] 'to put your Majesty in mind that the night after Culloden, in my Ld. Lovat's house, I gave your Majesty into his own hands a hundred and fifty guineas out of my private purse. I blush to be forced to this extremity.'

Though he had failed in the purpose of his mission, Elcho lingered in Rome through the summer. There was little enough to detain him. The city was almost deserted. Such few British visitors as were to be found there, with the excep-

---

[1] *Stuart Papers.* [2] *Ibid.*

tion of Lord Glenorchy, banned him from their society. He was a Jacobite outcast, exiled by an irony of fate for his devotion to a cause he had long ceased to support, and ostracised for a leader he had long learned to despise. His case justified pessimism. But he lived contentedly through the burning summer days, the tedium of his visit allayed by friendship with the French ambassador, the Marquis d'Aubeterre, and his mind diverted by the sights of the city, its churches, palaces, and works of art, for all of which he showed a ripening appreciation. He resisted the prevalent temptation of visitors, that of being painted by Pompeio Battoni, who at the rate of fifty sequins for a 'head' and a hundred for a 'full length,' had for many years been amassing considerable riches, mainly from the pockets of the English. Music, on the other hand, a taste for which at this epoch could be more easily gratified at Rome than in any other city, was his constant solace.

He took interest also in the frequent ecclesiastical functions, and narrates that on one occasion he attended as a spectator the tribunal summoned to decide upon the canonisation of a saint. Cardinals, bishops, and other functionaries sat in judgment, while learned theologians were present in a consultative capacity as technical assessors in the cause. It was necessary to prove the performance of some miracle by the proposed saint. Doctors and surgeons were called to give their opinion as to how far the alleged miracle might be accounted for by natural and physical causes. The consistory advocate, popularly known as the 'Devil's Advocate,' was there to test the validity of the claim.[1] In the case which Elcho heard, witnesses were called who gravely stated that they had seen the saint under discussion fly like a bird out of the window. He does not, however, state what view was taken by the medical experts, nor how far the consistory advocate thought it desirable to press his investigations. On another occasion, when less juggling with the supernatural was involved, he was present at a service held by the Jesuits. The sermon concluded, whips were handed to the congregation consisting of men, the lights were extinguished, and during a quarter of an hour of total darkness the more devout worshippers scourged themselves without mercy.

Naples, to which he migrated in September, proved a welcome contrast to the lethargy of

[1] *Voyage en Italie*, vol. v. p. 50.

Roman life. The presence of the Court gave distinction to society. The riches of the nobility were spent in entertaining. The attitude of the social world to foreigners was marked by none of the aloofness observable in the other towns of Italy. Living was cheap. Music, dancing, and the opera—Elcho's favourite diversions—could be enjoyed to the best advantage. The gaiety of the inhabitants, the charm and beauty of the surroundings, made him declare his preference for Naples over all the towns he had visited. He dined frequently with the French ambassador, M. de Choiseul. On one occasion he referred to Prince Charles. M. de Choiseul said he had never forgiven the Prince for visiting the Opera in 1746 when his adherents were perishing on the scaffolds of England, a circumstance which, it may be remembered, had excited angry protest at the time from Elcho himself.

In November the exile was once more on the move, posting across Italy to Venice. There he arrived in time for the last days of the Carnival. He saw the concluding festivities held in the presence of the Doge Moncenigo on the Piazza ; the head of an ox severed at a single blow ; a man raised by a cord from a gondola to the top of the

Campanile, and thence lowered to the feet of the Doge, to whom he presented a bouquet of flowers ; a pyramid formed by gondoliers standing in five tiers on each other's shoulders, which, though a mild acrobatic feat to the modern world, was one that excited the plaudits and astonishment of contemporary onlookers. At Venice he met many former friends : the patrician Priuli, recently liberated from the *piombi* ; Madame Morosini, now Madame Zenobio ; Madame Cornaro and her husband ; and the doctor Rigolini. There were the usual amusements : the opera, the theatre, and gambling at the Ridotto, pleasures for which he continued to show unflagging zeal. Since his last visit, theatrical performances had reverted or retrograded to their former character ; Goldoni had withdrawn to Paris, though keeping himself before the Venetian public with his *Genio buono e cattivo* ; Chiari had been beaten from the field ; for the moment the *Commedia dell'Art?* had revived, and Gozzi with his *Fiabe* was drawing crowded and enthusiastic audiences.[1]

In 1769, after uneventful wanderings over the

---

[1] *Mémoires of Carlo Gozzi* ; Vernon Lee, *Italy in the Eighteenth Century* ; *Mémoires of Goldoni.*

Continent, Elcho returned to Paris. In May 1770 he witnessed the arrival of Marie Antoinette before her marriage to the Dauphin, and attended the fêtes by which the event was celebrated. The most magnificent was, as usual, that given by the Spanish ambassador in the 'Vauxhall de Boulvart.' A supper was followed by a masked ball, to which eight thousand guests were invited. Four battalions of Swiss acted as waiters, and halls were set apart for faro, biribi, and trente-et-quarante. Elcho saw six thousand louis d'or staked on a single deal of trente-et-quarante, and eight hundred appears to have been a common venture. But gambling in Paris was carried to the verge of eccentricity. Goldoni relates the case of a lady at Versailles who remained at her post for thirty-six hours, eating her meals at the card-table, and in the case of the Spanish ambassador's party the play was continued till eight o'clock the following evening.

In July 1770 Elcho was presented by Louis xv. with the Order of Military Merit. In the same month Miss Walkinshaw, who was inclined to claim an enemy of Charles as a friend of her own, sent a message to Elcho, begging him to come and see her in a convent at Meaux, where she was

living with her daughter. Elcho went. She narrated her history, and told Elcho what she had
suffered in her life with Charles. She said that
she had received as many as fifty blows from him
in a day, and that he was so jealous that he would
surround the bed in which she slept with chairs
placed on tables, while on the chairs he would put
little bells which would sound if any one approached
during the night. He had refused subsistence for
her and her daughter, had even refused to write
the letter to the Duc de Choiseul which would
have secured for her support from the French
Court. He had driven her away by maltreatment,
and his vengeance had pursued her in her misfortunes. She appealed to Elcho to assist her,
and begged him especially to find a husband for
her daughter. He responded in a few weeks by
producing an Englishman, possessed of sufficient
wealth, who duly accepted the position of suitor
to the daughter of Prince Charles.[1] The marriage
was on the point of being arranged, but the young
lady's over partiality for the Jesuits led to a rup-
ture of the negotiations. The *Journal* does not

---

[1] In 1784 Charles summoned his daughter to Italy. He created
her Duchess of Albany, and she remained with him till his death in
1788.

give the name of the hypersensitive Protestant lover, but it is evident that his admiration must have been lukewarm.

In 1771 great festivities, to which Elcho was invited, were organised at Louisberg to celebrate the birthday of Charles Eugene, Duke of Würtemberg (1737-93). This licentious and capable Prince held a Court beside which the ostentation of Versailles was a thing of shadow and pretence. He was a specialist in festivals ; he had *la manie des altitudes* in shows and fêtes ; and though a more enlightened age would have deposed him as a monomaniac, in the epoch which he startled and adorned he was able to devote the revenues of the State and his entire income to fabulous entertainments. At ten in the morning he held a review of the flower of his army, after which the troops and the populace were admitted to the courtyard of the Castle, where the fountains were spouting wine, and bread and meat were distributed, and showers of silver coin were thrown among the crowd. In the meanwhile the numerous guests would be pursuing a more exact ceremonial, each being arrayed in robes of gold or silver silk, preparatory to dining with the Duke. At the dinner a row of pages—'all Counts or Barons'—were stationed behind the guests, while hussars and chasseurs formed a second, and the lacqueys of the Duke a third line of attendants. The waiting was carried on to a 'continual playing of trumpets, timbrels, drums, hautboys, bassoons, hunting-horns, and clarionettes.' Small wonder if in the Royal Palace the art of conversation was on the decline. After dinner the guests issued on to the Place St. Marc, an accurate reproduction of the Piazza of Venice, and promenaded in masks. The shops, the cafés, the casini, the diversions, and the whole turmoil of the Carnival were in full swing. In this way the Duke, who had been much in Venice, was enabled to gratify a whim and show his appreciation of the Queen of Cities. These, however, were not the only distractions provided for the guests. At his country house, La Solitude, the roof of which was a vast expanse of slates gilt at all the joinings, the Duke was able to develop the art of surprising to the greatest perfection. At dinner, says Elcho, 'the roof of the hall was suddenly thrown back, disclosing an orchestra of musicians dressed like gods and goddesses.' During supper 'the side of the hall opened, revealing an illuminated lake, into which the chasseurs had driven a number of big game, which they proceeded to shoot down before the spectators.' Movable roofs and walls indeed appear to have been one of the Duke's main resources. At the Opera the back of the theatre was unexpectedly withdrawn, exposing to view an illuminated country and the spacious spectacle of the royal troops engaged in a sham fight.

From these exhausting entertainments Elcho retreated to La Prise, where he resided intermittently for the next two years. In 1773 he is again attempting marriage, proposing for the hand of the daughter of the Vice-President of Neufchâtel, 'but,' he frankly says, 'as I wished a dowry of 200,000 livres, and the Vice-President would only give 50,000, I abandoned my suit, and the young lady some time afterwards was married to Baron de Bulach, to whom the Vice-President gave 40,000 livres.' Once more we find him pressing his claim for a pardon. His cause in this case was warmly taken up by the Margravine of Baden Dourlach, whose niece had married Prince Charles of Mecklenburg, brother of the English Queen.[1] But it was in vain. The English Ministry were relentless.

The remaining years of his life may be briefly

[1] See Appendix E.

dealt with. In 1776 he was at last successful in his matrimonial aspirations, and on September 9th, at the age of fifty-five, he was married at Beutal to a daughter of the Baron and Baroness d'Uxhull. With his wife he received a dowry of three thousand imperial florins. But financial considerations appear to have played a small part in the marriage, and a new era of peace and content seemed about to bring consolation to the later years of the exile. But it was short lived. In November 1777 Lady Elcho gave birth to a son. The child died within a few hours, the mother survived only a day. Elcho was once more alone and a wanderer. He was inconsolable. Their year of married life at his home in Switzerland had been attended with complete happiness. Lady Elcho had won the affection and goodwill of the neighbourhood, and on her demise there were public and genuine manifestations of sorrow. On the monument erected to her memory in the little church of Bôle there may still be read the following inscription—

'. . . épouse chérie du très-haut et très-puissant seigneur Milord Comte de Wemyss . . . née le 18 Août 1756, morte en couches le 26 Novembre

1777 et enterrée le 29 avec son fils
Milord Vicomte d'Elcho ; plus respectable par sa piété que par sa naissance
Elle faisait le bonheur de son époux
qu'elle a plongé par sa mort prématurée
dans une douleur profonde . . .'

Elcho himself resumed his former life of travel,
with occasional residence at his home, where, as
the municipal archives show, he continued to gain
the respect and esteem of the authorities and the
inhabitants among whom his estranging lot was
cast. He died in Paris in 1787 ; but in the town
of Bôle his memory is perpetuated by the bells
of the parish church, which before his death he
presented to the town in recognition of the
welcome extended to him by the Swiss.

It has often been said that Adam Smith thought
there was a Scotsman inside every man. In Elcho
there was little else. The political character of
his training made escape from the bond of nationality impossible. His fights as a boy at Winchester, his treatment as a young man in London,
the open hatred of the Union which he was
taught to develop in Scotland, all combined to
establish in him a deep-seated aversion to the
prevailing system of Anglicised government and

the dominance of what he considered a hectoring nationality. He was not one of the 'master spirits who have got the start of this majestic world.' In politics and the larger movement of national interests he was always at sea, and his soundings, when he took them, were invariably wrong. He was blind to the true significance of the Union. He totally miscalculated the forces opposed to a Stuart restoration. In war, when the watch-fires were kindling through Europe, he was unable to see beyond the clash of arms and the incidents of the campaign. In peace he never doubted of the permanence of the existing order of things. To the pent-up energy below and the liberating tendency of opinion above he was equally dead. Cast in a feudal mould, he carried into a new world of change and progress the outfit of a generation for whom there was no longer foothold. He had the bitterness of knowing that the supreme sacrifice of his life had been made on behalf of a lost cause and a worthless Prince; but to his credit he never repined. He had courage and resolution, and in the hand-to-mouth existence which he was forced to lead on the Continent he kept up a spirit of fortitude and a lively power of enjoyment. He was practical, and perhaps

sordid—so were his contemporaries. He was not
fired by any stirring aspiration—neither was the
generation to which he belonged. He took no
thought for the things of the mind. It is not on
record that once away from school he ever read a
book. It is true also that in his constant negotiations for marriage he displayed those practical
instincts which are conventionally said to be
Scottish characteristics. On the other hand, he
was candid and sincere. He was gifted with
soldierly qualities ; he played a distinguished part
in '45-'46, and he favourably impressed not a few
of those with whom he served. If his observation
of passing events was superficial, it was at least
accurate, and no more trustworthy account of
Charles's campaign is to be found than that contained in the Narrative. The sense of banishment
from the land to which his strongly marked
nationality was always drawing him was never
absent from his mind. This it was which produced the amazing restlessness of his disposition,
and made his postchaise an almost familiar object
on the great roads of France. The embassies
abroad, the Government offices at home, were the
unresponsive receptacles of his appeals for redress.
The liberty to return to his country was the real

object to which his life was dedicated. He failed, as we know, and with the one reflective outburst to which he gave utterance this sketch of his career may fittingly conclude. ' In the month of March 1778,' he writes, ' seeing that the English ministers were endeavouring to arrange terms of peace with the American rebels, I wrote a letter to Lord North, in which I remarked to him that since the government had come to treat with the rebels in America, they ought to extend a little of their clemency to me, a rebel Scot, and permit me to return to my native land and see my relatives after an exile of thirty-two years. The English are the most inconsistent and the most stern nation in the world when they have their enemies in their power. For thirty-two years I have vainly solicited leave to return to my native land. They have steadfastly refused it, although they know that I have neither seen Prince Charles nor held the least intercourse with him since my exile, and that he is despised by all those that have formerly acted under him. To-day they see that they cannot conquer the American rebels, who defeat them on every occasion. Thereupon they humble themselves before them and offer all sorts of terms of accommodation even to baseness, while

they treat their Scottish rebels with the utmost
haughtiness, hardship and cruelty after having
vanquished them. What difference is there between the Americans who wish to form themselves into a republic and renounce the sovereignty
of George III., and the Scots who renounced the
sovereignty of George II. and wished to recognise
a Prince of the Scottish house of Stuart in place
of the house of Hanover, which is German and
foreign? The Scots love liberty as much as the
English, and would not have endured arbitrary
power under a Prince of the house of Stuart. . . .
A generous Prince and people would have
pardoned the Scots for having shown attachment
for the race of their ancient Kings, seeing that
they were ready to abandon them on becoming
convinced of their incapacity to govern. . . . But
ferocious in prosperity and abject in adversity—
that is the national character of the English. . . .
Their hatred towards all nations of Europe is well
known. They cannot even tolerate their subjects
the Irish. Their conduct towards their subjects
in America brought upon them a civil war. Their
animosity against their own compatriots in Scotland is such that a turmoil arises when the King
appoints a Scotsman to be his Minister; yet with-

out Scotland what would they do ?   The Scots are
their mainstay in all their wars.   Take three years
of the war in America and see how the brave
Frazer, Agnew, Campbell, Abercrombie and
Pitcairn, all officers of rank and Scotsmen, have
laid down their lives, but not an Englishman
of rank has done so.   Their Howe and their
Clinton did nothing with their numerous troops,
and their Burgoyne with all his host laid down
their arms.'

With these embittered words the Narrative of
the lifelong wanderer and exile may well terminate.
Of those Jacobites who were saved from the
scaffold few lived a more unhappy existence than
Elcho.

LIST OF AUTHORITIES

THE following is a list of the Authorities most
frequently cited in the Notes to the Narrative, and the Abbreviations by which they
are indicated.

A. C. *Atholl Correspondence: Jacobite Correspondence of the Atholl
Family during the Rebellion.* 4to. Abbotsford Club,
1840.

A. P. *The Albemarle Papers: being the Correspondence of William
Anne, second Earl of Albemarle.* Edited with Intro-
duction and Notes by Charles Sanford Terry. 2 vols.
New Spalding Club, Aberdeen, 1901-2.

B. H. Browne's *History of the Highlands and of the Highland
Clans, including an Index of Stuart Papers.* 4 vols.
Glasgow, 1836.

Blaikie. *Itinerary of Prince Charles Edward Stuart*, by Walter
Biggar Blaikie. Scottish History Society, Edinburgh, 1897.

C. D. *The Clan Donald*, by the Rev. A. Macdonald, Minister of
Killearnan, and the Rev. A. Macdonald, Minister of
Kiltarlity. 3 vols. Inverness, 1896.

C. G. *History of the Clan Gregor from Public Records and Private
Collections*, by Amelia Murray MacGregor of Mac-
Gregor. 2 vols. Edinburgh, 1901.

G. C. T. *General Cope's Trial: Report of the Proceedings of the
Board of General Officers on . . . Lieut.-General Sir
John Cope, etc.* 4to. London, 1749.

G. E. C. Cokayne. *Complete Peerage.*

H. B. A. *A History of the British Army*, by the Hon. J. W. Fortescue.
2nd vol. London, 1899.

H. H. Home's *History. The History of the Rebellion in the Year
1745.* 4to. London, 1802.

H. P.   *Historical Papers relating to the Jacobite Period.* Edited
by Colonel James Allardyce. 2 vols. 4to. New
Spalding Club, Aberdeen, 1895-6.

H. R.   *The History of the Rebellion,* by Andrew Henderson.
5th ed. 1753.

J. M.   *Jacobite Memoirs.* Edited by Robert Chambers. Edinburgh, 1834.

L. M.   *The Lyon in Mourning, etc.,* by the Rev. Robert Forbes,
1746-75. Edited from his MSS. by Henry Paton,
M.A. 3 vols. Scottish History Society, Edinburgh,
1894-6.

L. P.   *Lockhart Papers.* 2nd vol. 4to. London, 1817.

L. P. R.   *List of Persons concerned in the Rebellion.* Edited by Lord
Rosebery and the Rev. Walter Macleod. Scottish
History Society, Edinburgh, 1890.

Michel.   *Les Écossais en France, les Français en Écosse,* par Fran-
cisque-Michel. 2 vols. London, 1862.

M. J.   *Memoirs of the Chevalier de Johnstone.* Translated from
the French by Charles Winchester. Aberdeen, 1870.

M. K.   Maxwell of Kirkconnel's *Narrative of Charles, Prince of
Wales's Expedition to Scotland.* 4to. Maitland Club,
1841.

M. M.   *Memorials of John Murray of Broughton.* Edited by Robert
Fitzroy Bell. Scottish History Society, Edinburgh,
1898.

M. R.   *The History of the Present Rebellion,* by John Marchant.
London, 1746.

S. M.   *Scots Magazine.*

T. G.   *Tales of a Grandfather.* Ed. 1893.

References are also made to—

S. P. Dom., i.e. 'Scotland, State Papers, Domestic, George II.,' from
the Record Office, London.

F. F. O. Documents in the French Foreign Office, of which Mr.
Blaikie has kindly lent me copies.

A SHORT ACCOUNT OF THE
AFFAIRS OF SCOTLAND
IN THE YEARS 1744, 1745, 1746

Charles Edward.
1745–6.

A SHORT ACCOUNT OF THE AFFAIRS OF SCOTLAND IN THE YEARS 1744, 1745, 1746

IN the Year 1743 there were two Gentlemen at Paris who's names were Lord Semple[1] and M[r] Macgregor,[2] *alias* Drummond of Bakaldie. They

[1] Francis Lord Sempil (described as the second Baron of the Junior Branch), grandson of the Hon. Archibald Sempil, and son and heir of Robert Sempil, created a Peer of Scotland by James III. and VIII. The first lord lived in Paris, where he died in 1737. Francis Lord Sempil continued to make his headquarters in France : probably the Francis Sempil who married the widow of the Hon. John Caryll. He died Dec. 9, 1748 : buried at St. Andrews, Chartres.

[2] William Macgregor or Drummond of Bohaldie or Balhaldies, son of Sir Alexander Macgregor of Bohaldie, a Jacobite baronet, his mother being a daughter of Sir Ewen Cameron of Lochiel; b. 1698 ; fought at Sheriffmuir 1715; escaped to France; married a daughter of Oliphant of Gask ; first appears as agent to James in 1740. Murray of Broughton speaks of him thus : 'the descendant of a cobbler, himself a broken butter and cheese merchant, a stickt doctor, a Jack of all trades, a bankrupt indebted to all the world, the awkwardest Porter-like fellow alive, allways in a passion, a mere bully, the most forbidding air imaginable, and master of as much bad French as to procure himself a w—— and a dinner' (*M. M.* 330). According to Murray, Elcho described Bohaldie as 'a low lifed fellow void of truth' (*Ibid.* 51). Throughout his career he was the object of mistrust. Murray accuses him of plundering the baggage at Sheriffmuir. In September 1744 Earl Marischal writing to James says : 'Can you desire that either the Duke of Perth or I undertake ever anything on the word of

were known to be ministers of the Chevalier de
St Georges, and by most people suspected to be
pensioners of the court of France. Mr Macgregor made frequent journeys to England,
Scotland, and to Rome, and they both gave out
they were trusted and employed by the friends
of the Family of Stuart in Great Britain. They
certainly were employ'd by the Court of France,
for Lord Semple went often to Versailles and
was always well received by the French Ministers.
In the Winter 1743 Mr Macgregor left Paris and
took with him one Mr Buchanan.[1]   They went

Lord Sempil and Balhaldy?' (*Stuart Papers*; *B. H.* ii. 476).   In
Feb. 1743 Lord John Drummond, writing to Edgar, says: 'Most
of the King's friends I meet within Scotland speak against him
[Bohaldie] and desired most positively that I should inform the
King from them that Bohaldy having alwise been in low life,
he trayed several different trades without success and obliged to
flay the country in danger of being taken up for a Fifty Pound
note, he had now for a recourse taken the management of the
Kings affairs' (*Ibid.* 446).   In March 1745 Charles was writing to
his father, 'I take the liberty to advertise you that there is no
believing anything they [Sempil and Bohaldie] say.'   On the
other hand James considered him 'an honest and sensible man,' and
trusted him throughout the protracted negotiations with the French
Court.   Readers of Stevenson will remember that it was Bohaldie
who received Catriona in Paris.

   [1] Buchanan lived in the house of Æneas Macdonald in Paris,
and acted as Jacobite messenger between France and England.
He accompanied Charles to Scotland.   In a manifesto issued at
Holyrood Charles speaks of his companions as numbering seven.
This would exclude Buchanan, but in *L. M.* i. 282 there is the
following note: 'Perhaps Mr. Buchanan (as I have heard suggested
by several persons) was reckoned amongst the Prince's domesticks.
Robert Forbes, A.M.'   See *ante*, p. 47.

by Switzerland to Rome, and soon after the
Prince, the Chevaliers Eldest son, left Rome
incognito and came to Genova. From thence he
embark'd aboard of a filucque for Antibes, and in
his passage pass'd through Admiral Mathews's[1]
fleet, which was then in those seas. From Antibes
he came to Paris, & Lodged at Lord Semples, in
the month of January 1744. He was a fortnight
at Lord Semples before it was known. At the
end of that time Lord Semple Came & invited
the Earl Marischall[2] & Lord Elcho, who were
then at Paris, to Come and see him. They went
seperately. He told them that the King of France
was to send him over to England from Dunkirk
at the head of 12000 men, that there was to be a
fleet to Sail from Brest to support that Embarkation, and that he was to land in the river Thames
as near London as they Could. He told the Earl
Marischall, who had the Chevaliers commission to
Command in cheif in Scotland, that he was to be
sent to Scotland with the Irish Brigade. He
desired the Earl Marischall and Lord Elcho to get

---

[1] Admiral Matthews (b. 1676, d. 1751), 'Il Furibondo.' In
1746 tried by court-martial for his conduct of the action against the
French and Spaniards off Hyères, Feb. 1744; dismissed the service
in 1747. See *ante*, p. 67.
[2] See Index for references to Lord Marischal.

ready and told them that he was to sett out for the sea coast in a Short time.   He Seemed very desirous his being at Paris Should be kept as secret as possible ;   Lord Caryle [1] came to him to Paris from England and it was given out he was sent by the Party in England who were to join the French upon their Landing.   The Prince left Paris in the Beginning of Febrewary 1744 and went to Graveline, where he remained incognito with his secretary Bakaldie untill the Embarkation was laid aside.   About the End of the same month the troops who were to Embark assembled at Dunkirk, and the Comte de Saxe,[2] who was to

list of the troops destined for the embarkation

Monaco	3	Batts:
D'Eu	2	„
Diesbach	2	„
la cour au chantre	2	„
Beauffremont	1	
Royal Corse	1	
Royal la marine	1	
Soissonois	1	
Languedoc	1	
Navarre	4	
Gondrin	2	
	20	

Mailly Cavalerie

Dauphin Dragons

[1] John Baptist Caryll, 3rd Baron Caryll of Durford, Sussex (b. 1713, d. 1788); son of Hon. John Caryll ; s. his grandfather 1736; became a member of Charles's household ; escorted Princess Louisa of Stolberg from Loretto to Macerata, where she was married to Charles, April 17, 1772 (L. M. iii. 265); subsequently quarrelled with and dismissed by Charles.   The Baronage was a creation by James, 1699.

[2] Maurice (b. 1696, d. 1750), natural son of Augustus II., King of Poland and Elector of Saxony, and Aurore de Koenigsmarck ;

Command them, arrived with the General officers
under his Command. There were large Ships
gott together in the road into which the troops
were to be putt, by means of Bilanders which lay
in y[e] harbour. About the Beginning of March
they Embarked the Duke D'Antin and the
Prince of Monaco with their Regiments. Mons[r]
de Roqufeuille,[1] who Commanded the Brest
Squadron, Came into the Channel & sent Mons[r]
de Barailh[2] with four men of war to protect the
Embarkation, and Sir John Norris[3] Came with a
large English Squadron into the downs. The
Embarkation went on but Slowly upon account of
the distance of the Ships from the harbour ; and
when their was about 6000 men embark'd, their
came on a violent Storm which putt a stop to
the Embarkation, and as the Storm continued for
15 days it drove most of the ships with the
troops Ashoare and a great Many men were

began military service at the age of twelve; present at Malplaquet ;
entered French service 1720; Marshal of France 1743; commanded
at Fontenoy 1745.

[1] de Roquefeuille (b. 1665, d. 1744), Admiral 1728. Bohaldie
was afterwards responsible for a totally unsupported assertion that the
Admiral had been bribed by the English Government (M. M. 73).

[2] Barailh, Jean André, Marquis de (b. 1671, d. 1762), present
at the battle of the Hague, where he greatly distinguished himself ;
Vice-admiral 1753 (Larousse, i. 722).

[3] Sir John Norris (b. 1660, d. 1749), known as 'foul weather
Jack'; Admiral and Commander-in-chief 1733; resigned 1744.

drownded. During the Storm Monsieur de Roc-
quefeuille came into Dungeness Bay : Sir John
Norris Stood into the Bay to him, but the Badness
of the weather prevented their engadging, and
Seperated them.   Monsr de Rocquefieulle died in
Dungeness Bay of an Apoplecthick fitt, & his
Squadron returned to Brest.   Sir John Norris
return'd to the Downs, and the French gave up
their Embarkation.   The Earl Marischall was all
the time at Dunkirk, but was not at all Consulted ;
and whenever he Ask'd about the embarkation
for Scotland, he was told it would take place after
the other was over.   The Prince sent for Lord
Marischall to come & see him at Graveline, and
proposed to him to hire a Boat[1] and to Go to
Scotland, where he Said he was sure he had many
friends who would join him ; but Lord Marashall
desauded him from thinking of it, and the Prince
return'd back to Paris, where he lived untill y^e
1745, not much frequented by French people of
Fashion but much by the Irish & Scots then
there.   My Lord Semple and Balkady had forgott to advertise the Duke of Ormond[2] of the

---

[1] ' Il dit dans sa lettre que s'il savait que sa présence seule fut
utile en Angleterre, Il s'y rendroit dans un canot ' (*F. F. O. Minute* ;
March 25, 1744).

[2] James, 2nd Duke (b. 1665, d. 1745).   In 1715 vote for his
impeachment carried in the House of Commons ; fled to France ;

Embarkation, but being told by some English Gentlemen that the Party in England had a great value for him & would take his not being with them amiss, they Sent for him. His Grace sett out for Dunkirk, but having heard of the affairs being over upon the road, he return'd back to Avignon. So soon as the Embarkation was over, ye French declared War[1] Against The King of England, Elector of Hanover, (as they termed it). The Embarkation Finish'd in ye End of March 1744. In the Month of August 1744 Mr Murray of Broughton[2] (who was the Chevaliers agent in Scotland) went to Paris, where he

same year landed at Plymouth to take part with the English Jacobites, but, finding no support, returned to France ; commanded the troops despatched from Spain 1719 to promote the restoration of James ; escaped to the Continent.

[1] France declared war March 20, 1744. This was followed on the 31st by a similar declaration on the part of England. Although Dettingen had been fought, England had hitherto been acting only as the ally of Austria.

[2] John Murray of Broughton (b. 1715, d. 1777), son of Sir David Murray of Stanhope, 2nd Bart.; matriculated at Leyden 1735; in 1739 appointed to succeed Colonel Urquhart as agent for James in Scotland; after the campaign of 1745-6 taken prisoner and conveyed to the Tower of London, where he turned King's evidence and obtained his pardon and a pension of £200 per annum in 1748 (S. M. x. 245). In the *Journal* Elcho says: 'Mr. Murray was a very well educated man, had travelled widely, and had spent a great part of his capital. As his affairs were disordered, he had good reason to encourage the Prince in his project of coming to Scotland, that he might have the chance of fishing in the troubled waters.' 'A well looking, little man, of a fair complexion' (H. P. ii. 351). See *ante*, p. 40 *et seq.*

Saw the Prince, and informed him that if he could prevail upon the French to give him 6000 men and 30000 lewis d'ors and ten thousand Stand of arms, that he was charged to tell him he would be join'd upon his landing by a great number of his friends, but if he Could not obtain these Succours it was impossible for them to do anything for him. Mr Murray returned from France in October 1744, and gave out,[1] in all the meetings he had with the Princes friends, that the Prince told him he would certainly be in Scotland next Summer whither the King of France assisted him or not. Most of the Gentlemen of that party look'd upon it as a mad project and were utterly against it. Mr Murray & some others who were in desperate circumstances certainly encouradged the Prince underhand ; others such as the Duke of Perth,[2] out of Zeal. There were likewise some gentlemen, who were against his Coming, used in their Conversations to Say that they would do all they could to prevent his Coming, but if he did

[1] See *ante*, p. 62.

[2] James Drummond, grandson of James, 4th Earl of Perth, created Duke by James II. at St. Germains. He was brought up in France, but had, Murray says, 'an over fondness of speaking broad Scots.' Elcho says of him, ' He was a very brave and gallant man, and devotedly attached to the house of Stuart ' (*Journal*). Escaped after Culloden, but died on the voyage to France, May 1746.

come & persisted in Staying, they believed they could not hinder themselves from joining in his fortune. Mʳ Murray in the beginning of the year 1745 sent over Young Glengary[1] to the Prince with a State of his Affairs in Scotland, in which it is believed he represented every body that had ever spoke warmly of the Stuart family as people that would certainly join him if he came. In the Beginning of this year the Prince had sent several Commissions to Mʳ Murray to be distributed amongst his friends in Scotland, which were all signed by himself, as his Father had made him Regent of the three Kingdoms; and in June Sir Hector Maclean[2] arrived with letters from the Prince, wherin he told he would be in Scotland in June. He beg'd his friends in

---

[1] Alastair Ruadh Macdonell (b. 1725, d. 1760), eldest son of John, Chief of Glengarry. Mr. Lang has identified him with Pickle the Spy (*ante*, p. 51). John Macdonell himself did not join Charles, but in August 1746 he was committed prisoner to Edinburgh Castle in consequence of an information signed by Barrisdale and six other Macdonells, wherein it was alleged that they had been forced to take up arms by their chief. Lord Albemarle suggested that this was 'another fetch' of Barrisdale's 'to save his sweet Bacon.' (*A. P.* i. 87 ; ii. 405.)

[2] 5th Bart. of Duart (b. 1704, d. 1751) ; arrested shortly after his arrival in Scotland ; conveyed to London; examined by Lord Tweeddale ; denied all knowledge of the letters found in his possession, but said that 'Captain Barclay' (*i.e.* Charles) mentioned in the letters, was a Captain Stewart who had been obliged to leave Paris on account of matrimonial difficulties (Craigie MSS., Marquis of Tweeddale to the Lord Advocate, July 27th). See *ante*, p. 69.

the Highlands to be in readyness to receive him, & desired if possible all the Castles & fortresses's in Scotland might be taken before his arrival. Every body was vastly alarm'd at this news, & were determinded when he came to endeavour all in their power to prevail upon him to go back; and the Gentlemen of the party then at Edinburgh sent Mr Murray to the Highlands to lett the Prince know their sentiments, but upon his not Coming all the month of June, Mr Murray return'd to the Lowlands.

In the Month of June 1745 The Prince Sett out from Navare, a Country house of the Duc de Bullions,[1] Attended by the Duke of Athole,[2] Sir Thomas Sheridan,[3] his old Governor, Sir John Macdonald,[4] a Captain in the Carabineers,

[1] Charles-Godefroid de la Tour d'Auvergne (Duc de Bouillon) (b. 1706, d. 1772); son of Marie-Charlotte Sobieski, Duchess of Bouillon, and thus cousin of Charles.

[2] William Murray, Marquis of Tullibardine, eldest surviving son of John, 1st Duke of Atholl; attainted 1715; escaped to the Continent; returned to Scotland with Spanish forces; present at Glenshiel, 1719, and again went abroad; came over with Charles from France July 1745, and carried his standard at Glenfinnan; surrendered, April 27, 1746, to Buchanan of Drummakill; conveyed to the Tower, where he died July 9, 1746. The dukedom and estates passed to his younger brother James in 1724, by special Act of Parliament.

[3] Tutor to Charles; accompanied him to the siege of Gaeta 1734; escaped after Culloden and retired to Rome; died Nov. 1746.

[4] An officer in the French service; surrendered at Culloden; 'a man of no extraordinary head as a councillor' (L. M. i. 283).

M^r O'Sulivan,[1] who was Marèchal Maillebois's[2] aid du camp in the wars of Corsica, Mr Kelly,[3] who had been a prisoner in the tower of London, Mr Strickland,[4] who had been about his Father, Mr Macdonald,[5] Banker at Paris, & Mr Buchanan,

1 Afterwards quartermaster-general of Charles's army. Both Elcho and Lord George Murray lay stress on his incompetence and the inefficient manner in which he carried out his duties.

2 Maillebois, S. B. F. Desmarets, Marquis de (b. 1682, d. 1762), Marshal of France, son of Desmarets, grandson of Colbert; commanded a division in Italy 1733; conquered part of Corsica 1739.

3 Rev. George Kelly (b. 1688), spent fourteen years in the Tower on suspicion of having been concerned in the Atterbury Plot; escaped 1736. He was recommended to Charles by Sempil. In 1748, when recriminations among the Jacobites were general, Sempil accused Kelly of being 'the ruin of the Cause.' Subsequently Charles dispensed with his services. May 11, 1744, Charles, writing to James, says that Sempil and Bohaldie had recommended Kelly as a man of 'tru sence & experience.' Kelly was then with the Duke of Ormond, and in a postscript Charles adds: 'I have seen a letter from Kelly in which he ses that my request for him will be very agreeable to his Duke because that he was a great constrent to his Amoors' (*Stuart Papers*). In Oct. 1745 Charles employed him to carry despatches from Scotland to the French Court. ' C'est tout ce qu'il y a de mieux autour du prince, et le seul homme après le Che$^{r.}$ harrington, qui connoisse un peu le gouvernement et la situation des choses en Angleterre' (*F. F. O.*, 1746-7, *Stuarts*, vol. 79, fo. 235).

4 Formerly companion to Charles in Italy; died in Carlisle after the surrender to Cumberland. James was suspicious of his influence. On Oct. 26, 1745, Charles writes to James saying that he will send Strickland away 'in all hest' (*Stuart Papers*). Dec. 19, 1746, Charles to James, 'I must own I am now entirely convinced F. S. [Francis Strickland] was an ill man' (*Stuart Papers* printed by Lord Mahon.)

5 Æneas Macdonald, brother of Kinlochmoidart; banker in Paris, where his house was a centre of Jacobitism. Sept. 10, 1745, he is found writing to Charles denying a charge brought against him of discouraging the troops (*S. P. Dom. George II.*, 1745,

that came with him from Rome.   From Navare
he went to Nantes where he met with M[r] Welch,[1]
a rich Irish merchant, who had prepared a little
vessel[2] of 14 Guns for him, & aboard of which
the Prince embark'd at a Villadge call'd la Vrai
Croix, a little below Pleinbeuf at the Embouchure
of The Loire.   They say Cardinal Tencin[3] was
the only one of the French Ministers that knew
of this expedition.   The Prince had on board
with him 4000 Lewis d'ors, 1000 Guns, and
Eighteen hundred broadswords, which he had
bought with his own money.   He was detain'd by
Contrary winds a week at Bell'isle, where he was
join'd by the *Elizabeth*, a 60 gun Ship Commanded by Captain d'O & fitted out for a Cruize by

B. 67, No. 83); surrendered to General Campbell 1746 ; conveyed
to London; gave evidence before the Duke of Newcastle but
betrayed little of importance; died in Paris during the Revolution.
Elcho in his *Journal* says: 'Without Mr. Macdonald he (Charles)
could have done nothing, not one of the Highlanders would have
acknowledged him, and it was Macdonald that persuaded his brother
[Kinlochmoidart] and Mr. Macdonald of Clan Ranald to take
arms for the Prince.'

   [1] Antony Walsh, descendant of an Irish family for many years
settled in France; b. 1703; created Earl Walsh by James Oct. 20,
1745.

   [2] This vessel was named the *Dutillet* or *Du Teillay*, after Du
Teillay, Commissary of the Marine at Nantes (*A Royalist Family
and Charles Edward Stuart*, 109).

   [3] Pierre Guerin de Tencin (b. 1678, d. 1758); French envoy to
the Vatican 1721; through the influence of James made a cardinal
1740; succeeded Fleury as minister of France 1743; withdrew to
his diocese of Lyons 1751.

M[r] Rutlidge,[1] an Irish Merchant at Dunkirk, who had given the Captain orders to Escort the Prince to Scotland. They Sail'd from Bellisle y[e] 8 of July,[2] & next day they fell in with the *Lion* man of war, Captain Brett, who bore down upon the *Elizabeth* & engadged her for five hours. In the Engadgement they were both much damadged & had a Great many men killed on both sides. The *Elizabeth* lost her first & Second Captains (Brothers) & went back to Brest to Refitt. The frigate in which the Prince was, & which had Lain by at a distance during the time of the Action, Steered away for the north west coast of Scotland, and about the middle of July made the isles of Barra. M[r] Macdonald was sent ashoar upon South Uist,[3] where he mett M[r] Macdonald[4] of Buisdale,

---

[1] Walter Rutledge, an Irishman and merchant at Dunkirk. He and Walsh had advanced the money which Charles had on board the *Doutelle* (about £3800).

[2] 'Thursday, July 15th [July 4th, Old Style]. Raised anchor from the Roads of Belle Isle in company with the *Elisabeth* Captain Deau about 5 in the morning.'—Log of *La Doutelle*. The engagement did not take place till July 20th (9th, O. S.) (*A Royalist Family*, 18, 19).

[3] The landing-place was on the west side of the Isle of Eriskay.

[4] Alexander Macdonald of Boisdale (b. 1698, d. 1768), son by his second marriage of Donald Macdonald of Benbecula, was the first of the Macdonalds of Boisdale; he not only discouraged Charles, but dissuaded many of his brother Clanranald's followers from joining (*L. M.* i. 148). In later times of peril, when Charles was a hunted fugitive, however, he rendered assistance; was carried as a prisoner to the Tower; regained his liberty July 1747.

Brother to Clanronald who told him he Came
from Sir Alexander Macdonald[1] and Macleod[2] to
beg that if the Prince was in that Ship he might
go back to France, for that it was a bad project
he came upon, and Could never be Attended with
Success. The Prince came and lay ashoar that
night upon south Uist[3] and held a Council with
the Gentlemen that came along with him what
was to be done ; they were all for Going back
again to France, except Sir Thomas Sheridan.
Even the Prince himself seemed for it,[4] but Sir
Thomas, as he had always a great deal to say with
the Prince, persuaded him to remain. So they
embark'd aboard ye Ship and Steer'd for the main
Land, and made the bay of Lochnanuagh in Arisaig, and they landed at a place call'd Borodale.[5]

[1] 7th Bart. of Sleat (b. 1710, d. 1746); sided with the Government ; he from the first had declared that he would only join if
Charles came with adequate support ; yet in Jacobite verse his
memory is thus celebrated—

> 'If heaven be pleased when sinners cease to sin ;
> If hell be pleased when sinners enter in ;
> If earth be pleased to lose a truckling knave ;
> Then all are pleased—Macdonald's in his grave.'—C. D. ii. 91.

[2] Norman, 19th of Macleod (b. 1706, d. 1772), sided with the
Government.

[3] i.e. Isle of Eriskay.

[4] The hesitation of Charles at this point is not spoken of elsewhere, and it certainly differs from his attitude at Arisaig, where he
said he would choose 'far rather to sculk among the mountains in
Scotland than to return to France,' and was single in his resolution
to land (L. M. iii. 51). [5] On July 25th.

The Arms, Money, and Amunition were Landed here, and some meal they had found in a Scots Ship they had taken upon the Coast. The Prince after having given M[r] Welch 500 Lewis d'ors & made him a knight, dismis'd him, and he saild back to France were The Chevalier made him an Irish Peer. From Borodale where they were join'd by Young Clanronald[1] with 300 Macdonalds, they went to Kienlochmoidart, where a great many highland Gentlemen Came to visitt him. M[r] Murray Came to him from the Lowlands, but it is believed he did not advise him to Go back as he was desired to do, but on the Contrary advised him to remain. It was here the first Guard was mounted upon him, and the whole Expedition Concerted ; Glenfinan was the place appointed for the General rendevous where the Standard was to be sett up.

About the 2 of August[2] they gott notice at

[1] Ranald Macdonald, younger of Clanranald ; educated at St. Germains in France ; served through the campaign ; escaped after Culloden ; obtained military employment in France ; returned to England 1752 ; kept prisoner in London till 1754 ; died 1777. ' Il est le premier écossois de nom qui ait joint le prince, et le seul montagnard qui à derby ait opiné de marcher à londres . . . c'est un fort honete homme, très doux et point antifrançais comme beaucoup de ses compatriotes ' (F. F. O. 79, fo. 235). Although probably written by D'Éguilles, this statement as to Macdonald's attitude at Derby must be accepted with reserve.

[2] See ante, p. 70.

Edinburg from fort William of the Princes being
Landed, and Lt Gen: Sir John Cope,[1] who at that
time commanded the Forces in Scotland, order'd
away arms and amunition to all the forts and
Castles in Scotland, put in two Companys of
Lascelles regiment into the Castle of Edinburgh and Stored it with provisions. He sent
Campbell of Inverau's Company away by Argyleshire to fort William and they arrived safe,
but two new raised Companys of the Royal
Scots, which he had Sent from Perth to the same
fort, were attack'd on the 16 of August 1745,
betwixt fort Augustus & fort William, by Macdonald of Keppoch,[2] and were after some resistance
taken prisoners. Two of the Soldiers were kill'd,
and Cap^{ts} Scot,[3] Tomson, L^{ts} Rose & Fergusson

[1] Sir John Cope, died 1760; gazetted to the Cavalry 1707; afterwards colonel of 7th Regiment of Foot; Commander-in-chief in
Scotland 1745. His conduct was subsequently inquired into by a
council of officers, who exonerated him from blame.

[2] Alexander Macdonald of Keppoch; educated at Glasgow
University; took part in the rebellion of 1715; escaped to France;
served in the French army; killed at or immediately after Culloden.
' At the battle of Culloden in the retreat Capt. Roy Macdonald saw
Keppoch fall twice to the ground, and knows no more about him,
but that upon the second fall, looking at Donald Roy Macdonald
he spoke these words: "O God have mercy upon me. Donald,
do the best for yourself, for I am gone "' (L. M. ii. 5). The
actual capture of the two companies was effected by Donald
Macdonald of Tiendrish (L. M. i. 36).

[3] Afterwards General Scott of Balcomie; one of the few
captured officers who kept his parole with the Highlanders. He was

and the Men were carried to the Prince, and released upon their paroles of honour not to serve against him. About the 8 of August a Camp was form'd at Stirling, Consisting of Lascelles's Regiment 8 Companys 560, Murrays Regiment Compleat 700, 5 Companies of Lee's 350, one Company of the old highland regiment 70 men, Gardners Dragoons 300 men, and Hamiltons 300, in all 1680 foot and 600 Dragoons, with some field pieces of Cannon and some Coehorns.

The 19 of August the Prince sett up his Standard at Glen-finan, Where was present the Duke of Atthole and Major General Gordon of Glenbuckett,[1] the Gentlemen that Came along with him, Mr Murray, Young Clanronald with 300 Macdonalds, Young Locheil[2] with 600 Camerons,

a member of that limited class of persons who have made a fortune by gambling. In June 1773 he m. Margaret, 3rd daughter of Lord President Dundas. His wealth was inherited by his two daughters, the Duchess of Portland (wife of the 4th Duke) and Lady Canning. (See Angus Macdonald, *Memoirs of the Macdonalds of Keppoch*, 63.)

[1] Glengarry's father-in-law. He raised 400 men from Banff and Aberdeen, and rejoined Charles at Edinburgh, Oct. 4, 1745; member of Charles's Council; escaped after Culloden; d. 1750. 'An old man much crouched.' 'He rode on a little gray highland beast' (*H. P.* ii. 353). See *ante*, p. 129.

[2] Donald Cameron (b. 1695, d. 1748), son of John Cameron of Lochiel, who was attainted for his share in the rising of 1715. He was severely wounded at Culloden; after hiding in the hills he escaped in the same ship as Charles; received the command of the

Macdonald of Keppoch with 300 Macdonalds, Macdonald of Glenco[1] with 150 Macdonalds, and Stuart of Ardshiel[2] with 250 Stuarts of Appin, in all 1600 men. Their was a paper drawn up[3] which they all Signed and swore to : the substance of it was that they would never abandone the Prince while he Stay'd in Great Britain nor never lay down their arms untill they had Establish'd the Family of Stuart, except with his consent. From Glenfinnan they march'd to Kien Lochyel [Kinlochiel], from thence by the north side of Loch Lochy to Invergary, where they were join'd by a

regiment of Albany in the French service. In the MacPharie MSS. there is a curious instance given of Highland discipline. Lochiel and Glencarnock were marching with their men to join Charles. Hearing the sound of firing, Lochiel said, What shooting can be on the hill ? Glencarnock said, I shall tell you that the Camerons are shooting sheep on the hill. 'God forbid,' said Lochiel ; 'it is the Macgregors.' The two then went in the direction of the firing. 'By great good fortune passing the head of the avenue, there was a Cameron with a sheep on his back; Lochiel fir'd at the fellow and shot him through the shoulder ; there he fell ; the two went on a good way, but they got not a Macgregor yet' (*C. G.* 366).

[1] Alexander Macdonald of Glencoe took part in 1715; m. (secondly) Isobel, daughter of John Stewart of Ardsheal ; member of Charles's Council ; surrendered after Culloden (*L. M.* i. 80); d. about 1750 (*C. D.* iii. 214).

[2] Charles Stewart, 5th of Ardsheal; attainted 1746; remained in hiding in a cave on his estate till Sept. 1746, when he escaped to France. 'A big fat man, troubled with a lethargy' (*H. P.* ii. 362). In Dec. 1746 Ardsheal House was sacked by Cumberland's soldiers.

[3] Murray says that the paper which he himself 'drew up' at Glenfinnan was not signed till Aug. 26th at Invergarry (*M. M.* 172).

Younger son of the family of Glengary[1] with 300 Macdonalds. On the 27 of August they march'd to the Corierg (Corrieyairack), where they gott intelligence of Gen: Copes coming to Attack them. Gen Cope and the Earl of Loudon[2] had arrived at the Camp at Sterling the 19, and the General order'd Gardners Dragoons to remain there, and Hamiltons to march to Edin[r], where they encamp'd first in S[t] Anes Yard,[3] then in Barefoot parcks,[4] and lastly on the links of Leith. He on the 20 march'd the rest of the army over the Bridge of Sterling to Creif, so to Tay Bridge, then to Dalnacardoch and to Dalwhiny. He had a thousand stand of arms to give to the people that would join him upon the root, but he was join'd by none. The 27 of August, as his Army had taken the road to the Corierg, he gott news of the Princes Army

[1] Angus or Æneas Macdonald, or Macdonell, of Glengarry, 'a modest brave and advisable lad'; accompanied Charles to Edinburgh; thence went north to raise men; he rejoined Charles at Bannockburn; was accidentally shot in Falkirk, Jan. 22, 1746, by a Macdonald of Clanranald's Regiment (*C. D.* iii 312). His elder brother was Young Glengarry (Alastair or Alexander, Pickle the Spy).

[2] John Campbell, 4th Earl (b. 1705, d. 1782); only son of Hugh Campbell, 3rd earl; entered the army 1727; s. his father 1731; Commander-in-chief in America 1756; superseded 1758; General 1770.

[3] Now partly enclosed in the gardens of Holyrood Palace.

[4] Bearford's Parks occupied the land of which to-day the site of Charlotte Square is the centre.

marching to attack him ; upon which he Call'd a Councill of War, wherin it was determin'd not to fight the Prince but to go to Inverness, upon which he order'd his army to file off from the rear, and after a very quick-march they Arrived the 29 at Inverness, where he was join'd by four Companies of Lord Loudouns regiment 280 men, and two Companies of Guises 140 ; and some Monroes,[1] who were the only highlanders not regulars, join'd him. The Prince detach'd part of his army to see & Come up with his rear, & they took some Bagadge, but could not come up with his army. He likewise detach'd 500 men [2] to See & gett before him to the Pass of Slachmuick (Slochd Mor), but he had passed it before they Arrived. The 28 the Prince halted at Dalwhiny, and his Army as usual lay in the open air rank and file. He sent off Major General Gordon of Glenbuckett from hence to raise men in the Braes of Mar. The 29 he march'd to Dalnacardich, and the 30 to Blair of Athole, where he halted two days. He was join'd

[1] Two hundred, commanded by Captain George Munro of Culcairn (*G. C. T.* 32). In August 1746 Captain Munro was mysteriously shot on the roadside while at the head of his detachment (*A. P.* ii. 216).

[2] Murray says this move was abandoned. But a small force was detached to capture the barracks at Ruthven, a venture which failed (*M. M.* 178, 184).

here by the Viscount of Strathallan,[1] who was made a Major General, M[r] Oliphant of Gask[2] and his son, M[r] Murray[3] Brother to the Earl of Dunmore, who was appointed vice Chamberlain of his household, and John Roy Steuart,[4] who Came from the French Camp in Flanders. He brought letters[5] to the Prince from the Comte de Saxe, the Duc de Bullion, and the Prince Campo Florido, the Spanish Ambassador then at Paris. The Duc de Bullion said

[1] William, 4th Viscount; killed at Culloden by Colonel Howard (*L. M.* iii. 12 ; Cumberland to Newcastle, *H. O. Scot.* xxxi., April 1746).

[2] Laurence Oliphant (b. 1691, d. 1767), laird of Gask; son of James Oliphant, laird of Gask, by Janet, daughter of the Rev. Anthony Murray of Woodend, Perthshire; took part in 1715; s. his father 1732. His son Laurence (b. 1724) also took part in 1745. Both father and son present at Falkirk and Culloden. Remained in hiding in Aberdeenshire for six months ; escaped to Sweden Oct. 1746.

[3] Hon. William Murray of Taymount (b. 1696, d. 1756); formerly an officer in the Royal Navy ; present throughout the campaign; in April 1746 he surrendered ; pleaded guilty and was condemned to death Dec. 1746; reprieved, but kept a prisoner for life, dying in Lincoln ; he succeeded his brother the 2nd Earl 1752. His eldest son John was page-of-honour to Charles at Holyrood.

[4] Formerly British cavalry officer, Quartermaster of Scots Greys ; later in French service. 'He goes always very gay, sometimes he had Highland cloathes and other times long cloathes on' (*L. M.* iii. 149). After Culloden he was despatched by Charles to France with news of the battle (*A. P.* i. 230). He rejoined Charles Sept. 13, 1746 (*L. M.* iii. 43).

[5] Copies of the letters from Bouillon and Campo Florido were sent by Cope to London from Aberdeen on Sept. 14th. Sir James Steuart, writing to Edgar, Aug. 16th, from Ghent, says that the letters had been given to *him* to transmit to Charles (*B. H.* iii. 443).

his Master was determined to Assist the Prince. The Spanish Ambassador promised money and arms from Spain, & the Comte de Saxe said he would do all in his power to prevent the English from sending men from Flanders to England. The 2 of Sep[t] the Prince march'd from Blair to Dunkeld, which the Duke of Atholes Brother had left some days before. Here he was join'd by Lord Nairn,[1] who was made a Brigadeer General, and his Brother, M[r] Mercer of Aldie.[2] The Prince left the Duke of Athole here to raise the Athole men. The 3 of Sep[t] the Prince dinn'd at the house of Nairn, and at night arrived at Perth, where he proclaimed his Father and had a new Provost and Magistrates chosen upon the old ones refusing to Act. Here he was join'd by the Duke of Perth with 200 men, & L[d] George

---

[1] Nairn, Lord (b. 1691, d. 1770), son of Margaret Baroness Nairn and Lord William Murray, son of 1st Marquis of Atholl; took part in 1715; taken prisoner at Preston; pardoned; marched into England at the head of a Lowland regiment in 1745; escaped on a Danish vessel to Sweden, Oct. 1746 (A. P. i. 316). 'C'est un honnête homme d'environ 60 ans très borné, un peu grossier, qui n'a plus rien au monde, que le prince a toujours negligé, et qui cependant luy est attaché au point detre un de ses braves sil en était question' (F. F. O. 79, fo. 235).

[2] i.e. Hon. Robert Nairn, son of the second Lord Nairn; assumed the name of Mercer on marrying the heiress of Aldie; served in the Prince's army, at first as a colonel in the Atholl Brigade, afterwards as a volunteer; killed at Culloden.

Murray.[1] (There had been a Warrant out to Seise his Grace some weeks before this, and he narowly Escaped being taken at his own house by a Party and had been obludged to keep private always untill he joined the Prince.) Both the Duke and Lord George were made Lieutenant Generals. Lord Ogilvy[2] who was made Lord Lieutenant of Angus and sent there to raise men, Robinson of Strowan[3] with about 50 men, Mʳ Smith, Brother to Methven. There happen'd a Circum-

---

[1] 5th son of John, 2nd Marquis and 1st Duke of Atholl by Lady Catherine Hamilton, eldest daughter of Anne, Duchess of Hamilton (b. 1694, d. 1760) ; served in 1st Royals 1712-15 ; joined the Earl of Mar, and commanded a battalion in 1715; wounded at Glenshiel 1719 ; pardoned 1726. Sir Walter Scott calls him ‘ the soul of the undertaking’ (Scott, *Jl.* i. 115). ‘ He alone was capable of conducting our army’ (*M. J.* 18). He figures prominently in ‘ The Gathering of Atholl’ :—

> ‘ Wha will ride wi’ gallant Murray ?
> Wha will ride wi’ Geordie's sel’ ?
> He 's the flower of a’ Glenisla,
> And the darling o’ Dunkell.’

See Index for further references.

[2] David, eldest son of 4th Earl of Airlie (b. 1725, d. 1803); after Culloden escaped to Norway; became Lieut.-General in the French service; pardoned 1778.

[3] Alexander Robertson (b. 1670, d. 1749), 13th Baron of Strowan; joined Dundee in 1689; took part in 1715 with 500 of his clan; escaped to France; obtained a remission from the Government 1731. In 1745 the Robertsons were not out as a clan; Robertson himself joined with a number of his tenants; authorities differ as to the number of his men: 200 (*M. K.* 33); 100 (*H. H.* 117). After Prestonpans he was driven back to his house in Cope's carriage, with the general's furred nightgown as a trophy (Ramsay, i. 34). A volume of his poems was published in 1785.

stance here at Perth that was ever after very detri-
mental to the Princes affairs and was the chief means
of breading any jealousies that happen'd afterwards
in that army. M[r] Murray of Broughton, who the
Prince had made his Secretary,[1] had gott a Great
deal of his masters Ear, and it was Supposed he
aim'd at having the chief direction of all that
concerned Military affairs as well, as he had
already the administration of all moneys belonging to the Prince and every thing that concerned private Correspondence. To Effectuate
this Scheme it was necessary to remove a great
obstacle, which was to deprive Lord George
Murray of the Princes favour, which would in
Consequence lessen his Command, as he knew
Lord George would not be directed by him and
in the main had no regard for him, and he
hoped as the Duke of Perth would then Command to have more to Say with him and Consequently have more the direction of Military
affairs. To bring this about he told the Prince
that Lord George had taken the oaths[2] to the
Government, and that he had been looked upon

---

[1] At Moy on Loch Lochy, Aug. 25th.

[2] Lord George had visited Cope at Crieff, Aug. 21st, together
with the Duke of Atholl and Macdonald of Glengarry (*G. C. T.*
6). He had also written the day before this visit to the Lord
Advocate, giving particulars of what had already occurred in the

for some time past as no friend to the Cause, and in Short his Opinion was, that he had join'd only out of an intent to Betray the Affair. What Mr Murray said to the Prince upon this Subject had such weight that he ever afterwards suspected Lord George which did his Affairs great harm, as Lord George by his behaviour gained the Esteem and Confidence of the whole Army. The Prince sent a party[1] from Perth to proclaim his Father at Dundee. Both at Perth and Dundee the Manifesto's which he had brought with him were read : one of them was a Commission of Regency appointing the Prince Regent of The three Kingdoms until the arrival of his Father ; the others were declaring that both the father and son were willing in a free parliment to Grant the Nations all the Securities they Should demand for their rights and priviliges & for the Churches at that time Established by Law. Their was a pardon Granted for all past Offences to all those that would accept of it, and the Union was declared Nul, as having been made to prevent the house of Stuart from

Highlands, finishing his letter in these words : ' It is very leat, so shall end with my best wishes that these troubles will soon be over ' (Omond's *Lord Advocates*, ii. 15).

[1] Under Keppoch and Clanranald.

their right to the Crown. The town of Edinburgh, when the Princes army lay at Perth, were making great preparations to defend themselves, least he Should march that way. Their * Of 60, or train'd bands, Consisting of 16 Companies,* were 100 men each. armed and mounted guard, their City guard was Augmented to 180 men, and they were raising a regiment which was to Consist of 1000 men to be Commanded by Provost Stuart ;[1] besides 400 Voluntiers Commanded by George Drummond, and 200 Seceders by Mr Bryce of Kennet.[2] They Planted Ship Cannon upon the Walls of the town, and threw up Entrenchments before the Gates and in a great many other places. General Guest[3] retired to the Castle, where

[1] Archibald Stewart, the Lord Provost, Elcho says in his *Journal*, was a 'zealous supporter of the Prince,' and contrived that the arms in the city should not be sent to the Castle but eventually fall into the hands of Charles's troops. 'The Provost's conduct cast a damp upon all, he was slow in his deliberations, bacward in executing things agreed' (*Woodhouselee MS.* 15). Stewart was tried in Oct. 1747 for neglect of duty, but acquitted after a prolonged trial, and after being fourteen months in prison. During the trial the jury represented that 'the Court had now continued upon this Trial without any respite since Tuesday morning at 8 o'clock, being upwards of forty hours . . . that the assize could not imagine it to be the Intention, either of Prosecutor or Pannel, to kill or destroy them; which behoved to be the consequence, should they insist on finishing the trial at one sederunt.' The appeal was allowed, and an adjournment made for eight hours (*Trial of Archibald Stewart*, 102).

[2] Probably Alexander Bruce, seventh of Kennet; d. 1747.

[3] Joshua Guest (b. 1660, d. 1747), enlisted 1685 ; cornet in Colonel Carpenter's Dragoons (now 3rd Hussars) 1704; served in Flanders; lieutenant-general 1745 ; buried in Westminster Abbey.

Lieutenant General Preston[1] commanded, and the Banks and Some of the inhabitants most valuable effects were sent there. On the 11 of Sep[t] the Prince marched from Perth to Dumblain and halted all the next day. On the 13 they pass'd the Forth at the Frews[2] and halted at Touch. Gardners dragoons, who were at the Frews, retired to Falkirk. The Princes Army, when it pass'd the Forth, Consisted of 2000 foot —the half Compleatly armed, the others with pitch forks, Scythes, a sword or a pistol, or some only a Staf or Stick—a troop of 36 horse which was afterwards call'd the Perthshire Squadron, and one field piece of cannon. The 14, as the army pass'd by Sterling, the Castle, where General Blakeny[3] Commanded, fired upon it but hurt

[1] George Preston (b. 1659, d. 1748), captain in service of States-General 1688; accompanied William of Orange to England; wounded at Ramilies; colonel of the Cameronian (26th) Regiment 1706; Commander-in-chief of the forces in Scotland 1715; superseded by General Guest as governor of Edinburgh Castle 1745, but is said to have prevented surrender of the Castle: 'Every two hours a party of soldiers wheeled him in an armchair round the guards that he might personally see if all were on the alert' (Grant's *Edinburgh Castle*, 231).

[2] The Ford of Frew, a ford in the river Forth, a few miles above Stirling.

[3] William Lord Blakeney (b. 1672, d. 1761), served in Flanders under Marlborough; colonel 1737; major-general and lieutenant-governor of Stirling Castle 1744; Governor of Minorca 1747; forced to capitulate to the French at the commencement of the Seven Years' War; buried in Westminster Abbey.

nobody. That night they halted at Falkirk, and
Colonel Gardner[1] with his regiment retired to
Linlithgow. The Prince order'd Lord George
Murray to march with 500 chosen men[2] and
attack his Camp in the night, but he gott notice
of it and removed his Camp to Kirkliston. The
15 the Princes army halted three miles south
of Lithgow, and Collonel Gardner retired to
Corstorphin and from thence to the Colt bridge,
where he was joined by Hamiltons Dragoons and
a detachment from the Garison of Edinbourgh ;
and they gave out they were to fight the highlanders next day.

On the 15 Sir Steuart Threapland[3] joined the
Prince and told him that it was his friend's
opinion at Edn^r he should march and attack the

[1] James Gardiner (b. 1688, d. 1745), wounded at Blenheim
1704 ; lieutenant-colonel Inniskilling Dragoons 1730 ; commanded
Light Dragoons (now 13th Hussars) 1743-5 ; in youth notorious
for his dissolute life ; when in Paris he was suddenly converted by
a vision, while waiting for an assignation. At Prestonpans he was
killed within sight of his own house.

[2] Cf. J. M., *Marches of the Highland Army*, 31.

[3] Sir Stuart Threipland, 3rd Bart. of Fingask (b. 1716, d.
1805) ; served through the campaign and ultimately escaped to
France with Charles ; on Nov. 8, 1745, James, writing to Charles,
says : ' With regard to Cluny and Threipland, in those gentlemen
I have entire confidence, and I design to create them barons, the
first Lord Clanchattan and the last Lord Fingask ' (Chambers,
The Threiplands of Fingask, 42) ; returned to Scotland under the
amnesty of 1747 ; President, Royal College of Physicians, Edinburgh, 1766. He succeeded to the Baronetcy 1746.

town. On the 16 the Princes army march'd on the high road to Edinburgh with a designe to attack the Dragoons, but they, whenever they perceived the Highlanders, were struck with such a pannick, that they wheel'd about and galloped away in the greatest confusion, pass'd by the town of Edn[r], droping their Bagadge and arms upon the road ; and a great many of them never stoped untill they gott to Haddington, which is fourteen miles off. They were Commanded in this retreat by General Fowkes. The Princes Army after the Troops fled halted at Grays mill, where he was joined by Lord Elcho, who brought the Prince 1500 Guineas, which was very acceptable as their was not 50[1] remaining of what he had brought with him. The Prince made him his first aid de Camp.

At Eight of the Clock at Night The Prince sent a messauge to the Magistrates of Edinburg to Demand the keys of the Town and to tell them he intended to Enter it either that night or next day, and if their was any resistance made, whoever was found in Arms should be Severely

---

1 'When the Prince came to Perth he had but one guinea left, which he showed to Mr. Kelly and told him it was all he had left in the world' (*M. K.* 31). Murray says that in the early part of 1745 Francis Charteris had contributed a bill for £1500 payable the following Whitsuntide (*M. M.* 121.) See *ante*, p. 77.

treated ; and besides, he Could not answere but
if the town was taken by Storm his Soldiers
would plunder it.   At ten at night,[1] their came
four of the town Councill out to the Princes
quarters to beg he would give them time to
think on his demand.   This was a messauge
contrived to gain time, for they expected
General Copes Army every hour to land at
Leith from Aberdeen, and in case he landed time
Enough, they intended to wait the Event of a
Battle.   The Prince, after they had kiss'd his
hand, told them that he was going to send of a
detachment to Attack the town and lett them
defend it at their peril ; that if they did the
Consequences would be bad, and if they did not
he intended no harm to the old Metropolis of
his Kingdom.   As Soon as they received this
answere the Prince order'd Young Lochiel with
800 men to March & attack the town.   Their
Came out sometime after another deputation of
Six Counsellors: Provost Coots was one of them.
They Gott the same Answere as the first, and
the Prince did not See them.   The Coach that
they came out in went in at the West port and
sett down the Company, and as they were letting

[1] See *ante*, pp. 76, 77.

out the Coach at the Netherbow [1] Lochiels party
who were arrived their rush'd in, seized all the
Guards of the Town, who made no resistance, and
made themselves masters of Edinburgh whihout
firing a Shot. They Establish'd Gaurds at the
Gates, Guard house Weigh house,[2] and Parliment
house. Notwithstanding of the towns being in
this way taken without any Capitulation, the
Highlanders did no mischief. The Prince Gott
the news of Edn^{rs} being taken the next morning
17 of Sept as he was upon his March and of their
having seized 1000 Stand of Arms, which Gave
him & his Army a Great deal of joy as they
Stood in need of them. When the Army Came
near town it was mett by vast Multidudes of
people, who by their repeated Shouts & huzzas
express'd a great deal of joy to See the Prince.
When they Came into the Suburbs the Croud
was prodigious and all wishing the Prince prosperity; in Short, nobody doubted but that he
would be joined by 10,000 men at Edinburgh

---

[1] *i.e.* on its way back to the Canongate, where at that time the
hackney coaches used to be kept.

[2] The city Weigh House or Tron stood at this time opposite the
West Bow, at the west end of the Lawnmarket, and was chosen by
Charles as a suitable position to menace the Castle. It was the scene
of several contests during the blockade between the Highlanders and
the garrison. Taken down in 1822.

if he Could Arm them. The Army took the road
to Dediston, Lord Strathallan marching first at
the head of the horse, The Prince next on horse-
back [1] with the Duke of Perth on his right and
Lord Elcho on his left, then Lord George
Murray on foot at the head of the Colum of
Infantry. From Dediston the Army enter'd the
Kings park at a breach made in the wall. Lord
George halted sometime in the Park, but afterwards march'd the foot to Dediston, and the
Prince Continued on horseback always followed
by the Croud, who were happy if they could
touch his boots or his horse furniture. In the
Steepest part of the park Going down to the
Abey he was oblidged to Alight and walk, but
the Mob out of Curiosity, and some out of
fondness to touch him or kiss his hand, were

---

[1] A bay gelding presented to him by the Duke of Perth (*ante*,
p. 78 ; Henderson, *History of the Rebellion*, 5th ed., 50). 'He [the
Prince] was a slender young Man, about five feet ten inches high,
of a ruddy complexion, high-nosed, large rolling brown Eyes, long
visage: his chin was pointed and Mouth small, in Proportion to his
Features: his Hair was red, but at that Time he wore a pale Peruke:
he was in Highland Dress, with a blue sash wrought with Gold
coming over his Shoulder, red velvet Breeches, a green velvet Bonnet
with a gold Lace round it, and a white Cockade which was the
Cross of St. Andrew. He likewise had a silver-hilted broad Sword,
was booted, and had a Pair of Pistols before him. His Speech was
shy, but very intelligible; his Dialect was more upon the English
than the Scottish Accent, seem'd to me pretty like that of the Irish,
some of whom I had known ' (*Ibid.* 50).

like to throw him down, so, as soon as he was
down the hill, he mounted his horse and road
through S[t] Anes yards into Holyroodhouse
Amidst the Cries of 60000[1] people, who fill'd
the Air with their Acclamations of joy. He
dismounted in the inner court and went up
Stairs into the Gallery, and from thence into
the Duke of Hamiltons Apartment, which he
Occupied all the time he was at Edinbourgh.
The Croud Continued all that night in the outward Court of the Abbey and huzza'd Every time
the Prince Appeared at the Window. He was
joined Upon his Entring the Abby by the Earl
of Kelly,[2] Lord Balmerino,[3] M[r] Hepburn of

---

[1] The population of Edinburgh in 1747 is estimated by Maitland
in his *History of Edinburgh*, 1752, p. 220, at 50,120, and in Brown's
Guide to Edinburgh at 82,000 in 1775.

[2] Alexander, 5th Earl of Kellie, s. his father Feb. 4, 1743;
d. 1756. The Lord Justice-Clerk, writing (after Lord Kellie had
surrendered) July 10, 1746, to the Duke of Newcastle, says: 'I
have no knowledge of him but by reputation being a Person who,
notwithstanding his quality, lived obscure and little regarded by
any Body, his Fortune small, and his Understanding of an inferior
size, not many removes from the very lowest.' 'He had no command. . . . I never heard he was an idiot. . . . I can't say how far
he was disordered by drinking' (Deposition of James Logie, *H. P.* ii.
339-340). No proceedings were taken against him beyond including
his name in the Bill of Attainder.

[3] Arthur Elphinstone, 6th Lord Balmerino (b. 1688, d. 1746),
colonel of Charles's second troop of Life Guards; succeeded to the
title on the death of his brother, Jan. 5, 1746; surrendered after
Culloden; executed Aug. 18, 1746 (*ante*, p. 91). 'His memory for

Keith,[1] M[r] Lockart younger of Carnwath,[2] M[r] Graham younger of Airth,[3] M[r] Rollo Younger of Powhouse,[4] M[r] Sterling of Craigbarnet,[5] M[r] Hamilton of Bangore[6] and Younger of Kilbrackmont,[7] Sir David Murray,[8] and Several other

his years was wonderful, the more so for its not being in the least impaired by his hard drinking—his sole and predominant passion ' (Daniel's *Progress*).

[1] An East Lothian gentleman; took part in 1715; supported the Stuarts as the only means of repealing the Union. As Charles was about to enter the Palace, Hepburn stepped out of the crowd, and, drawing his sword, preceded him to his apartments (*H. H.* 101). 'He bore the highest character as the model of a true Scottish gentleman ' (*T. G.* ch. lxxi.).

[2] George Lockhart (b. 1726, d. 1761), escaped after Culloden ; died in France without being pardoned. Three generations of the family had been zealous supporters of the Stuarts.

[3] James Graham, younger of Airth, described as 'lurking' in May 1746 (*L. P. R.* 56). Elcho had been engaged in marriage to his sister (*ante*, p. 66).

[4] David and James Rollo of Powhouse, Stirlingshire, sons to the Laird of Powis; carried arms till Culloden; in May 1747 'lurking' (*L.P.R.*58). The laird himself was arrested Aug. 23, 1745, by warrant of the Lord Advocate, on suspicion of treason. See *post*, p. 322 n.

[5] James Stirling of Craigbarnet; served in the Prince's Life Guards.

[6] William Hamilton of Bangour, Linlithgowshire (b. 1704, d. 1754); Jacobite poet; contributor to Allan Ramsay's *Tea Table Miscellany* 1724-27; was the earliest translator of Homer into English blank verse; d. at Lyons ; poems issued by Foulis 1749.

[7] Robert Hamilton, younger of Kilbrackmont, Kilconquhar, Fife.

[8] David Murray, 4th Baronet of Stanhope, nephew of John Murray of Broughton, sixteen years of age when he joined; made aide-de-camp to Charles and captain of hussars; prisoner in York 1746; tried there and sentenced to death, but reprieved on condition of leaving Britain 1748 ; joined the Prince in France, and died there *circa* 1769 (*G. E. C.* iii. 343 ; Macbeth Forbes, *Jacobite Gleanings*). ' On ne scauroit trop plaindre et trop louer ce jeune homme qui m'a paru avoir supérieurement toutes les qualités du cœur et de l'esprit ' (*F. F. O.* 79, p. 235).

Gentlemen of distinction, but not one of the Mob[1] who were so fond of seeing him Ever ask'd to Enlist in his Service, and when he marched to fight Cope he had not one of them in his Army. The Princes first orders in Edinburgh were to Cause his Father to be proclaimed and his Manifestos to be read, which was done by the pursuivants in their habits from the Cross by Sound of Trumpet and all the Usual Ceremonies used at a proclamation. There was a paper likewise given about here which had been wrote in the highlands Upon the Princes hearing that the Lords of the regency had put a reward upon his head of 30000[pd].[2] This paper offer'd the like sum to any body that would secure the person of the Elector of Hanover (as his Majesty was at the time of the Princes Landing Abroad but Arrived at London soon after). At night their came a Great many Ladies of Fashion, to Kiss his hand, but his behaviour to them was very Cool : he had not been much used to Womens Company, and was always embarrassed while he was with them.[3] The 18 in the morning the Prince sent Lord Elcho to the Magistrates

---

[1] 'In ye afternoon a Drum beat up for volunters when a good many entered the Duke of Perth's regiment' (*M. M.* 198).

[2] Aug. 31st.

[3] *Ante*, p. 28.

who were Assembled at provost Steuarts, to demand under pain of Military execution (if not Comply'd with) 1000 tents, 2000 targets, 6000 pʳ of Shoes, and 6000 Cantines. The Magistrates Agreed to it, and the workmen were immediately sett to work. It was imagined when the Highlanders left Edinburgh to fight Cope that the Castle would have made a Sally to have putt a Stop to the peoples working, but all Sallies from the Castle were prevented by a Common Soldier of the princes Army getting drunk the night his Comrades left the town to meet Copes Army; for next morning when he Appeared alone upon the Street, being Ask'd why he was not with the rest of the highlandmen, the fellow said that their were 300 more highlanders in town lurking in cellars to cut of any Sally from the Castle. The thing was believed, so the Castle made no Sally, the workmen Continued working, and the fellow Escaped being taken. The 18 Lord Nairn arrived at Dediston with a thousand Athole men :[1] the Laird of Maclauchlan was along with

---

[1] This agrees with the number given by Sir Walter Scott (*T. G.* 400). It also agrees with a report received by the Government (*S. P. Scot.*, Oct. 29, 1745). Cf. Lord George Murray: 'I sent about a thousand of these knapsacks to Crieff, to meet the men that were coming from Atholl' (*J. M.* 31). William Duke of

them. The Prince, attended only by his aid du Camp, went and pass'd them in reveiw.

General Cope, who had march'd from Inverness to Nairn, Forres, Elgin, Fochabers, Cullen, Bamf, Tureff, old Meldrum, and to Aberdeen, where he embarked his army, had landed at Dunbar the 17th, where Brigadeer Fowkes join'd him with the two regiments of Dragoons. A great many from Edn[r] went and join'd him, particularly the Earl of Home,[1] Lord Napier,[2] Lord justice Clerck,[3] the lords of the Session Drummore,[4] Elchies,[5] &

Atholl, writing to Lord George Murray, Sept. 16th, says: ' I went to Dumblain with my Lord Nairn and about 1000 men he brings up to the Prince' (*A. C.* 19). On the other hand Lord George Murray writes to the Duke of Atholl, Sept. 25th : 'Nothing vexes me at present so much as that your men are much fewer in number than was expected' (*Ibid.* 25). But this letter probably refers to the men from Atholl as distinguished from those belonging to other clans, but included in the 'thousand Atholl men.'

1 William Home, 8th Earl, joined the army in 1735; d. at Gibraltar in 1761; a General in the British army.

2 Francis Scott, 6th Lord Napier of Merchiston; served as a volunteer in the Allied army 1743; d. 1773.

3 Andrew Fletcher, Lord Milton (b. 1692, d. 1766); Lord of Session 1724 ; Lord Justice-Clerk 1737; resigned office 1748, but ' retained the charge of superintending the elections, which he considered as his masterpiece' (Ramsay's *Scotland,* i. 89). Tweeddale's letters to the Lord Advocate show but little confidence in Lord Milton. Writing June 27, 1745, he says: 'He [Lord Milton] is not to be trusted with secrets butt is only to be employed as itt shall be thought necessary for his Majesty's service' (Craigie MSS.).

4 Drummore—Hon. Sir Hew Dalrymple (b. 1690, d. 1755), Lord of Session as Lord Drummore 1726 ; Lord of Justiciary 1745.

5 Lord Elchies—Patrick Grant (b. 1690, d. 1754); advocate 1712; raised to the Bench 1732 ; Lord of Justiciary 1737.

Arniston [1] the Advocate, and Solicitor,[2] Mr James
Lesly,[3] and Mr Charles Hope [4] & many more of
less note; but they did not all remain with him
when the prospect of an Engadgement drew nigh.
The 19 General Cope march'd his Army [5]—which
Consisted of 2100 regular foot, 300 Volunteers,
600 Dragons, 6 Cannon, and some Coehorns—and
Encamp'd in a field west of Haddington.[6] The 18

[1] Dundas—Robert Dundas (b. 1685, d. 1753), son of 2nd Lord
Arniston; Lord of Session 1737-48, when he s. Duncan Forbes of
Culloden as Lord President.

[2] The Lord Advocate at this time was Robert Craigie of Glendoick (b. 1685, d. 1760); Lord President 1754. The Solicitor-
General was Robert Dundas, younger of Arniston (b. 1713,
d. 1787), who resigned this office in 1746 owing to differences with
the Justice-Clerk (Lord Milton).

[3] Probably the Hon. James Leslie of Milndeans, son of 7th Earl
of Rothes; passed Advocate 1726; one of the Commissaries, Edinburgh; Solicitor of the Exchequer, and afterwards, on the abolition
of the Hereditary Jurisdictions, Sheriff of Fife 1748; d. 1761
(Douglas, *Peerage*, ii. 433).

[4] Probably Hon. Charles Hope (b. 1710, d. 1791), 3rd son of
1st Earl of Hopetoun. He was elected Member for the County of
Linlithgow 1743; and appointed Commissary-General of Musters in
Scotland 1744.

[5] '. . . the army being reinforced by 200 Highland levies under
Lord Loudon, and by the 13th and 14th Dragoons, the force was
raised to a total of 2300 men with 6 guns' (*H. B. A.*, iii. 130).

Johnstone gives the number as 4000 men (*M. J.* 21).

Murray   „   „   2700 men (*M. M.* 200).

Maxwell   „   „   2300 foot 600 horse (*M. K.* 41).

Cope   „   „   1400 foot 600 horse + a small
number of the Highland regiment (*G. C. T.* 43).

[6] Dr. Carlyle records a curious circumstance connected with
Lord Elcho's younger brother. He says: 'On Wed. (Sept. 18th)
the army was encamped to the west of Haddington, they (the
dragoons) were thrown into confusion by an alarm. The army,

the Prince order'd Lord Nairn after the review
to relieve the Guard of the town with his 1000
men—which was the Usual Guard ever after—100
men at the Abby, 50 at the Cannon gate guard, 50
at the City Guard, 100 at the Weigh house, and
25 at the foot of the Bow. The rest were Lodged
in the parliament house and Assembly room.
The 19 the Princes Army Evacuated Edinburgh
and went to Dediston [Duddingston] ; the Army
lay out rank and file in one line and the Prince
and the Principal officers lay in houses and Barns.
The Prince held a Councill of War at Dediston
and sent Officers [1] beyond Musselburgh to recon-
oitre the Ground, and upon their reports it was
determined to fight Gen Cope about Musselburg
bridge in Case he was near their next morning,
but if not to advance and meet him. Their were

however, was drawn out immediately, and it was found to be a
false alarm. The hon[ble] Francis Charteris had been married the day
before at Prestonhall to Lady Francis Gordon, the Duchess of
Gordon's daughter, who was supposed to favour the Pretender. . . .
How that might be nobody knew, but it was alleged *that the alarm
followed their coach*, as they passed to their house at New Amisfield '
(Carlyle, *Autobiography*, 134).

[1] Roy Stewart and George Hamilton. At Musselburgh they
captured Francis Garden (afterwards Lord Gardenstone, a Lord of
Session) and Robert Cunninghame (afterwards a general in the
Government forces). These ' were taken prisoners at Crystall's inn,
west of Musselburgh, where they were seated at a regale of white
wine and oysters at an open window when observed by one of the
Prince's lifeguards, who were riding past ' (*Ibid.* 136).

several reports of his being at tranent that night. The Prince had a pretty just account of his horse and foot, but none of his Cannon : some people call'd them 20, others 16, and none under 12. The Cannon & the Cavalerie were what the high-landers seemed most to dread, for the foot they did not mind upon account of their having Shun'd fighting in the Highlands. On the 20 at six in the morning the Princes army march'd away [1] from Dediston in one Colum ; at Pinkie house the horse that were advanced brought intelligence that they had seen parties of the dragoons about Tranent, and by what they Could learn Gen: Copes army was thereabout. Upon which The Princes army Struck to the right, and in two Colums, which was the line of Battle, Gain'd the top of Carberry hill which goes to Tranent, Where they plainly descried Gen. Copes Army drawn up in Line of Battle in the plains below Tranent, his foot in the Centre and the Dragoons on the Wings with a small Corps de Reserve, Colonel Gardners park walls on his right, his bagadge on his left, a broad ditch

---

[1] It was at the moment of moving off from Duddingston that Charles, drawing his sword, said: 'Gentlemen, I have flung away the scabbard ; with God's assistance I don't doubt of making you a free and happy people ' (*Caledonian Mercury*, Sept. 23, 1745).

in his front, and the town of Preston pans in his
rear. The Princes Army remained sometime in
View of Mr Copes to See what he would do, but
upon his making no motion it was judged he
intended to be upon the defensive, which encouradged the highlanders ; for Certainly M^r
Cope Ought to have sought them out. As his was
regular troops, he ought to have look'd upon
them as militia and never show'd the least fear
for them, but Attack'd them wherever he met
them, and his always Showing an inclination to
decline the combat was the Greatest fault he
Comitted, for every motion he made to Shun
an Engagement added so much courage to the
Princes Army. The Prince after having had
Tranent reconoitred, order'd the army to advance
towards it, & the Church Yard to be taken
possesion of by 300 men, but as it lay Exposed
to Mr Copes Cannon which they fired Briskly
upon it, and wounded some men, it was abandon'd. Upon General Copes never moving out
of his place, the army Grew so keen to Engage
that they offer'd to Cut fascines to Carry with
them and attack him notwithstanding of the
broad ditch in his front, and upon some of the
Officers alledging he intended to Gett into Edn^r

without fighting, Lord Nairn with the Second line
was order'd to March down Upon his right flank,
leaving Colonel Gardners parks between him and
it. Upon Which Mr Cope fil'd of to the left and
drew his right further from the inclosures, and
fronted again as he was; at this which the Highlanders attributed to fear, Their Spirits rose prodigiously, and their Common Conversation was
how to Catch Cope. About eight at night, after
having been in view of Mr Cope six hours, Lord
George Murray march'd the first line through
Tranent and halted, and fronted Mr Cope, with
Tranent on the left. The Army lay upon Shaves
of Corn every man on his post, rank and file, and
the Prince with the principal officers in the centre
of the line: there were advanced Guards upon the
right and left and all along the front. All that
day people ran great risk of being shot by the
highlandmen, for as they think it Ominous [1] to
lett hogs or hares pass their lines, they kill'd
severals of them to the great risk of Everybody
that was near. General Copes Army, which lay
on their arms all night at half a miles distance
from the Princes with the broad ditch betwixt

[1] 'No prosperity could attend a journey at the outset of which a
pig or hare was encountered' (Campbell's *Superstitions*, 254).

them, kept great fires, and threw off one Coehorn, which fell short in a direct line where the Prince was. About ten o'clock at night Lord Nairns Colum fired a good deal at some dragoons who were patrouling and kiled some of them.

As the Conversation amongst the Officers where the Prince was, run mostly Upon what was to be done next morning and whow to Gett at Mr Cope, their was one Mr Anderson, an East Lothian Gentleman, said he knew of a road that was upon the right, but as it was a narrow defilèe, if it was guarded it would be difficult to pass. Every body immediately agreed to try to march that way next morning, before day light, and an aid du camp was sent of to order Lord Nairn to join the Army which he did, and the Army march'd of from the left in one Colum (this was done in order to Give the Macdonalds who were on the left the right). The Duke of Perth Commanded the right wing and Lord George Murray the left. The first line was Composed of the following regiments, viz Clanronald 250, Glengarry 350, Kepoch and Glenco 450, Perth 200, Appin 250, and Lochyell 500. The Prince himself Commanded the second line, which was Composed of three regiments, viz. Lord

George Murrays 350, Lord Nairnes 350, Menzies of Shians[1] 300, and Lord Strathallan with his troop of 36 horse was orderd to remain near Tranent in order to take prisoners in case of a Victory.

The first line pass'd the defillèe before day without being perceived, for the defillèe was not Guarded. Their was one Embrazure in a wall but no Cannon at it. As the Second line was passing, Sir John Cope fired an Alarm Gun and formed so as to front the Princes Army, the Broad ditch upon his right, the town of Preston pans on his left, and Gardners and the house of Prestons parks in his rear: a Great many breaches were made in the park walls which were of Great use to them on the defeat. He sent his Badgage to a house at Cockeny, where there was a court with a wall about it, and it was Guarded by all his highlanders. He formed his army the foot in

1 Sir Walter Scott's figures have clearly been taken from Elcho's Narrative. Elcho's analysis of the second line leads to the supposition that the 1000 Atholl men under Lord Nairn included the men from Atholl brigaded as Lord George's regiment, Lord Nairn's regiment, which probably comprised the Maclauchlans and Robertsons, and thirdly, the Menzies of Shian (cf. *M. K.* 41). In favour of the view that the Menzies had joined before the battle, there is a letter from Lord G. Murray to the Duke of Atholl, Sept. 26th, in which he says: 'This goes by Sheen Menzies, who, with a hundred men, guards so many of our prisoners to Lougaret' (*A. C.* 30).

the Centre and the dragoons on the right, left, & corps de reserve ; he placed his Cannon on his right advanced before Gardners dragoons and Supported them with 100 foot. His Army Commanded by himself & under him by Brigadeer Fowkes, Consisted of Murrays regiment 700, Lascelles 560, 5 Companies of Lees, and 2 of Guises 490, Gardners on the right and Hamiltons dragoons on his left : these two last Corps were 300 men Each. Both Armies were alike in Number.* When the Two Lines of the Princes Army were pass'd the Defilèe they wheel'd to the left and fronted General Copes and marched forwards in line of Battle. When they Came so near as plainly to Discover his line, for it was just at the dawn of Day, they sett up a hideous noise and run in as fast as they Could. In the running in, the first line broke in the Middle, but Copes Army did not perceive it, for the Second line was so Close to the first it Appeared to them as one. General Copes Battery fired one round, and as they were going to Charge Again, Lochyells Regiment seized it. The Princes first line closed Again, and Continued running in, when they Came near enough ; the right & left firr'd upon

*including those that guarded Gen: Cope's baggage.

the dragoons, who immediately Broke, turned their Backs, and run Away; the Centre firred upon the foot & received a very regular fire from them, but as the highlanders (notwithstanding of their fire) Continued to run in upon them sword in hand (for After firing they threw away their Guns) they likewise Broke, threw down their Arms, & run Away. The Highlanders in running in were pretty much a la Debandade, some places 10 deep, others one or two. Whoever their was always the Appearance of a line. As Soon as the pursuit began all the Principal Officers Mounted on horseback in order to Save and proteck Gen. Copes Officers as much as they Could, and had not they done it, Their would have been a great many of them kill'd, but as it happen'd their were very few. The foot Soldiers run to Gett through the Breackes in the walls that were behind them, and through which the Dragoons [1] had Escaped, but they were either cutt down or taken by the Highlanders, who in a pursuit are very nimble, and had it not been for the breaches in the walls their would not have a Soul Escaped either horse or foot; and as it was,

---

[1] With regard to the continuous panic of the dragoons, Tweeddale, on Sept. 24th, wrote: 'The dragoons have no excuse but that they are from Ireland' (Craigie MSS.).

Battle of Gladsmuire or Preston Pans

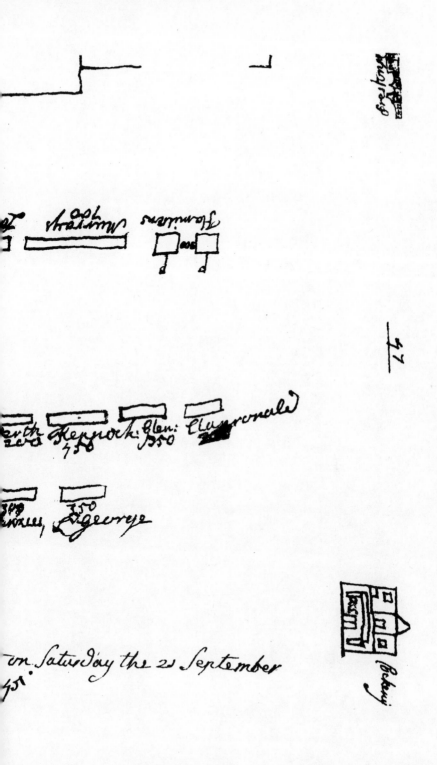

47

on Saturday the 21 September
451

most of the foot were either kill'd or taken prisoners. General Cope at some distance from the field of Battle rallied 400 dragoons and Marched them by Lauder to Berwick. The Earls of Home and Loudon were along with them.

In the pursuit the Princes first line went into the Greatest Confusion, some pursuing their Enemy wherever they saw them running, others were employ'd in pilladging the dead and taking the locks of the Guns: the Second line kept in order. Their was a report a little after the deroute that the Dragoons had rallied and were returning to the field, upon which Lochyell order'd his pipes to be played and a good many men Came to them. The Prince order'd Lord George Murray to March down with y^m, to the house at Cockeny where their Bagage was, Guarded by five Companies 350 men; Lord George sent Lt Colonel Halket (who was a prisoner) to Summon them to Surrender, which they accordingly did; by which means the Prince became master of their Military Chest, in which their was 2500^{pd} & all their Bagage. Their was a great Many Colours and Standards taken in the battle and some horses: their would have been a great many more

taken, had it not been for a notion the Highlanders had that the horses fought as well as the
men, which made them kill a great many of them
after their riders were dismounted. The Prince
had killed, Capt[s] Stuart of Appins and Macdonald
of Keppochs[1] and L[t] Cameron and Ensigne
Cameron of Lochyells, and about 50 private men
and 80 wounded. Cap[t] Macgregor[2] of Perths was
much wounded, Sir John Cope lost Collonel
Gardner, Capts. Steuart of Lascelles's, Braimer &
Rogers of Lee's, Holwell of Guises, Bishop and
Ens: Forbes of Murrays, Killed, and the following is a list of the officers taken prisoners. A 'w'
is at the names of those that were wounded.

[1] Archibald Macdonald, third son of Coll.

[2] Malcolm Drummond or Macgregor, eldest son of Donald
Murray or Macgregor ; wounded in five places, he died shortly after
the battle ; he commanded a section of Macgregors from the Perth
estates, and has been frequently confused with James Mor, son of
the famous Rob Roy ; being 'whimsical and singular,' says
Johnstone, 'he called out to the Highlanders of his company (after
he had been wounded), ' My lads, I am not dead, and, by God,
I shall see if any of you does not do his duty' (*C. G.*, ii. 373 ;
M. J. 24). Elcho makes no mention of the Macgregors, but in
Duncan MacPharie's MSS. it is stated that besides the company
from the Perth estates there was a body of Macgregors under
Glencarnock ; probably, however, the two sections were brigaded
with Perth's battalion and Ardsheal's Stewarts. (Cf. *C. G.* ii. 373 ;
Blaikie, 91.)

Gardners	Guises	Murrays
Lt Grafton : w :	Capt Pointz : w :	Lt Col : Clayton
Quarts Young	Lts Cuming	Maj : Talbot
„ Bouroughs: w:	Paton	Capts Reid
„ West	Ens Wakeman	Cochran
	Irwine	Scot
Hamiltons	**Lees**	Leslie : w :
		Blake : w :
Lt Col: Wright: w:	Lt Col : Halket	Lts Sir Tho: Hay: w:
Major Bowles : w :	Capts Cochran	Disney : w :
Corns Jacob : w :	Chapman	Wale
„ Nash	Tatton	Wry
Quarts Nash	Lts Sandilands : w :	Sims : w :
	Drummond : w :	Ens Sutherland
Ld John Murrays	Kenedy	Lucey
	Hewitson : w :	Haldane : w :
Capt Sir Pa : Murray	Ens Hardwick	Birnie
Lt Farquarson	Archer	L'Estrange
Ens Campbell	Dunbar	Adj : Spencer
Lascelles's	**Loudons**	**of ye Artilery & Volunteers**
Maj : Severn	Capts Mackay	Maj : Grieffiths
Capts Barlow	Monro	**Volun :**
Forester	Stewart	Lt Col Whiteford : w :
Anderson	Lts Macnab	Lt Carrick
Corbet	Reed	
Collier	Ens Grant	**Doctors**
Drummond	Ross	Trotter
Lts Swiney : w :	Maclaggan	Young
Johnston		Drummond
Dundass		Hunter
Hewon : w :		Mr Wilson
Ens Stone		quarter master
Cox		to Lees
Bell		
Gordon		
Goulton		

Their were 500 private men kill'd, 900 wounded,
and 1400 taken prisoners, including the wounded;
which undoubtedly made it one of the most Compleat Victorys[1] ever was Gained, for all the
artilery, Consisting of six piece of Cannon and
some Coehorns, was also taken. Lord Strathallans
troop took some of the Dragoons. Their was
instances of 16 of them Surrendring to one
person. Whoever Mr Threapland[2] had the misfortune, in Attempting to overtake some that were
running away, to be kill'd, his horse fell, and an
Officer of the dragoons seeing he was alone, turn'd
about and shot him. As most of General Copes
Surgeons had run away, the Prince Sent into Edn^r
for Some, and the wounded were taken very good

[1] Cope himself reached Coldstream that night, a distance of
forty miles, preceded by Fowkes, Lascelles, and another officer. To
Berwick he is said to have been the first to bring news of his defeat
(see Skirving's ballad, 'Hey, Johnnie Cope.') Writing to Lord
Tweeddale (S. P. Dom., Sept. 21, 1745), the evening of the battle,
Cope said: 'I cannot reproach myself: the manner in which the enemy
came on was quicker than could be described, and (of which the
men have long been warned) possibly was the cause of our men
taking a destructive panic. I cannot give any account of the
numbers killed and wounded, the whole baggage taken, and the
military chest and papers belonging to it. The fatigue and concern
I have had render me incapable of being more particular.'
    For Charles's own account of the battle, written on Oct. 7th,
see Lang's Charles Edward, 167: 'Of ye horse only to hundred
escaped like rabets, one by one.' He awards no praise and mentions
no names in describing his victory.
    [2] David Threipland (b. 1694), 3rd son of Sir David and half-
brother of Sir Stuart Threipland.

care of. This Battle, which the Princes army call'd Gladsmuir and other people Preston, was fought on the 21 * of Sep^t 1745, and was ended just as the sun gott up : it did not last full a quarter of an hour. The Prince from this Battle entertained a mighty notion of the highlanders, and ever after imagin'd they would beat four times their number of regular troops. After the necessary orders were given for Burying the dead, The Prince marched away to Pinkie house where he lay all night. He did not Carry many men with him that night, for they were pretty busy in picking up what they Could find, and some of them went home from the field of Battle with their plunder. The Prince left orders with their officers to Assemble them at Dediston next day ; The Officers prisoners were order'd to Musselburgh, and those that were wounded were left at Colonel Gardners house. The 22 he March'd into Edinburgh with about 800 foot Carrying the trophies of the victory, he himself and all his principall officers on horseback. When he Came near the town he was mett by a multitude of people who huza'd him quite into the palace. Next day The Cannon and Bagage arrived, and it was putt into a yard by the Abbey, which was

afterwards call'd the Artilery parck. The rest of
the army that had not gone home came to Dediston, where they pitch'd tents and form'd a Sort
of Camp ; the Officers prisoners were that night
Confined in the Duke of Queensboroughs[1] house,
but Gott the liberty of the town next day upon
parole. Lord Strathallan being made governor
of Perth and Oliphant of Gask Lt Governor,
they were sent to Perth after having given their
paroles of honour not to Go above two miles from
the town without leave, never to take arms
Against the Prince while the affair lasted, and to
deliver themselves to him when Call'd for, all
which they most Scandalously broke sometime
afterwards. Suppose[2] Lord Strathallan had been
so indulgent as to allow all those that were Scots
to go home to their own houses, and the others to
Go to Lesly, Glamis, or in a manner to whatever
place they Chose, the Soldiers that would not
inlist with the Prince were sent to Athole under

[1] Queensberry House in the Canongate, now a house of refuge
for the destitute.

[2] Elcho uses ' suppose ' for ' although ' throughout the Narrative. In Wright's *Dialect Dictionary* ' suppose' is stated to be an
obsolete conj. signifying ' although.' ' Cf. Suppois. Suppose conj.
although.' ' I believe that the use of this word *suppose* for *though*
is still common in Scotland.—Tooke's *Divers. Purley*, i. 188 '
(Jamieson's *Scottish Dictionary*).

the Escorte of Colonel Menzies of Shian. The Highlanders were sent home upon parole not to take arms Again, but most of them followed the Example of their officers : those that inlisted mostly all deserted.

It was thought by most people that had the Prince immediately after this battle been in a Situation to have march'd directly up to London the affair might have Succeeded, and he certainly Could have done it, had all the people join'd him at first that he had afterwards at the Battle of Falkirk, but when he returned to Edinburgh from Preston he Could not have assembled 1500 men, which Certainly was not Sufficient for Such an Enterprise, Considering the Government had order'd their Troops from Flanders and a Considerable body of them had landed at London, Newcastle, and Berwick. The Dutch had likewise sent 6000 Auxilaries under the command of Prince Maurice of Nassau ; but as they were Friench prisoners of war and Could not act[1] against the French or perform any military duty whatever

---

[1] By treaty, Jan. 30, 1713, the States-General were bound to despatch 6000 men, when required, for the defence of His Britannic Majesty. The troops sent were part of the garrison of Tournay, and had been released on the surrender of that town (June 20, 1745) to the French, on condition of not bearing arms against Louis or his allies before January 1747 (Blaikie, *Itinerary*).

untill ye 1747, The French Ambassador at the Hague reclaimed them, and it was thought they durst not have fought.

The Dutch regiments that came to Britain were Hersler Swiss 3 Batt : Holstein Gothorp 3 Batt : Villets 3 Batt : Patot 3 Batt : Brackell 1 Batt : and La Rocques.

The Prince issued out Several proclamations upon his arrival at Edn^r, viz. one on the 23 to prevent any publick demonstrations of joy for the Victory as it had been obtained over his fathers Subjects, who's blood he was sorry to have been oblidged to Spill. Suppose, he said, they were in Rebellion in Another, he order'd all the Ministers to Continue their worship in their Ususal way, and not to Abandone ^{1} their kirks as they had done, and Assured them they Should not be molested.

One was issued dated ye 24, granting protection to all farmers within five miles of Edn^r who would enact themselves to be ready on twelve

---

^{1} Only three ministers were found to obey this direction. One of them, Mr. M'Vicar of St. Cuthbert's, delivered himself of the often quoted prayer, in which, after praying that God would bless the king, he added, ' Thou knowest what king I mean. May the crown sit long easy on his head. And for this man [Prince Charles] that is come amongst us to seek an earthly crown, we beseech thee in mercy to take him to thyself and give him a crown of glory ' (Ray's *Rebellion*, 45).

hours warning to transport the baggage to Berwick or as far on another road. The Same day a pardon was Granted to all such of the Volunteers as would appear in twenty days at Secretary Murrays office and promise never more to take up arms Against the Prince. On the 25 their was one issued promising protection to the banks if they would Come to town and Act as Usual. Whoever they remained in the castle, but paid all the notes the army was possess'd of. Their was a great many proclamations to prevent thefts & robberies. The Highlanders no doubt committed some, but a great Many more were done by people who putt on white Cockades for that end, and did not at all belong to the Army; but at last their was a trusty officer and a party putt into all the villages about Edn^r in order to put a Stop to it. Letters were Sent to all the Officers of the publick revenues and to the factors of the forfeited Estates to Come and pay their money to Secretary Murray, who in a Short time after offer'd to Lend out money at 5 per cent, which was very Suspicious as every one knew he was not worth 100^{pd} before this Affair. Their was a party sent to Glascow to demand 10,000^{pd}, and they Compromised the Matter for 5500^{pd} ; their

were partys sent as far as Douglass and Hamilton
and all up and down the Country to Search for
horses and arms ; the Goods of the Custom house
at Leith were sold for the Princes use, and Ardsheils Battalion was order'd to East Lothian to
facilitate the levying of the publick money in that
County.

The tents, targets, Cantines, &ca, order'd from
ye town of Edn^r were deliver'd and distributed to
the different Corps at the Camp at Dediston.
The Prince order'd a great many Officers to the
Highlands to see and recruit more men and bring
back those who had gone home with their plunder.
After the Battle of Preston a great many people
of fashion joyned the army, particularly Lord
Ogilvy and Glenbuckett with 300 men Each; the
Prince pass'd them in reveiw on the links of Leith
and Sent them to quarter in Leith; Lord Pitsligo [1]

[1] 4th and last Lord Forbes of Pitsligo (b. 1678, d. 1762), took
part in rebellion of 1715; escaped to France ; returned to Scotland
1720. Published *Essays : Moral and Philosophical* in 1734. He
kept up a correspondence with the Quietists in France. He con-
fessed that he joined without enthusiasm from a considered fidelity
to the House of Stuart. He addressed his troop of horse, ' O Lord,
thou knowest that our cause is just. March, Gentlemen.' After
Culloden, was a fugitive in the Highlands. As late as March 1756
he was still an object of search ; had many romantic escapes (*Thoughts
Concerning Man's Condition*, by Lord Forbes of Pitsligo, 1763, also
Chambers's *Eminent Scotsmen*, ii. 36-8).
' A little thinn fair man a great schollar and fond of study, of
the primitive Stamp, and fitter to have been a martyr in the days of

with a Squadron of 180 Aberdeen and Bamffshire Gentlemen and their servants, They were order'd to Dalkeith. Lord Lewis Gordon,[1] who was made Lord leiutenant of Aberdeenshire and sent there to raise men; the Earl of Nithsdale,[2] the Earl of Kilmarnock,[3] who gott a comission to raise a troop of horse Grenadieers, but in the mean time was appointed to Command the Perthshire 120 horse Squadron; Sir Alexander Bannerman[4] of

Nero than to live in an age of villany and corruption . . . not beloved but adored' (*M. M.* 226). 'In his letters on that subject he usually called the young Pretender by the name of the Amiable young Stranger' (MS. in the possession of Mr. Blaikie).

[1] Youngest son of the 2nd Duke of Gordon; lieutenant in the Royal Navy; declared for Charles; defeated the laird of Macleod near Inverury, Dec. 23, 1745; escaped to the Continent; attainted 1746; d. 1754 at Montreuil. 'Il est très brave, très etourdi, et fou quelquefois jusqu'à se faire enfermer; il s'est presque brouillé avec le prince qu'il ne voit guère' (*F. F. O.* 79, fo. 235).

[2] Son of William Maxwell, 5th Earl of Nithsdale; d. in London 1776. After visiting Holyrood he retired to the country, 'where nothing but the most dreadful scene of axes, Gibbets, and halters presented themselves to his weaking and sleeping thoughts . . . he continued crazy for some time' (*M. M.* 228).

[3] William Boyd, 6th Earl of Kilmarnock (b. 1705, d. 1746). He surrendered or was taken prisoner after Culloden; tried at Westminster, and beheaded on Tower Hill Aug. 18, 1746. His appearance and speech at the trial, when he pleaded 'guilty,' moved the spectators to tears (see Walpole's *Letters,* Aug. 1746). On the morning of his death he said 'Amen' to the prayer of the official, 'God save King George.' On the same occasion Balmerino added the words, 'God save King James.'

[4] 3rd Bart. of Elsick; m. Isabella, heiress of the Trotters of Horsley, in Yorkshire; raised a regiment and commanded it at Culloden on the left of the second line; escaped to France; died in Paris 1747; his mother was a daughter of Sir Donald Macdonald of Sleat.

Elsick who was made Lord Leiutenant of the
Mearns; David Fothringham, Esqr,[1] who was
made Governor of Dundee, as Lord Kelly was of
Lochleven; and Macgregor of Glengyle of Down,[2]
who had taken for the Prince before the battle the
fort of Inersnaat [Inversnaid] & made the Garison,
Consisting of a Leiutenant and his Command,
prisoners of war.   John Roy Steuart was order'd
to raise a regiment, and he inlisted a great many
of Copes Soldiers, but they mostly all left him.
The rest of the Gentlemen that join'd the Prince
were Grant of Glenmorisden with 100 men—they
join'd Glengarys, Mackinnin of that ilk [3] with the

---

[1] Merchant of Dundee, 'was governor for the rebels and was
very active, managed in a Tyrannical manner' (*L. P. R.* 213).

[2] Gregor Macgregor of Glengyle (b. 1689, d. 1777), afterwards adopted name of James Graham; signed the Bond electing
Bohaldie as Chief of the Macgregors 1714; active for the Stuart
cause 1715; towards the end of August 1745, together with his
cousin James Drummond, he captured the Fort of Inversnaid and
eighty-nine soldiers. 'Glengile and sixty men had been placed upon
Castle of Doune as Commander-in-Chief in Scotland, being an old
man. . . . I know Glencarnock was a very sensible man, and did
not choose to rise Glengile's corruption as he was sometimes stark
mad' (MacPharie MSS., *C. G.* ii. 368).

[3] Mackinnon of Mackinnon came in response to a summons
conveyed by Alexander Macleod of Muiravonside, which represented
that Charles was expecting immediate succour from France and
Spain. 'Mr. M'Kinnon of M'Kinnon joined him from the Isle of
Skey with about 120 men, realy brave and honest, inured to fatigue,
and patient to undergoe any thing that tended to the service of their
Masters, and might according to the litteral Sense of the word, be
called Solgers' (*M. M.* 223; Blaikie, 18).

Like number who join'd Keppochs, Sir William Gordon of Parck,[1] Sir William Dunbar of Duirn,[2] Gordon of Cowbardie,[3] Gordon of Carnousie,[4] Gordon of Halhead,[5] Gordon of Drumlethie,[6] Irvin of Drum,[7] Hay of Ranas,[8] Rollo of

[1] Eldest son of Sir James Gordon by Dame Helen Fraser; attainted; estates forfeited; abroad 1751. 'Very active in distressing the country by levying money, using very violent measures' (*L. P. R.* 29, 369). He acted as lieut.-colonel of Lord Ogilvy's regiment (*H. P.* 352).

[2] 3rd Bart. of Durn, d. 1786.

[3] James Gordon of Coubardie, Banffshire (*ante*, p. 129).

[4] Arthur Gordon of Carnoussie — 'An officer in the rebel army' (*L. P. R.* 30). Yearly rent of estate £9000 [Scots] (*Ibid.* 308). 'Carnusy and Cupbairdy's journey was a great surprise. The latter had no manner of tincture that way but being a rambling young lad was determined mostly by comradeship and something too by the high regard he had for Pitsligo. Carnusy was esteemed a wise, solid man and some one not at all wedded to kingscraft. But as many debts of his never heard of formerly, are appearing, this somewhat unravels the mystery' (MS. in the possession of Mr. Blaikie). Coubardie escaped to France; pensioned by Louis (Michel, ii. 441).

[5] George Gordon of Halhead, son and heir of Robert Gordon of Halhead by his wife Isabel Byres; secretary to Lord Pitsligo (*L. P. R.* 10). He m. Amy Bowdler, an English lady. In a letter to her sister Mrs. Gordon describes the visit of General Hawley to her house in Aberdeen, in Feb. 1746. The general, she says, had packed up her possessions and despatched them by sea to Edinburgh directed to himself. 'The flutes, musick, and my cane he made presents off' (*L. M.* iii. 170). Gordon escaped to France; pensioned by Louis (Michel, ii. 447); *ante*, p. 129.

[6] Alexander Gordon of Darlathis or Dorlathers (Banff). (*L. P. R.* 30, 178, 308).

[7] Irvine of Drum—carried arms during the whole rebellion (*L. P. R.* 12); taken prisoner after Culloden; died of wounds June 1746 (*L. M.* iii. 60).

[8] Andrew Hay, younger of Raness, 'major of horse to Lord Pitsligo's regiment' (*L. P. R.* 30); petitioned the Crown for pardon after the rebellion (*H. P.* ii. 489).

Powhouse,[1] Stirling of Keir[2] and Two of his Sons
and two Cousins, Hunter of Burnside,[3] Tomson
of Ffield,[4] Cuming of Pitulie,[5] Halden of Lanerk[6]
Father and son, Hay of Restalrig,[7] Hamilton
factor to the Duke of Gordon, Cochran of Fer-
gusslie,[9] Fletcher of Benchie,[10] Fothringham of

[1] Rollo. See note 4, p. 260.

[2] James Stirling of Keir—'A zealous ffriend for the Pretender's
Interest was in the rebellion of 1715. he was closs with the rebels
at Glasgow and prompted them to vex and oppress the inhabitants.'
Taken prisoner with his son Hugh on shipboard while making for
Holland, and lodged in Dumbarton Castle in May 1746. His son
William escaped (L. P. R. 276). James Stirling was mentioned by
Lord George Murray as being a member of Charles's Council (A.C. 25).

[3] David Hunter of Burnside, captain in the Prince's Life
Guards from Preston to Culloden. 'Prisoner at Bergen' (L. P. R.
218); ante, pp. 109, 129.

[4] Alexander Thomson of Feichfield, Aberdeen; recruited men
for the Prince. Yearly rent of estate, £200 (L. P. R. 99).

[5] William Cumming of Pittully, Pitsligo, Aberdeen. Yearly
rent of estate, £300 (L. P. R. 89, 302); ante p. 123.

[6] John Halden of Lanrick and his son Alexander both escaped
to the Continent. John Halden d. in Paris 1765 (L. P. R. 373).

[7] Hay of Restalrig during the illness of John Murray acted as
secretary to Prince Charles; escaped to France after Culloden (ante,
p. 105); afterwards knighted at Rome by the Chevalier de St. George
(L. M. iii. 218); ante, p. 200 et seq.

[8] John Hamilton, afterwards governor of Carlisle; surrendered
the town, Dec. 30, 1745, to the Duke of Cumberland; executed
at St. Margaret's Hill, Nov. 15, 1746. 'Hamilton undoubtedly
was a noted Jacobite, but reckoned too selfish to meddle in such
undertakings, so that the reason of his commencing adventures was
generally imagined to be owing to the disorder of his affairs' (MS.
in the possession of Mr. Blaikie).

[9] William Cochran of Ferguslie, Renfrew. Yearly rent of
estate, £100. Escaped after Culloden (L. P. R. 292, 326).

[10] Robert Fletcher of Benchy, Jun., major in Lord Ogilvy's
regiment; imprisoned at Bergen (L. P. R. 212).

Banden,[1] Riddle of Lathrick,[2] Auchinleck of Kunucky,[3] Halkston of Rathilet,[4] Maxwell of Kirkconnel,[5] Hamilton of Red House,[6] and a Great
many others, the viscounts of Kenmore[7] &
Dundee.[8] The Prince formed such as did not
belong to other Corps into two troops one of
Seventy, which he Gave the Command of to Lord
Elcho who he had made Colonel of his Guards

[1] Thomas Fotheringham of Bandaine—served in the Prince's
Life Guards (*L. P. R.* 212).

[2] Probably Riddle of Grange in Fife; escaped to France;
pensioned by Louis.

[3] Andrew Auchenleck. From Preston to Culloden. 'Not
known' (*L. P. R.* 62).

[4] Heleneas Haxton or Halkeston, gentleman, Rathehills, Kil-
minny, Fife. 'Lurking in the country' (*L. P. R.* 64). Sold the
estate of Rathehill about 1772 (Anderson, *Scottish Nation*, ii. 394).

[5] James Maxwell of Kirkconnel (b. 1708, d. 1762); served in
the Prince's Life Guards under Elcho, with whom he escaped to
France. Author of a narrative of the Rebellion. See Index.

[6] George Hamilton of Red House; tried at York, Aug. 21,
1746; executed Nov. 1, 1746. He was Deputy Quartermaster-
General of the Highland army. Seventy prisoners were condemned to
death at the assizes held at York. It was significant of the prevailing
temper that the High Sheriff's chaplain, preaching before the judges
in the Cathedral, chose as his text Numbers xxv. 5: 'And Moses said
unto the judges of Israel, Slay ye every one his men that were joined
unto Baal-peor.'

[7] Second son of Lord Kenmure, who was beheaded in 1716. His
elder brother died in 1741. Like Lord Nithsdale he withdrew to
his home. He subsequently wrote to the Lord Justice-Clerk to
excuse himself for having visited Holyrood (*M. M.* 229).

[8] 6th titular Viscount, 'Writer in Edinburgh,' son and heir
of 5th Viscount; was attainted as 'James Graham of Duntroon,
taking on himself the title of Viscount of Dundee.' He afterwards
had a company in the French service in Lord Ogilvy's regiment;
d. at Dunkirk 1759.

upon the field of Battle of Preston, and Since
Lord Leiutenant of Fife ; the other * he Gave
first to Lord Kenmore, and upon his not joining
at Carlisle, to Lord Balmerino, they formed a
Squadron of 150 horse including their Servants,
and the Prince order'd them to wear Blue turned
up with red and the Squadron to be Under Lord
Elcho's orders.   Mr Murray the Secretary raised a
troop and had them dress'd like Hussars.   The
Command of them was afterwards given to Mr
Bagot an Irishman.

* Consisting
of 30.

The Prince formed a Council which mett
regularly every morning in his drawing room.
The Gentlemen that he Call'd to it Were The
Duke of Perth, Lord Lewis Gordon, Lord
George Murray, Lord Elcho, Lord Ogilvy,
Lord Pitsligo, Lord Nairn Lochyell, Keppoch,
Clanronald, Glenco, Lochgary,[1] Ardshiel, Sir
Thomas Sheridan, Coll, OSulivan, Glenbuckett
& Secretary Murray.

The Prince in this Councill used Always first
to declare what he was for, and then he Ask'd

[1] Eldest son of John Macdonald of Lochgarry; in June 1745
lieutenant in Lord Loudon's Highland regiment, but joined Charles ;
wounded at Clifton ; commanded the Glengarry regiment; escaped
to France with Charles ; was concerned in the abortive plot to
restore the Stuarts in 1752 ; m. Isabel, daughter of Gordon of Glenbucket ; died in Paris.

Every bodys opinion in their turn. Their was one third of the Councill who's principals were that Kings and Princes Can never either act or think wrong, so in Consequence they always Confirmed whatever the Prince Said. The other two thirds, who thought that Kings and Princes thought sometimes like other men and were not altogether infallable and that this Prince was no more so than others, beg'd leave to differ from him, when they Could give Sufficient reasons for their difference of Opinion. Which very often was no hard matter to do, for as the Prince and his Old Governor Sir Thomas Sheridan were altogether ignorant of the Ways and Customs in Great Britain, and both much for the Doctrine of Absolute monarchy, they would very often, had they not been prevented, have fall'n into Blunders which might have hurt the Cause. The Prince Could not bear to hear any body differ in Sentiment from him, and took a dislike to Every body that did, for he had a Notion of Commanding this army As any General does a body of Mercenaries, and so lett them know only what he pleased, and they obey without inquiring further about the matter. This might have done better had his favourites been people of the Country, but as they were Irish And had nothing at Stake, The People of Fashion that had their all at Stake, and Consequently Ought to be Supposed to Give the best advice they were Capable of, thought they had a title to know and be Consulted in what was for the Good of the Cause in which they had so much Concern; and if it had not been for their insisting Strongly upon it, the Prince, when he found that his Sentiments were not always approved of, would have Abolish'd this Council long ere he did.

Their was a very Good paper sent one day by a Gentleman in Edn[r] to be perused by this Council. The Prince when he heard it read said it was below his dignity to Enter into such a reasoning with Subjects, and order'd the paper to be Laid aside. The Paper afterwards was printed [1] under the Title of The Princes declaration to the people of England and is Esteemed the best Manifesto was published in those times, for the ones that were printed at Rome and Paris were reckoned not well Calculated for the present Age.

The Prince Created a Comittee for providing the army with forage. It was Composed of Lord Elcho President, Lord Dundee, Sir Will: Gordon

---

[1] It is dated October 10, 1745, in margin of original.

of Parck Hunter of Burnside, Haldane of Lanerk
and his son, Mr Smith and Mr Hamilton. They
issued out orders in the Princes name to all the
Gentlemens houses who had employments under
the Government to Send in Certain quanties of
Hay, Straw, and Corn upon such a day under the
penalty of military execution if not Complyed
with, but their orders were very punctually obey'd.

Their were court martials satt every day for
the discipline of the Army, and some delinquents
were punish'd with death.

The Prince having had information that provisions were Scarce in the Castle, and that they
were dayly supplied from the town, issued out a
proclamation making it death for any body to
Carry provisions into them, and on the 29 of Sep^t
order'd it to be Block'd up, with orders to fire
upon Every body they Should see going in or
out. Upon which General Preston sent word to
the City that if they did not Send up provisions
to the Castle as Usual he had orders from court
to fire Upon the town. The Citizens sent to the
Prince to beg he would raise the blocade, but
their request was not Granted. General Preston
gave them a rispite for 6 Days to send to
London to See and gett his orders mitigated.

The 1th of October The Castle fired their Great
Guns upon the Weigh house and wherever they
saw any of the Princes Soldiers. There was some
of the towns people kill'd & some houses
damadged. On the 3 a Party Came down by
ropes from the Castle and Surprised a Guard of
the Princes at the West Kirk, kill'd one man &
took Capt Taylor prisoner, and putt the rest to
flight. The 4 at noon their was a terrible fire from
the Castle both of Cannon and small arms, and at
Night a Party Sallied out, took possession of
some houses on the Castle hill & Schirmish'd
with the Princes Gaurd who were about the
reservoir, sett fire to Some houses, and made a
trench across the Castle hill. Their were several
townspeople kill'd this night, and the whole town
was in Such Consternation that poeple began to
Abandon their Effects and run out of it. The
Prince Sent a Message to General Preston that if
he did not discontinue from firing upon the town,
he would Cause burn his house [1] in Fife. He made
answere that if he did, the fox man of War then
in the road had orders to burn Wemyss Castle,
which as the Earl of Wemyss was not with the
Prince was an odd sort of a reprisal. The next

---

[1] Valleyfield.

day the firing Continued, and a great many houses were much damadged and nobody Could be seen on the Streets, the bullets going every where very thick: the Earl of Dundonald[1] coming in at the West Port had his Servant kill'd, and Sir Robert Myrton of Gogar[2] his horse shot under him. Their were some more of the towns people kill'd, but in the Afternoon upon the Princes raising the Blocade, the firing ceased, and they only fired afterwards where they saw any of the Princes army. The Prince had 5 or 6 men kill'd in this affair, and found that he Could not think of Getting possession of the Castle without Battering Cannon and Bombs. The Parliment of Great Britain was summon'd to meet on the 17 of October. The Prince issued out a proclamation forbiding the Peers and Commoners of Scotland to pay any obedience to the Summons. About the same time the Parliment of Ireland offer'd a reward of 50'000 pd to any person that would Seize the Prince dead or alive in Case he landed in that Kingdom.

1 William Cochrane, 7th Earl of Dundonald, s. his father 1737; officer in the British army 1745; captain in Stewart's Scots Regiment in service of States of Holland 1750; captain in 17th Foot 1757; fell at siege of Louisburg, America, July 9, 1758.
2 2nd Bart. of Gogar, co. Edinburgh; b. 1720, d. 1774, when the baronetcy became extinct.

On the 7 of October their arrived a Ship at
Montross from France which brought 5000 ᵖᵈ
money, and 2500 Stand of Arms.   Their Came in
this ship Monsʳ de Boyer, Marquis D'equilles ¹ son
of a President of the Parliment at Aix, The Mʳ
of Strathallan,² Capᵗ Brown,³ who the Prince afterwards made a Colonel & his aid du Camp, and
Mʳ Sheridan Sir Thomas's Nephew, who he made
master of his horse.   Monsʳ du Boyer arrived at
Ednʳ on the 14, was vastly well received by the
Prince and treated by every body with a Great
deal of respect.   The Pr. gave out that he
brought letters to him from the King of France,
wherin the King promised him assistance, but
the Prince never show'd these letters ⁴ to his

¹ Alexandre de Boyer, Marquis d'Éguilles.   In the secret instructions which he received from Maurepas, he was told to veil, as far
as possible, his official position, and to occupy himself chiefly with
reporting to the French Court the progress of events and the prospects
of success (*M. M.* 435; *Les Écossais en France*, ii. 430; Pichot,
Histoire de Charles Édouard, ed. 1833, ii. 399).   'In his conversations
with us, however, he gave us to understand that it was all one to
France whether George or James was King of England, but that if
the Scots wished to have a King for themselves, then the King of
France would help them to the utmost of his power ' (Elcho, *Journal*).

² Eldest son of Lord Strathallan.

³ Captain in the regiment of Lally (Michel, ii. 431).   Left in
Carlisle, he escaped after the surrender; later he carried news of
Falkirk to France.

⁴ According to the secret instructions of the Marquis d'Éguilles,
Charles alone was to see the letter written to him by Louis (Pichot,
ii. 399).

Councill. The Prince told likewise that the King had sent Monsr du Boyer to reside with him as a Minister, he gave out publickly every where, that The French were to send over to England The Duke of York[1] (who had arrived at Paris) at the head of a number of Troops. This news gave the princes Army great Spirits as they expected to hear of a French Landing dayly. The Prince upon Mr du Boyers' arrival, sent of Mr Kelly with dispatches to France.[2] Towards the End of the month of October their Came three more Ships to Montross and Stonehive from France; their Came Several Irish officers in them who the Prince Gave all high Comissions to, six brass Cannon of four pound each, and twelve Cononeers. The Prince made Mr Grant[3] an Irish officer Colonel of his Train. Each Ship brought 2500 Stand of Arms and 1000 Money. The Arms and Cannon were first sent to Dunkeld and Then

---

[1] The Duke of York visited Louis at Fontainebleau Oct. 24th. At an embarrassing interview, Louis gave promises of support (Luynes, vii. 106). On the same day a treaty had been signed by d'Argenson on behalf of Louis and by O'Brien on behalf of Charles, whereby Louis pledged himself to aid Charles in his enterprise (*S. P. Dom. Geo. II.*, May 10, 1746).

[2] Charles's answer is given by Mr. Fitzroy Bell: 'Papers from French Foreign Office' (*M. M.* 513): it is dated Oct. 15th.

[3] 'An eminent mathematician who had wrought during a long time with M. Cassine in the observatory of Paris' (*M. J.* 35).

brought to Dalkeith by Higgins nook, where their was a battery raised to proteck the Passage. Rear Admiral Byng[1] hearing of the arrival of these ships upon the Coast of Scotland came into the firth and cast anchor in Leith road on the 26 of Oct[r], with the Glocester 50 Guns, Ludlow Castle 40, Fox 20, Happy Janet 20, the Hazard Sloop of war & some transports. Ever after a Party of Lord Elcho's Troop was order'd to patrouille at Nights betwixt Cramond and Musselburgh. The Men of War fired often asshoar but never kill'd any body. Mons[r] du Boyer was always Expecting to have news of an Embarkation,[2] and told the

---

[1] John (b. 1704, d. 1757), 4th son of George Byng, Viscount Torrington; Rear-Admiral 1745; tried by court-martial and sentenced to death for neglect of duty in the defence of Minorca (1756); executed at Portsmouth.

[2] See *ante*, p. 106. In the Record Office there is an abstract of a letter from the Duke of York to Charles, dated Bagneaux, Nov. 26, 1745: 'Overjoyed at the good news Kelly and his companions brought; Gordon's arrival has done good; d'Argenson assures that the troops for the expedition into England shall be ready by the 20th Dec.; French King resolved upon it; Ministers come to see the Duke of York *sans façon*' (Papers found after Culloden, *S. P. Dom. Geo. II.*, May 1746). Elcho says the embarkation was abandoned Jan. 6th. In December the Paris journals were already writing that the expedition would not be undertaken (Barbier, ii. 478). Many people regarded it merely as a feint to embarrass the English (Barrière, vol. ii.), and in conjunction with the rebellion it certainly did cause the British forces in the Low Countries to be withdrawn for the defence of England (*H. B. A.* ii. 123). On Sept. 4th Tweeddale had written to Craigie: '10 battalions of our Troops are ordered to embark for England directly, and now if the

Prince that it was his master the King of France's advice not to push things too fast, or to run the risk of a battle without being oblidged to it, for that if he kept his Army intire the French would certainly Assist him, Wheras if he was defeat before they Landed they certainly would not Send troops into the Country. Monsr du Boyer Likewise proposed Sending the Officers that were prisoners over to France by way of hostages for those of the Princes that might be taken, but it was not taken notice of by the Prince, so it dropt. About the middle of October, as the weather was cold, the army had Struck their tents and had gone into Cantoonments to Musselburgh, the Inch, & other Villages about Edn^r. It was a very irregular sort of a Camp, for the High-landers chose as soon to Lay without the tent as within, and never had them Rightly pitched. The Prince lay always in the Camp & never Strip'd. He Used to come into town early and Assemble his Council, after that he dined with his principal officers in publick. After dinner he road out with his Guards and review'd his Army, Came back & sup'd in town, & after Supper went

young Pretender should embark tomorrow he has effectually saved France and more than repaid her all the expence of the expedition ' (Craigie MSS.).

& Sleep'd in the Camp. Sometimes he sup'd in the Camp ; About the End of Otober their were reports every day [1] in town that Sir Alexander Macdonald, the Laird of Macleod at the head of their Clans, and the Frazers, Mackintoshes, and Mackenzies, were in arms and upon their march to join the Prince. Sometimes they were brought the length of Creif, but all these reports proved false. Suppose it is certain that they all had an inclination to joyn the Prince. Sir Alex. Macdonald, it is Said, promised it upon Conditions the Prince brought Troops with him, and Macleod had always expressed himself more warmly for that cause than Sir Alexander. Their was always a Great rancour against those two Gentlemen in the Princes Army, but it was more upon Account of their taking arms Against him than for not joining him. It was thought that had Lord Lovat [2]

[1] These rumours were spread by Murray in order to encourage others to join (*M. M.* 216).

[2] Simon Fraser, 12th Lord Lovat (b. 1667, d. 1747), son of Thomas Fraser, 3rd son of 8th Lord Lovat ; educated at King's College, Aberdeen ; one of his earliest exploits was his forcible marriage with Emilia, widow of the 10th lord, after failing to marry her eldest daughter, who had assumed the title of Baroness Lovat ; for this he was condemned to death (1698); took refuge in Skye, defied all attempts to arrest him; obtained a pardon, 1700 ; withdrew to France ; returned to Scotland and sided with the Government in 1715 ; in 1719 professed friendship and proffered aid to the Jacobites, but armed his clan for the Government; in 1745 he again intrigued with both parties; on Aug. 24th he wrote to

taken Arms all these people would have followed his Example, and if they had joined the Prince upon his Landing, as their were very few troops in the Island[1] at that time, they might have marched Straight to London and might possibly have Succeeded, but it is not Strange at all that they did not join the Prince at his Landing, Considering the Equipage he brought with him. If he had Solicitated[2] the Court of France for Troops they would have Given him a few by way of making a diversion in favour of their arms, & those few Landing in Scotland would have made

Craigie : 'I thank God I could bring 1200 good men into the field for the King's service, if I had arms and other accoutrements for them. . . . I hear that mad and unaccountable gentleman has set up a standard at Glenfinnan' (Craigie MSS.) ; to Duncan Forbes he wrote that he was in despair at his son joining Charles. In June 1746 he was arrested ; in March 1747 he was sentenced, and on April 9th he was beheaded. His coolness is illustrated by the well-known story of his drive to the Tower after receiving sentence at Westminster. His coach being halted for a moment, an ill-favoured old woman screamed out, 'You'll get that nasty head of yours chopped off, you ugly old Scotch dog.' 'I believe I shall, you ugly old English b——,' was his reply (Hill Burton, *Life of Lord Lovat*, p. 262).

1 'On the 6th of September a bounty of no less than six pounds was offered to every recruit who would join the Guards before the 24th, and of four pounds to any enlisting between the 24th and the 1st of October. . . . The gentlemen of Yorkshire raised a Royal Regiment of Hunters, first germ of our present Yeomanry, which served without pay' (*H. B. A.* ii. 133).

2 Charles had resolved on the expedition without consulting the Ministers of France, and only informed Louis of his resolution in a letter written June 12th (printed *M. M.* 507).

these Gentlemen in the highlands join, and very propably The thing might have succeeded. The President Duncan Forbes[1] receiving a present of Twenty Companies of 100 men each to distribute amongst the Highland chiefs as he pleased, intirely putt a Stop to most of these Gentlemens balancing, as a Great many that the Prince Counted upon accepted of them. They were given to Sir Alexander Macdonald, the Laird of Macleod, Lord Seaforth,[2] the Earl of Sutherland,[3] Lord Rea,[4] Sir

---

[1] Duncan Forbes of Culloden (b. 1685, d. 1747); studied law at Leyden; Lord Advocate 1725; President of the Court of Session 1737. He was owner of Stoneyhill, near Edinburgh, once the property of Elcho's grandfather, Colonel Francis Charteris. When the latter was condemned to death in London for a criminal assault, Forbes was instrumental in procuring a pardon on the ground of the weakness of the evidence. He was the first to suggest the formation of Highland regiments. At the time of the rebellion he did much to arrest the spread of disaffection, and was opposed to harsh measures of repression. Cumberland described him as 'that old woman who talked to me about humanity' (Omond, *Lord Advocates*, i. 363). He himself received no recognition from the Government in connection with his services at the time of the rebellion.

[2] Kenneth Mackenzie; styled Lord Fortrose—the attainder of his father had placed the title in abeyance; M.P. for Inverness 1741, Ross-shire 1747-54; d. 1761; buried in Westminster Abbey.

[3] William, 18th Earl of Sutherland (b. 1708, d. 1750); M.P. for Sutherland 1727; m. 1734 Lady Elizabeth Wemyss, eldest daughter of David, 3rd Earl of Wemyss, and aunt of David, Lord Elcho.

[4] George Mackay, Lord Reay, son of the Hon. Donald Reay; s. to the peerage on the death of his grandfather, and took his seat 1700; he supported the Government and raised his vassals 1715, 1719, 1745; d. at Tongue 1748.

Robert Monro,[1] the Master of Ross,[2] and the Laird of Grant,[3] to Give to Gentlemen of their Clans, and about the end of October the Companies assembled at Inverness, and the Earl of Loudon Arrived to take the Command of them. The Prince Got news that Maréchal Wade[4] had Assembled an Army of English and the Dutch auxilaries at Doncaster upon the 19 of October, and that he intended to march them to Scotland, and about the end of October he reveiw'd his own Army at Dediston and found them to be 5000 foot and 500 horse.[5] A day or two after the review he proposed to his Council to March the Army into England, where he Said he was sure all the Country would join him. His reasons for Thinking so were that in his Youth his Governors

[1] B. 1684, d. 1746; served in Flanders; gained distinction at Fontenoy; M.P. for Wick Burghs 1710-41; Governor of Inverness Castle 1715; killed at the battle of Falkirk Jan. 17th.

[2] An officer in the Hanoverian army; s. his father as 14th Lord Ross 1754; died the same year.

[3] Ludovick Grant—advocate 1728; M.P. for Morayshire 1741-61; d. 1773.

[4] George Wade (b. 1673, d. 1748), served in Flanders; lieut.-colonel 1703; M.P., Bath, 1722-48; in 1725 sent north to disarm the clans; carried out the construction of 250 miles of road in Scotland; Field-Marshal 1743; Commander of the Forces in Flanders 1744; Commander-in-chief in England 1745; superseded 1746. George II. said of him that 'he was timid, and had always black atoms before his eyes' (*Diary of Hugh, Earl Marchmont*, i. 9).

[5] Corresponds with the estimate of Patullo, Muster Master ot the Highland Army (cited *H. H.* 331).

and Flatterers amongst his Fathers Courtiers had always talk'd of the Hanover Family as Cruel Tyrants hated by every body, and only kept possession of the crown because they had enslaved the poeple, and that if he or any of his Family were ever to appear in Britain that they would flock to him & Look upon him as their deliverer and help him to chase away the Usurpers family (as they call'd him). The way he had been received upon his Entring Edn^r, and the success he had had against Gen: Cope, not only Confirm'd him in all the ideas he had when he came into the country, but he likewise now believed the regular troops would not fight against him, because of his being their natural Prince. As these were the arguments he Generaly used in his discourse, it was no wonder his Council[1] sometimes differ'd from him in Opinion, and upon his now proposing Going to England they differ'd from him for the following reasons: First, that as the

[1] The following information was conveyed to the Lord Justice-Clerk by a spy: ' He was also informed that they held a Council of War on Tuesday the 22nd wherein some of them proposed a retreat to the Highlands: But others were for going forward That it was put to a Vote and was carried to go forward by two votes viz. Lord Elcho and Perth. . . . The Informer's Author was told this by one of the Rebel's Officers who at the same time damned these two Lords " Because in an action they would be the last to appear "' (*S. P. Scot.*, Oct. 27, 1745).

army Consisted only of 5500 men, it was not possible to force the English to accept of him for their Prince, Therefore it would be time enough to March into England when his friends in That Country sent for him, either to join them or to Favour their rising in arms. Secondly, that as Marèchal Wade was marching most of the troops in England down to Scotland, it was better to lett him come because it left England free for The French to land in, and when they landed, which Monsr du Boyer expected daily, it was time enough likewise to march to England to join them. · The Prince proposed that day too to march and fight Wade, for he Said he was sure he would run Away. The Answere his Councill gave to that was that it was his interest at that juncture (as the King of France had advised him to it) not to search a battle immediatly, Especialy in England, where if his Army was beat, The affair was Ended, but at the Same time if Mr Wade came to Scotland they were ready to fight him upon his arrival, because Suppose of a defeat the thing might be begun again, and the French might Land. The Prince finish'd this days Councill by Saying he was sure a great body of English would join him upon his Entring their Country, that

the French would be Landed before he could
join them, and that in Short every body in
London was for him and would receive him as
they had already done at Edn^r. The Answere to
that was that Every body wish'd it might be so,
and wish'd that he might soon have Authority for
Saying so. The Prince in the Councill next day
told them that he would go to England and was
resolved upon it; but as he Saw they were not
for it no more than the day before, he then seem'd
to drop it, and proposed marching the Army
from Edinburg to the Borders, because the Army
would be employed and Every body learn their
business better Than in Edn^r, where the inaction
of the Army began to Cause a desertion. This
proposition was unanimously agreed to, and the
Prince Gave out orders for the Army to be ready
to march upon Command, and Caused putt about
that he was Going to join his English friends and
The French Landing. Dalkeith was Appointed
to be the first place of Rendezvous.

   That night the Prince Assembled a great many
of the Principal Officers of his army in his room,
and proposed again Going up the East road and
fighting Wade. Lord George Murray and the
rest of them were Against it, for the same reasons

as formerly. The Prince said, I find, Gentlemen
you are for Staying in Scotland and defending
Your Country, and I am resolved to Go to England. Lord George Murray and the rest of the
Gentlemen, finding they Could not prevail upon
the Prince to remain & fight Wade in Scotland,
and finding that if they marched on and fought
Wade and were beat and so the Affair Ended,
as their would have been no retreat, Then The
French would have Said, Had these people waited
a little we would have landed, and the English
we would have joined, but their own impatience
ended them. Lord George, to bring a medium
betwixt all these reasonings, proposed to the
Prince Since he would Go to England to go to
Cumberland, where, he Said, he knew the Country,
That the Army would be well Situated to receive reinforcements from Scotland to join the
French when they Landed, or the English if they
rose, and that it was a Good Country to fight
Wades Army in, because of the Mountanious
Ground in it which is the fittest for the Highlanders, and then his (Wades) Army would be
fatigued after a winters march across a bad
country. The Prince was against the proposal
but Came into it afterwards at Dalketh.

On the 30 of October King George the seconds
birthday was celebrated by the Castle and the
fleet, with firing of Guns and the other Usual
Ceremonies. At Perth the Mob rose, made bonfires and rung the bells, and oblidged Mr Oliphant
of Gask, the Deputy Governor, to retire into the
councill house, where they besieged him with fire
arms ; and their was several men kill'd on both
Sides. Upon some highlandmen Coming from
Athole next day to Mr Oliphants Assistance the
quiet of the place was restablish'd. The mob
rose likewise on the same day at Dundee and
oblidged Mr Fothringham, the Governor, to quit
the town. The Prince before he left Edn^r issued
out a proclamation to All Officers in the Govern-
ments service, offering them in Case they would
join him the same if not a higher rank, and to
all soldiers or sailors a reward of a years pay.
Many Gentlemen during the Princes Stay at
Edn^r suppose they never joined him, yett sent
him presents of Considerable sums of money,
horses, & other things. The Prince lived in
Edn^r from the 22 of Sep^t to the 31 of Oct^r,
with Great Splendour and Magnificence, had
Every morning a numerous Court of his Officers.
After he had held a Councill, he dinn'd with his

principall officers in publick, where their was
always a Crowd of all sorts of people to See him
dine. After dinner he rode out Attended by his
life guards and review'd his Army, where their
was always a great number of Spectators in
Coaches and on horseback. After the review, he
Came to the Abey, where he received the ladies
of fashion that came to his drawing room. Then
he Sup'd in publick, and Generaly their was
musick at Supper, and a ball afterwards. Before
he left Edn^r he dispatched Sir James Steuart to
France to manage his Affairs in that Country and
to Solicite Succours. On the 31 of October 1745
ye Prince march'd out of Edn^r at Six at night at
ye head of his Guards and Lord Pitsligo's horse,
and lay that night at Pinckie house. Next
day he went to Dalkeith, where he learnt that
Marechal Wades Army was Arrived at Newcastle. The Greatest part of the army rendevous'd at Dalkeith and Newbattle, and The Train
of Artilery arrived, Consisting of 13 piece of
brass Cannon. Clunie Macpherson [1] joined the

[1] Evan Macpherson, younger of Cluny, eldest son of Lauchlan
Macpherson ; in 1743 had been in correspondence with James ; at
the time of Charles's landing held a commission in the army of
King George, and was intrusted with a warrant for the arrest of
Alastair Macdonell (Craigie MSS.) ; it is said that Charles despatched
' 100 Camerons under the silence of the night to apprehend Cluny '

Prince at Dalkeith with 300 as handsome men
as any in his Army.   The Dukes of Athole and
Perth were order'd to march part of the army by
Peebles, Moffat, and Ecclefechin, and the whole to
Assemble at Carlisle.   That part of the army
Consisted of the Athole Brigade, Perths, Ogilvy's,
Roy Stuarts, Clunies, & Glenbucketts foot, Kilmarnocks and the Hussars horse, all the bagage
and the arteliry.   At Ecclefechin they were
oblidged to leave some of the bagage for want
of horses & Carriages to transport it, Notwithstanding of the vast number of horses the Prince
had Commanded, for from some parishes their
was 100 horses order'd. The people of Dumfries,
after the army had pass'd, took possession of it ;
after the army left Edn^r, the people of the castle
came & took possession of it & insulted &
Abused every body that had appear'd the Princes
friends ; & it was said they Used some wounded
men the Prince left behind very inhumanely.[1]

(*L. P.* ii. 443, *M. M.* 191) ; subsequently he was prevailed upon to
engage, and was sent to raise his clan (*ibid.*) ; in 1746 took an active
part in the hiding and escape of Charles, and devised a refuge
known as Cluny's cage in Ben Alder ; to him was confided the
distribution of the money sent from France in May 1746 ; in 1754
Charles summoned him to France ; d. at Dunkirk 1756.

[1] 'Some parties came out of the Castle and searched for arms.
Among other places they went to the Infirmary, where, finding a
few arms, they were a little rude to some of the Highlanders, and
took a few trifles from them ' (*S. M.* vii. 1745).

The 3 of November the Prince march'd the Colum of the army he and Lord George Murray commanded to Lauder : it Consisted of Lochyells, Glengarys, Clanronalds, Keppochs, and Ardshiels regiments of foot, and Elcho's and Pitsligo's horse. The 4th they marched to Kelso, the 5 they halted, & y[e] 6 the foot pass'd the Tweed and march'd to Jedburgh, and the horse remained draw'n up on a hight near Kelso, & Sent out scouts to Gett intelligence of M[r] Wades army, who was reported to be on his march from Newcastle & to have parties at Wooler ; the horse march'd afterwards to Hawick, where they halted next day. The 7 the Prince marched the foot to Holyhaugh. The 8 The foot march'd to Strangarside & Redens, and the horse to Longtown. The 9 the whole army pass'd the Esk [1] in Two Seperate bodies, the Princes Colum pass'd the Water that runs by Carlisle, & quarter'd at Brugh and the Villages about. The Duke of Atholes Colum that had come by Moffat quarter'd in the

---

[1] There appears to be some confusion at this point. The army crossed the Esk Nov. 8th ; the Eden Nov. 9th (*M. M.* 238, *M. K.* 62, *H. H.* 141). ' It was remarkable that this being the first time they entered England, the Highlanders, without any orders given, all drew their swords with one consent upon entering the river, and every man as he landed on the other side wheeled about to the left and faced Scotland again ' (*M. M.* 238). When drawing swords ' Lochiel cut his hand, which was onlooked as a bad omen ' (*L. P.* 455).

villages about Rowcliff.   The poeple in England
seemed mightily afraid of the army and had
abandon'd all the villages upon its approach.
When any of them was gott & ask'd why they
run away so, they said they had been told that
the army murder'd all the men & children &
ravish'd the women, and when they found themselves well used, they seemed mightily surprised.
Their was an old woman remained in a house that
night where some officers were quarter'd.   After
they had sup'd, she said to them, Gentlemen, I
Suppose You have done with Your murdering to
day, I should be Glad to know when the ravish-
ing begins.[1]   That night the Castle of Carlisle
fired several shot at parties of the army that went
near it.   Upon this march both Columns of the
army had a prodigious desertion, and it was computed at 1000 men : for the Army at leaving
Edn[r] was 5500 & at Carlisle only 4500.   The
Common poeple were quite averse to Going to
England, & only carried on by the Princes assuring them every day that the English would join
them & the French would Land.   The 10th the
town of Carlisle was invested by the Princes
colum on the south and west, and by the Second

---

[1] Cf. Byron, *Don Juan*, canto VIII., cxxxii.

Colum on the north and east, and a written
messuage signed the Prince of Wales sent into
the Mayor [1] to demand admittance, in answere to
which the army was fir'd upon from all sides of
the town. The army lay that night in the villages
round the town, and next day, upon intelligence
that Marèchal Wades army was upon their
march from Newcastle to Carlyle, the Army
march'd to Brampton, which was so far on the
road to meet him. It was a mighty convenient
position in the first place to fight him, then the
road on the right was open for the English to
join, and for the Prince to go & join the French
in case he had had news of their Landing ; and
Again the road on the left was open for the
succours that were daily expected to join the
army from Scotland, for the Frazers, Macken-
toshes, Mackenzies, and Lord Lewis Gordons
men to the number of 2000 men were in arms,
and were daily expected. The Prince was in such
a hurry to leave Scotland he would not wait for
them, for he was fully persauded That the regular
troops would not fight against him, and that all
England was in their hearts Convinced of his just

---

[1] The negotiations were conducted by the Deputy-Mayor,
Thomas Pattinson.

right, and in consequence for him, so he thought that he had nothing to do but to appear and Succeed. The 12 Some horse that were sent towards Newcastle to gett intelligence of Wades army brought word [1] that he was not within thirty miles, and by what they could learn had not moved, upon which in a councill of war held before the Prince it was resolved [2] to besiege Carlisle with part of the army while the Prince remain'd at Brampton with the rest.

All the Cumberland and Westmoreland militia were in Carlisle to the number of 2000 foot and 100 light horse, and their was Cannon mounted upon the Parapet all 'round the town. In the Castle, which is a very Strong place and cant be taken without battering cannon, of which the prince had none, their was 80 invalids Commanded by L[t] Colonel Durand,[3] a french man and 20 Canon nine pounders mounted. Whatever the town might be brought to do by threating to burn it or Scale the walls, the Castle was impregnable to the Princes army. The Duke of Perth

---

[1] The intelligence was brought by Kerr of Graden (L. P. 455).

[2] This plan was proposed by Lord George Murray (J. M. 48).

[3] Durand was tried by court-martial for surrendering the town, and acquitted Sept. 1746.

marched away from Brampton to Command the
Siege the 13 with the following troops under his
command, viz. the Athole Brigade, Ogilvys, Roy
Stuarts, Glenbuckets, and Perths Battalions, and
Elcho's, Pitsligo's, and Kilmarnocks Squadrons.
These troops were that night devided into three
bodies and sent to invest the English, Scots, and
Irish gates, and the trenches were open'd that
night betwixt the Scots and English gate within
less than Muskett shot of the wall : the Besieged
all the time kept a constant fire of Cannon &
Small arms, but their was but one man & an
officer kill'd. All the next day they likewise kept
a close fire, but at five o clock at night, seeing the
trenches pretty near them and the Cannon (which
Consisted only of 2 & 4 pounders) ready to be
mounted upon a battery, they hung out a white
flag, and demanded to Capitulate for the town ;
but the Duke of Perth who was in the trenches,
refused to Capitulate with the town unless the
Castle was to be included. They then demanded a
cessation of arms untill next day to think upon it,
which was agreed upon, and they were told, to
frighten them the more (Suppose their panick
was Sufficient enough), that the battery would fire
red hott bals upon the town next day if they did

not Surrender. The 15 they agreed to capitulate [1]
both for the town and Castle, so the troops
marched & took possession of the town, & the
Duke of Perth signed the Capitulation, which was
that the militia should deliver up their horses and
arms and take an oath never to take up arms
again either against the Prince or any of his
Family. Which all they that were in town did,
for a great many of them had gott over the walls
and run away home. The Mayor of the town
was to meet the Prince at the gate, to deliver him
the keys of the town, and to Congratulate him
upon his arrivall. The Duke promised that the
Prince would proteck the liberties and religion
of the inhabitants, and would prevent his troops
from doing any mischief. The Mayor and
Aldermen in their robes were to proclaim the
Princes Father king and read all his manifesto's
at the Cross; all which was performed. Every

---

[1] The militia passed the following curious resolution : ' The militia
of the Countys of Cumberland and Westmoreland having come
voluntarily into the City of Carlisle, for the defence of the sd Citty
and having for six days and six nights successively been upon duty,
in expectation of relief from His Majestys forces, but it appearing
y^t no such relief is now to be had, and ourselves not able to do
duty or hold out any longer, are determined to capitulate, and do
certify that Colol Durand, Capt Gilpin, and the rest of the Officers
have well and faithfully done their duty.—14 Nov. 1745' (Mounsey,
Carlisle in 1745, 89).

thing in the Castle was to be deliver'd to the
Prince; the Garison to march out with their arms
and drums beating, and to Ground their arms
when they were out of the Gate; Colonel Durand
and the rest of the officers to give their parolles
of honour not to serve against the Prince for a
year; all which was performed, and the Duke of
Perths regiment took possession of the Castle.
Most of the arms in the Castle were hid, and as the
army had plenty, they were not much sought after.
As for the horses, they were devided amongst
the four corps of horse. The 17 the life Gaurds
went out to meet the Prince, and he Enter'd the
town; the mayor and aldermen in their robes
mett him at the Gate, and the Mayor made him
a Speech Complimenting him upon his Success.
The Prince rode first to the Castle, where he was
Saluted with a round of all the Cannon; from
thence he came to his quarters in town. Their
happen'd a thing at Carlisle which was a
consequence of the false accusation given by
Secretary Murray at Perth against Lord George
Murray. The Prince had always shown a great
shighness for Lord George, and had always Affected to give all sort of Commands to the Duke
of Perth; and just now again at the Siege of

Carlisle, where people thought it would have been
more proper for Lord George as he was a protestant to have signed the Capitulation in which
their was question of Securing the people in the
enjoyment of their religion, than the Duke of
Perth,[1] who was a R: Catholick, and even the
people of Carlisle talked of it. Lord George
during the time of the siege wrote a letter to the
Prince, wherin he told him he was very sorry to
see that their had been very little confidence put
in him all along, and Suppose he was a Lieutenant General he found he was seldom or never
to be employed, for which reason he believed he
could be of as much service being a Volunteer,
so he beg'd the Prince to Accept of his Comission. The Prince immediately wrote him back
word that he did, which was precisely what Secretary Murray wanted. The Army when they heard
of this were very much alarmed, as their was
no other Leiutenant General but the Duke, and
as they had a much Greater opinion of Lord
Georges capacity than of the Dukes, Suppose

[1] Murray says that this episode 'compleated the dryness that
had almost from the beginning subsisted betwixt them' (Perth and
Lord George) (M. M. 243).

In the postscript of his letter to Charles, Lord George says, 'Lord
Elcho has the command till you please appoint it otherwise.' The
letter is printed in J. M. 50

their was nobody Braver or had the cause more at heart than his Grace. The Principal people of the army mett, and when the Prince came to Carlisle deliver'd a petition to the Prince, beging that he would discharge all Roman Catholicks from his Councill because it might be a handle for his enemies to make use of against him, as they had lately done in news papers where they said all his Councills were directed by R: Catholicks, and Compared Sir Thomas Sheridan to Father Peter [1] his Grand Fathers confident. They likewise beg'd that when their was any question of Signing Capitulations wherin their was mention made of Securing the Liberties of the church of England, that Protestants might be employed to do it preferable to R: Catholicks, and they Concluded by desiring that Lord George Should be desired to take back his Comission. The last article the Prince agreed to, which at present intirely defeated secretary Murrays Schêmes ; to the other demands he gave no answere. The Prince gott intelligence [2] at Carlisle that Marechal

[1] Edward Petre, an English Jesuit ; Vice-Provincial of the Order ; favourite of James II. ; Clerk of the Closet and a member of the Privy Council. Macaulay says : 'Of all the counsellors who had access to the Royal ear he bore perhaps the largest part in the ruin of the House of Stuart.' Petre preceded James II. in his flight to France ; later became Rector of St. Omer ; d. 1699.

[2] On Nov. 22nd.

Wade had moved with his army and had been at
Hexham on the 17, but upon finding the roads
extremly bad had returned back to Newcastle.
The Prince gott intelligence likewise before he
left Carlisle That the Justice Clerk, Lords of the
Session, & the Sheriffs of the Lothians had returned back to Edn^r attended by a great number
of other gentlemen, that they had reassumed the
goverment of the town, & had order'd the 1000
men formerly agreed upon, to be Levied and to
be under the command of the Commander in
cheif in Scotland. That Lt General Handasyde[1]
had marched on the 14 into Edn^r with Price and
Legoniers foot and Hamiltons and Ligoniers
(Late Gardners) Dragoons, and that the town of
Glasgow was raising their militia to be under the
Command of the Earls of Home and Glencairn.[2]
The towns of Sterling, Paisley, & Dumfries were
likewise raising their Militia, and General Campbell[3] was arrived at Invereray in order to raise the

[1] General Handasyde succeeded Cope as Commander-in-chief
in Scotland.

[2] William Cunningham, Earl of Glencairn, s. 1734; entered
the army 1729; major 52nd Foot 1741; lieut.-colonel 9th Foot
1747; Major-General 1770; d. 1775.

[3] John Campbell of Mamore (b. 1693, d. 1770), afterwards
4th Duke of Argyll; lieut.-colonel at the age of nineteen; colonel
of Scots Fusiliers 1738; Brigadier-General at Dettingen 1741.
When the rebellion broke out, was appointed to the command of the
troops and garrisons in the west of Scotland; arrived at Inveraray

Argyleshire militia. Lord Loudoun was at Inverness, so that Scotland was devided in the Following manner. Lord Loudoun Commanded all to the north of Inverness together with the Shires of Nairne & Moray, General Campbell had Argyleshire, and the Goverment posses'd all to the south of Forth. Lord Lewis Gordon commanded in Bamff & Aberdeenshire for the Prince, and as he was Lord Lieutenant of the county had raised three battalions by obliging every body to furnish so many men for so much valued rent. The three regiments were Abuchies Gordon[1] of 300 men, Farquharson of Monalterys[2] 200, and More of Stonywoods[3] 300. Sir James

Dec. 21, 1745; joined the Duke of Cumberland at Perth Feb. 9, 1746 ; colonel of the Scots Greys 1752 to 1761.

[1] John Gordon of Avochy. 'Mr. Gordon of Avochy, Glenbucket's Nephew, a very resolute active lad, assisted him considerably in his Levys about Strathboggy, where he had a small estate. He, Glenbucket, had also two sons joined him, but the eldest having drunk himself blind, could not attempt to march along, and was of little use to him at home : the other too, was but an insignificant creature ' (MS. in the possession of Mr. Blaikie).

[2] Francis Farquharson of Monaltrie, second son of Alexander Farquharson of Monaltrie. The family had supported the Stuarts in 1689 and again in 1715. Francis joined the Prince's army in Edinburgh with a few men, then went north to raise more recruits. He was taken prisoner after Culloden ; tried in London in Sept. 1746 ; condemned to death ; reprieved on the evening preceding the day fixed for his execution. Not allowed to return to Scotland for fifteen years.

[3] James Moir of Stonywood (b. 1712, d. 1782), 3rd laird of that name ; after months of hiding escaped abroad ; lived on the Continent till 1762, when he was allowed to return.

Kinloch[1] had raised by Ld Ogilvys orders in the same way a regiment of 600 men and posses'd Angus : the remainder of the Princes Troops lay at Perth. They raised the publick money in Perth and Fifeshire as the others did in Angus Merns, Aberdeen & Bamfshire. They Consisted of the following men, viz. The Master of Lovat[2] with 300 Frazers, Macgilvray of Drumaglash[3] with

The Earl of Cromarty and his son Ld Macleod with 200 men

200 Mackintoshes, Farquharson of Bamurel[4] with 200 Farquharsons, Macdonald of Barsdale[5] with 200,

---

[1] 3rd Bart. of Kinloch, co. Perth ; taken prisoner with his two brothers. All three were condemned to death, but reprieved. Sir James was eventually pardoned on condition of his residing in appointed places (*S. M.* x. 353). He commanded the 2nd Battalion of Lord Ogilvy's Regiment.

[2] Simon, eldest son of Simon, 11th Lord Lovat; he was pardoned in 1750; in 1757 he raised a regiment of 1800 men for the Government, the 78th, disbanded in 1763 ; he accompanied them as their colonel to America, and distinguished himself at Louisbourg and Quebec ; afterwards colonel of the 71st Regiment, disbanded 1783 ; Lieut.-General 1777 ; M.P. for Inverness 1761-82 ; d. 1782.

[3] Alexander MacGillivray of Dunmaglass, killed at Culloden. ' He was collonell of the Clan Chatton, the Mackintoshes, in this country. I may add many have not produced a finer youth ': Answers of Rev. James Hay, Inverness (*L. M.* iii. 55). The clan was raised by Lady Mackintosh, her husband having joined the Government.

[4] James Farquharson of Balmurle (now represented by Balmoral) ; kinsman of the Laird of Monaltrie ; wounded at Falkirk.

[5] Coll Macdonald, or Macdonell, of Barisdale, cousin of Glengarry. Charles made him a colonel, and gave a major's commission to his son Archibald.

a son of Glengary with 100 Macdonalds, Macleod of Raasa[1] with 100, 150 Macdonalds of Clanronald, Glenco with a 100, Steuart of Inernoyel[2] with 150 of Appins men, and Cameron of Torcastle[3] with 300 Camerons, all which putt together made 3400 men fully as

Coll was present at Prestonpans, and knighted on the field (Sutherland MSS.); member of Charles's council; later sent north to raise men; on March 20, 1746, he took possession of Dunrobin Castle, and detained Lady Sutherland, who was an aunt of David Lord Elcho, as a not unwilling prisoner; on leaving he addressed her in a letter published by Mr. Lang (*Companions of Pickle*, 112), as 'My Faire Prisoner.' He arrived with his men too late to take part at Culloden. On June 10th he and his son surrendered to Ensign Small; they obtained a 'pass-port' on promising, it is said, to deliver up Prince Charles. In Sept. 1746 he and his son visited Charles on board *L'Heureux*; they were placed in irons; conveyed to France, and imprisoned at Morlaix on a charge of treason; Coll was also accused of having carried off some of the money sent from France (*A. P.* ii. 272). In 1749 he returned to Scotland, and died a prisoner in Edinburgh Castle 1750. His son was tried and condemned to death in 1754; respited, he remained a prisoner till 1762, when he was released. (See *Stuart Papers*, Warren to James, *B. H.* iii. 463).

[1] Malcolm Macleod of Rasay; at Falkirk and Culloden the Macleods were brigaded with Glengarry Macdonalds (cf. *L. M.* i. 145 *et seq.*); Malcolm acted as Dr. Johnson's pilot in Skye in 1773. Boswell says that he was the most perfect representative of a Highland gentleman he had ever seen.

[2] Alexander Stewart of Invernahyle; engaged in the rebellion of 1715; Sir Walter Scott visited him as a boy and 'saw him in arms and heard him exult in the prospect of drawing his claymore once more before he died' when Paul Jones threatened a descent on Edinburgh 1779; after Culloden was long in hiding in a cave not far from his own house; cf. the story of Bradwardine (*Life of Sir Walter Scott*, i. 140).

[3] Ludovick Cameron of Torcastle; subsequently agent for Cluny in the distribution of part of the 'Arkaig Treasure'; escaped to France; awarded a pension by Louis (Michel, ii. 447).

good as the Prince had with him, and it was a
most extrodinary thing not to wait for them.
Whoever at Carlisle the Prince dispatched Colonel
Maclauchlan of that ilk with orders for them to
march and join him.[1] Macgregor of Glengyle
Commanded Doune Castle with 50 Macgregors
and kept that whole Country and the castle of
Sterling in great Awe. The reasons they gave
afterwards for not joining the Prince were that
they wanted money for such a march; then again,
as the Prince had left Carlisle & was making
forced marches every day, they Could have no
thoughts of overtaking him.   Lord John Drum-

---

[1] Lord Macleod's Narrative (385) states that at Derby an
answer was received from Lord John Drummond refusing to comply
with the order conveyed by Maclachlan, on the ground that the
directions given by the French Government did not permit of his
doing so. But the directions printed in the Appendix to Browne's
History contain no such prohibition ; and at the time that Maclachlan was despatched from Carlisle Lord John Drummond's arrival
from France was unknown to Charles. Cf. the more probable
account in *L. M.* ii. 209: 'He (Maclachlan) attended the Prince at
Gladsmuir, and marched with him to Carlyle, from whence he was
detached by the Prince . . . to lead on to England the 3000 men
that lay then at Perth. But my Lord Strathallan (who was Governor
of Perth) refus'd to comply with the Prince's orders.' The
Highlanders were for marching at once, and hostilities between the
parties seemed imminent when Rollo of Powhouse arrived with an
order from Charles (dated Dumfries) to Lord Strathallan to hold
himself and his forces in readiness to join on receipt of further orders
from Glasgow (*H. H.* pp. 115, 116). At Culloden Maclachlan commanded a regiment of Maclachlans and Macleans, at the head of
whom he was killed.

monds arrival afterwards from France putt an intire Stop to their thinking of it. Had the Prince had them with him in England he might very possibly have beat the Duke of Cumberlands army and gone on to London.

The Prince held a Councill at Carlisle, wherin he proposed Going Straight to London. The answere that was made was that the army came up to join his English friends or a French Landing, but could not pretend putting him in possession of the crown of England without either, and that it was better to wait at Carlyle for the reinforcements Colonel Maclauchlan had gone for then to think of taking any Step before their arrival. The Prince said he was sure all his English friends would join him in Lancashire. Mr du Boyer assured every body of a French Landing daily, and Mr Murray, who was tresorer as well as Secretary, said that it was impossible to stay longer at Carlisle for want of Money, so every body agreed to March on. The Prince flatter'd himself every body would receive him with joyfull hearts, and that he would meet with no opposition, and the rest of The Gentlemen were determined to carry him to the utmost bounds of Lancashire, that people might not say afterwards had the army march'd to Lancashire the English would certainly have joined, and the French being sure of meeting friends would have been encouraged to Land. The Princes army that marched from Carlisle into the heart of England consisted of The troops in the opposite plan. The Government had order'd all the militia in England to be raised: Wades army was computed 12000 foot & 1200 horse, and the Duke of Cumberlands 10'000 men. The 18 of November the Guards marched to Penrith, and next day to Lowther hall. The 20 Lord George Murray marched with the Athole Brigade, Ogilvys, Glenbucketts and Roy Stuarts.

The 21 the Prince marched to Penrith with the rest of the army; Perths Regiment and the artilery went by Warwick Bridge and arrived at Penrith the 22. The Prince left a small garison at Carlisle and appointed Mr Hamilton factor to the Duke of Gordon Governor both of the town & Castle. All the People both of that town and county show'd a great dislike to the Princes cause. Kilmarnocks horse were sent from Penrith to gett intelligence of Marechal Wades Army, and brought back word that they were still at Newcastle. At Penrith the people did not seem

The Prince

Pitsligo
150

Hussars
70

Lochyel
500

appin
150

Clunie
300

Ella

Ogilvy
200

R: Stuart
200

Glenbucket
200

Perth
300

Total 4000 feet 50

+ + + + + + + + +
13 Cannon
Colonel G

Lochyel
Keppoch
Clanronald
Ardshiel
Lochgarry
Robert Menzies
John Ogilvy
Roy Stewart
Clunie

Grant Colonel of Artillery

O Sullivan Quarter master
general

Pitslio Commissary General

ny that marched to Derby

Keppoch   Glengary
150   500

guards Ld Elcho
150

n Thian   Ld G: Murray   Kilmarnock
300   350   perthshire sq:
ms & 58 Cannon   530

129

Principal Officers

Lt Generals
The Prince general
The Duke of Athole
Lord George Murray

Major General Gordon of Glenbucket

Brigadeer et
the Attolebrigade Lord Nairne

Colonels of
Horse
Lord Elcho
Lord Balmerino
Earl of Kilmarnock
Lord Pitsligo
Mr Murray

so much affraid of the army as the poeple in the neighbourhood of Carlisle had been, for they had heard they did not either murder or ravish. The Army did no manner of mischief the whole march up to Derby; the Soldiers were lodged and gott their Victuals for nothing, and the Officers payed for every thing they Gott, and very often very extravagantly which they did rather than disoblidge the poeple.[1] At Penrith they did not like the cause more than at Carlisle. Their was one M[r] Saunderson from Northumberland joined the army at Penrith : he was a Roman Catholick Gentleman. The 21 Lord Elcho's Squadron march'd to Kendal, Lord George Murray with one colum the 22, and the Prince with the other the 23. Perths Regiment with the bagage and the artilery went by Barrowbridge, as the straight road was bad and too hilly, so they did not arrive at Kendal untill the 24. At Kendal the poeple were civiler than in Cumberland, but none of them joined. The 23 the Guards and the Athole brigade marched to Burton, where their was a report that the poeple of Lancaster intended to

---

1 'When the Prince happened to be a night or so in any gentleman's house, the ordinary custom was to give five guineas (at least) of drink-money to the servants' (L. M. ii. 117).

hold out the Castle, upon which Lord Elcho wrote to the Mayor informing him that part of the army would be their next day, & told him if their was no resistance made, no harm would be done to the town. Lord George Murray march'd the Athole brigade in the morning of the 24 into Lancaster ; the Guards went about by Hornby castle and arrived at night at Lancaster. Next day, 25, Lord George with the Athole Brigade and the Guards advanced to Garstang, and the Prince with the rest of the army arrived at Lancaster, where his Father was proclaimed and all the manifesto's read, but the people testify'd no joy and Seemed all against the cause. It was the custom, as soon as any of the troops came into a market town, to proclaim the Princes father and read all the manifesto's from of the Cross, and it was done in all the Towns both in England and Scotland where any of the Princes troops ever pass'd. Lord George had an acquaintance in that country who procured him two Spies, who he dispatch'd, the one into Yorkshire, the other into Staffordshire, to gett intelligence of Marèchal Wade and the Duke of Cumberlands armies, and the 26 he march'd and took possession of Rippel Bridge a mile beyond Preston, and the

Prince with the rest of the army came the same
night to Preston,[1] only the Baggage with an
Escort halted that night at Garstang and arrived
next day. The poeple of Preston show'd more
joy upon seeing the Prince Than they had done
any where else, and their were for the first time
in England several huzza's, and next day when
the manifesto's were read the people ask'd for them
and seemed keen to read them. M[rs]. Morgan
and Vaughan,[2] two Welch gentlemen joined
the Prince at Preston ; The Prince gave M[rs].
Brown and Goehagan,[3] two Irish Gentlemen and
French Captains, comissions to raise English regiments in this Country, and Upon their drums
beating up for recruits for them in this town a
great many of the officers of the army went to
the Prince and told him that as it was known

---

[1] The furthest limit reached in 1648 and 1715. 'Preston, so
fatale to the Scots that they never coud get beyond it, but Lord
George Murray, in order to evade the freet (or superstition which
the Highlanders are full of) cross'd the bridge and quarter'd a great
many of the men on that side of the water' (*L. P.* 457).

[2] William Vaughan and David Morgan joined Elcho's troop
of Life Guards. 'Morgan was seen very busy amongst the rebels
with a white cockade in his hat' (*H. P.* ii. 448). 'He was reputed
to be the Prince's Counsel' (*Ibid.* 451). He had been called to the
bar ; executed July 30, 1746.

[3] Probably Sir Francis Geoghegan, a French officer, afterwards
captured at Carlisle; he was a captain of Lally's regiment (*S. M.*
vii. 580).

that these gentlemen were Roman Catholicks (as they wore the cross of St Lewis), if he had a mind to raise English regiments, which was quite needless as no volunteers offer'd themselves, that he had better give them to protestants, because it would be more suitable to the genious of the people. So the scheme was laid aside. In Preston as well as in all the towns the army march'd through, the Militia, who were all in arms quit the town upon the Armys approach. The Officers of the army began here to doubt of being joined, and to Say they had marched far enough, but upon the Prince Assuring them they would be joined by all his English friends at Manchester, and Monsr de Boyer offering to lay considerable wagers that the French were either landed or would land in a week, these discourses were laid Aside. Lord Georges Spies return'd to him here and brought him word that Marèchal Wade had march'd his army straight south upon the London Road, to Doncaster, and that their was rumours of his marching across the country into Lancashire ; the other said that Sir John Legonier[1] was

[1] Jean Louis Ligonier, a Frenchman born at Castres (b. 1680, d. 1770); served as a volunteer in Marlborough's army 1702 ; in 1703 purchased a company in Lord North and Grey's regiment ; in 1720 appointed colonel of the 8th or Black Horse, now the

forming an army, about Litchfield and Coventry to Consist of ten Thousand men, and that the Duke of Cumberland was expected from London every day to take the Command of it. The 27 the Prince road through the town of Preston with his guards dress'd in Lowland cloaths in order to Show himself to the poeple. Usualy he wore the highland habit, and March'd all the way to Derby on foot at the head of one of the Colums. He never dinn'd nor threw of his cloaths at night, eat much at Supper, used to throw himself upon a bed at Eleven o clock, & was up by four in the morning. As he had a prodigious strong constitution, he bore fatigue most surprisingly well. All the Prisoners that w^r in jails upon suspicion of Jacobitry were always released, and the publick money was raised[1] in all the towns the army was in, and if their had been any Sub-

7th Dragoon Guards; Brigadier-General 1735; at the battle of Dettingen he was made a Knignt Banneret by George II.; at Fontenoy commanded the British Foot; commanded the troops sent home to deal with the rebellion; Commander-in-chief and Viscount 1757; buried in Westminster Abbey.

[1] 'They levied all the taxes and all the public money destined for the Government not only here, but wherever they went in England, and this money served to pay the army during its sojourn in England, for the Prince brought back to Scotland all the money that he had taken with him' (Elcho, *Journal*). The pay of the Army was at first as follows: Capt., 2s. 6d.; Lieut., 2s.; Ensign, 1s. 6d.; Private, 6d. per day. Latterly the men were paid in meal (*H. H.* 138; *L. P.* ii.). See *post*, p. 398.

scriptions for money to raise men for the use of the government as their was in most of the towns, the very poeple were oblidged to pay to the Prince the indevidual sum they had subscribed for, suppose very often they had paid it before to the government. The 28 of November Pitsligo's horse march'd to Manchester, where they were very well received, and a mob appeared publickly for the Prince, and Several of them show'd an inclination to inlist. The Same day Ogilvys, Roy Stuarts, and Elcho's horse march'd to Leigh, and the Prince with the rest of the army to Wigan. The road betwixt Preston and Wigan was crouded with people standing at their doors to see the army go by, and they generaly all that days march profes'd to wish the Princes army Success, but if arms was offer'd to them and they were desir'd to Go along with the army they all declined, and Said they did not Understand fighting. The 29 when the Prince arrived with his army at Manchester the Mob huzza'd him to his Lodgings, the town was mostly illuminated, and the Bells rung, their were several substantial people came and kis'd his hand, and a vast number of people of all sorts came to see him supp. Their were likewise some Clergymen

of the Church of England came and waited upon
him, & one of them joined, and ever after in all
the towns or villages where the army was and
where their was a Church he used to Say prayers
and Pray publickly for the Prince and all his
family. After all these proceedings it was natural
enough to imagine that their would be a great
joining, but every body was astonish'd to find
that all that was to join was about 200 Common
fellows who it seems had no subsistance, for they
used to Say by way of showing their military
inclination, that they had for sometime been resolved to inlist with whichever of the two armies
came first to town. Their was one or two
Gentlemen and about 15 or 20 twenty merchants
likewise joined, the Prince formed them into a
Regiment which was Called the Manchester regiment and gave the command of it to Mr Townly [1]
a Roman Catholick. The Prince was so far de-
ceved with these proceedings at Manchester of
bonfires and ringing of bells (which they used to
own themselves they did out of fear of being ill

---

[1] Francis Towneley (b. 1709, d. 1746), formerly in the service
of Louis xv.; when the Highland army withdrew to Scotland
he was left at Carlisle; taken prisoner; executed July 30, 1746
(H. P. ii. 373). 'The Manchester Regiment never exceeded 300
men' (M. J. 44).

Used) that he thought himself sure of Success, and his Conversation that night at Table was, in what manner he should enter London, on horseback or a foot, and in what dress. The reason he thought himself so sure of Success was, he himself knew nothing of the Country, or the Strength that was Against him, and as he Could not bear to hear that the Goverment had any friends, his favorites, who were mostly the Irish, and who knew that at the worst as they were French officers they would be quit for a month or two's imprisonment, Used to represent the King as a hated Usurper who would be deserted by every body upon the Princes appearing ; and as for his armies, they made the Prince believe they were small, dissaffected, and ill provided with every thing. The Principal officers of the army who thought otherwise upon these topicks, mett at Manchester and were of Opinion [1] that now they had marched far enough into England, and as they had received not the least Encouragement from any person of distinction, the French not landed, and only joined by 200 vagabonds, they had done their part ; and as they did not pretend

[1] 'I have been very well informed that a retreat was talked of at Manchester' (*M. K.* 70).

to put a King upon the throne of England without their consent, that it was time to represent to the Prince to go back to Scotland. But after talking a great deal about it, it was determin'd to March to Derby, that so neither the French nor the English might have it to Say, the army had not marched far Enough into England to give the one Encouragement to Land and the other to join. On the 30 St Andrews day,[1] the Prince road through the town with his life Guards, and that day the people of the Country were employed in making and repairing bridges over the rivers which the Government had order'd to be broke down. The 1 of December Elcho's & Pitsligo's horse march'd to Altringham, and the rest of the army to Maclesfield :[2] at both of

[1] 'Saturday 30th: St. Andrew's day ; more crosses making till twelve o'clock ; then I dressed me up in my white gown and went up to my aunt Brearcliffe's, and an officer called on us to go see the Prince, we went to Mr. Fletcher's and saw him get a-horseback, and a noble sight it is, I would not have missed it for a great deal of money ; his horse had stood an hour in the court without stirring, and as soon as he gat on he began a-dancing and capering as if he was proud of the burden, and when he rid out of the court he was received with as much joy and shouting almost as if he had been king without any dispute, indeed I think scarce anybody that saw him could dispute it ' (John Byrom's *Remains*).

[2] At Macclesfield they learnt that Cumberland, who had taken the command of Ligonier's army, was on the march, and that his forces were quartered at Lichfield, Coventry, Stafford, and Newcastle-under-Line. Lord George Murray moved westward to Congleton ; this forced Cumberland to fall back on Stone, thus leaving the road clear for Charles's advance.

these places their was parties of Dragoons who
retir'd upon aproach of the Army; at Maclesfield the people seemed mightily against the Prince
and vast numbers of people had run away from
their houses. At one o clock next morning the
body at Altringham was order'd to join the army,
and that day the Prince halted at Maclesfield and
Lord George Murray march'd to Congleton with
the Athole Brigade and Elcho's & Kilmarnocks
horse. The Duke of Kingston[1] upon Lord
George's coming near the town left it with his regiment of horse, and Lord George gott the dinner
that was prepared for his Grace. Lord George
Sent on the Earl of Kilmarnock with the Perthshire
Squadron and fifty foot to Ashbury (a village
betwixt Congleton and Newcastle) to Gett intelligence of the Duke of Cumberlands army. Their
was Sixty Dragoons in the Village, who retir'd to
Newcastle, but they took one Weir, a famous Spie;
and the party might Likewise have been taken
had the foot march'd in before the horse, for it
was the noise of the horses feet that first gave
the alarm. This Weir had from the time of the
Princes Landing always kept within ten miles of

---

[1] Evelyn Pierrepont (1711-73), 2nd Duke of Kingston. He
married his mistress, Elizabeth Chudleigh, who in 1776 was convicted of bigamy.

his army and had given the goverment the best
accounts of his motions. Weir informed Lord
George that the Dukes Cavalery with two regiments of foot were at Newcastle, nine miles from
Congleton, some of the army at Stone, and the
rest with the Duke at Stafford. But that night
the Corps that was at Newcastle retired to Stone.
and the Duke march'd to it, & Assembled the
army their next day. Weir gave Lord George a
list of the Dukes army which he had with him
and which was, viz.

	Horse	
	Horse	
General officers. The Duke	Ligoniers Montagu's : new	Bligh's
Sir John Ligonier	Kingston's : new	Skeltons
		New Foot
Lᵗ Genˢ : Duke of Richmond	Dragoons	Gowers
Sᵗ Claire		Montagu's
Major Genˢ : Howard	Blands	Halifax's
Skelton	Cobhams	Granby's
Bland		Cholmondeleys
	Foot	total
Brigadeer Genˢ Lord Sempill	3 Battˢ : of yᵉ guards	8250 foot
Bligh	Howards	
Douglass	Sowles's	2200 horse
	Johnstons's	
30 piece of	Douglass's	10450
Cannon 68 3	Sempills's	
pounders		

The 3 Lord George march'd from Congleton by Leek to Ashburn. The Prince march'd to Leek, but as the Duke of Cumberland had moved from Stone towards Newcastle, and their was a cross road so that the Duke might have march'd in betwixt Leek & Ashburn and so seperated the two colums of the army, the Prince march'd from Leek at Night & joined the Colum at Ashburn early in the morning of the 4th: the Princes Army was by that march nearer London by a good many miles than the Dukes. All betwixt Maclesfield and Ashburn the people seemed much afraid of the Princes army, and the tops of the hills were crouded with men on horseback, who were often pursued but never came up with as they were well mounted. The 4 of December the whole Army marched into Darby. The Duke of Devonshire[1] had left the town with his regiment the day before; the Dukes army were that night at Stafford and the next at Litchfield.[2] The

[1] William Cavendish, 3rd Duke of Devonshire (b. 1698, d. 1755).

[2] While Cumberland's army of five regiments of cavalry and eleven battalions of infantry had reached Lichfield Dec. 5th, Wade's, comprising seven regiments of cavalry and eleven battalions of infantry, was on the same day at Wetherby, and moved the following day to Ferrybridge (Blaikie, 95, citing newspapers and official histories of regiments; MS. General Orders of Marshal Wade's Army).

5 in the morning Lord George Murray and all
the Commanders of Battalions and Squadrons
waited upon the Prince, and Lord George told
him that it was the opinion of Every body
present that the Scots had now done all that
could be Expected of them. That they had
marched into the heart of England ready to join
any party that would declare for him, that none
had, and that the Counties through which the
Army had pass'd had Seemed much more
Enemies than friends to his Cause, that their
was no French Landed in England, and that if
their was any party in England for him, it was
very odd that they had never so much as Either
sent him money or intelligence or the least advice
what to do, but if he Could produce any letter
from any person of distinction in which their was
an invitation for the army to go to London, or to
any other part of England, that they were ready
to go. But if nobody had either invited them or
meddled in the least in their affairs, it was to be
Supposed that their was either no party at all, or
if their was they did not chuse to act with them,
or else they would ere now have lett them know
it. Suppose even the Army march'd on and beat
the Duke of Cumberland yett in the Battle they

must Lose some men, and they had after that the
Kings own army consisting of 7000 men near
London [1] to deal with. On the contrary, if either
of these armies beat them, their would not a man
Escape, as the militia, altho they durst never face
the army while in a body, yett they would have
courage enough to putt an end to them if ever
they were routed. And so the people that were
in arms in Scotland would fall an Easy Sacrifice to
the fury of the Government. Again, Suppose the
Army was to Slip the Kings & Dukes army and
gett into London, the success of the Affair would
intirely depend upon the mobs declaring for or
against it, and that if the Mob had been much inclined to his Cause, since his march into England,
that to be sure some of his friends in London would

---

[1] An exact estimate of the troops concentrated on Finchley
Common is difficult to arrive at. Mr. Blaikie quotes the following
entry from the *Gentleman's Magazine*, 10th Dec. : 'The guards and
other regiments sent on 7th to Highgate, Enfield, and Barnet in order
to form a camp at Finchley Common were countermanded ' (p. 96).

'Orders were issued Dec. 4th for the regiment of Scots Highlanders
and some other Regiments of Foot and Horse, that were quartered
about Deptford in Kent, to march to Finchley Common to encamp
there. A few days after, a Train of 32 Pieces of Cannon with
Powder, Carriages, Waggons, etc., were drawn out of the Tower'
(*M. R.* 237).

'The gentlemen of the law formed themselves into a regiment
under the command of the Lord Chief-Justice Willes to be denomin-
ated The associated regiment of the law, for the defence of the
Royal family, and the preservation of the constitution in church and
state ' (*S. M.* vii. 581).

have fall'n upon some method to have lett him
Know'n it, but if the Mob was against the Affair
4500 men would not make a great figure in
London. Lord George concluded by Saying that
the Scots army had done their part, that they
Came into England at the Princes request, to join
his English friends, and to give them Courage by
their appearance to take arms and declare for him
publickly as they had done, or to join the French
if they had Landed ; but as none of these things
had happened, that certainly 4500 Scots had
never thought of putting a King upon the
English Throne by themselves. So he Said his
Opinion was they Should go back and join their
friends in Scotland, and live and die with them,
and the French (who at Derby the Army Learned
had landed in Scotland with Lord John Drummond but did not know their numbers but believed 4000 men). After Lord George had spoke
he desired all the rest of the Gentlemen present
to Speak their sentiments, and they all agreed
with Lord George except two,* who were for * Duke of
going to Wales to see if the Welch would join. Perth Sir Will:
Gordon.
It was urged too that Wades Army, who was
following, must likewise be fought with as the
other two armies would certainly Stop the

Princes by fighting or other Methods, which
would give Wade time enough to come up.
The Prince heard all these arguments with the
greatest impatience, fell into a passion and gave
most of the Gentlemen that had Spoke very
Abusive Language, and said that they had a
mind to betray him.[1] The Case was he knew
nothing about the country nor had not the
Smallest Idea of the force that was against him,
nor where they were Situated. His Irish favourites to pay court to him had always represented
the whole nation as his friends, had diminished
much all the force that was Against him, & he
himself believed firmly That the Soldiers of the
Regulars would never dare fight against him, as
he was Their true prince. For all the Success he

[1] Charles's own account of what occurred states that *all* the
members of the Council except himself were of opinion that the
retreat was absolutely necessary (*H. H.* Appendix, 340), but cf.
Examination of John Murray.

'Lord George Murray, Lord Elcho, and everybody present, except
Lord Perth, declared their opinion for marching back to Scotland'
(*M. M.* 432).

Of John Murray's conduct on this occasion, Maxwell says
(*M. K.* 75):—

'The little knave appeared plainly in his conduct on this occasion.
He argued strenuously for the retreat, because he thought it the only
prudent measure, till he found it was carried by a great majority and
would certainly take place, and then he condemned it to make his
court to the Prince, to whom it was very disagreeable, and lay the
odium upon other people, particularly Lord George, whom he
endeavoured to blacken on every occasion.'

had had as yett he attributed more to the mens
Consciences not Allowing them to fight against
him, than to The power of the Broad Sword, and
he always believed he Should enter St James's
with as little difficulty as he had done Holyrood
house. He Continued all that day positive he
would march to London ; the Irish in the army
were always for what he was for, and were heard
to say that day that they knew if they escaped
being killed the worst that could happen to them
was some months imprisonment. The Scots were
all against it ; so at Night the Prince Sent for
them and told them he consented to go to Scotland, And at the same time he told them that for
the future he would have no more Councills, for
he would neither ask nor take their Advice, that
he was Accountable to nobody for his Actions but
to his Father ; and he was as good as his word, for
he never after advised with any body but the Irish
Officers, Mrs Murray & Hay, and never more
summons'd a Councill.[1] The 6 the army march'd
back to Ashburn ; that morning the Dukes
march'd to Meriden common near Coventry, so

[1] 'I think there was but one council of war call'd aftir they
return'd to Scotland and that was near Crief the day after the retreat
from Stirling ' (*L. P.* ii. 534).

if the Prince had march'd forward the two armies would have mett at Northampton. The inferior officers of the Princes army were much Surprised when they found the army moving back and imagined some bad news had been received, but when they were told every thing, & found the army had marched so far into England without the least invitation from any English man of Distinction, they blamed their Superiors much for Carrying them so far, and Approved much of Going back to Scotland; they had all along imagined they were marching to join the English, and were Acting in concert with them. To the Common men it was given out the Army was Going to meet their friends from Scotland and to prevent Marèchal Wade from getting in between them (who's army was at Wetherby and Doncaster). The Prince, who had march'd all the way to Darby on foot at the head of a Column of Infantry, now mounted on horseback,[1] and road generally after the van of the Army and appear'd to be out of humour. Upon the Armies marching out of Darby Mr Morgan an English Gentle-

---

[1] Charles, who had marched afoot at the head of the men all the way, was obliged to get on horseback, for he could not walk, and hardly stand (as was always the case with him when he was cruelly used) (John Hay's account of the Retreat, *H. H.* 339).

man came up to Mr Vaughan who was riding in the life Guards, and after saluting him said Damn me, Vaughan, they are going to Scotland. Mr Vaughan replied, Wherever they go I am determined now I have joined them to go along with them.* Upon which Mr Morgan Said, By God I had rather be hanged than go to Scotland, to Starve. The army march'd on the 7 from Ashburn to Leek, and Elcho's & Pitsligo's horse, Ogilvys & Roy Stuarts foot advanced that night to Maclesfield where the people were every moment expecting Marèchal Wades army. The 8 the troops in Maclesfield advanced to Stockport and the rest of the army came to Maclesfield. All the Country people were arm'd, and at Stockport they fir'd from a Village in the night upon the patrouilles and killd some of them : the rest sett fire to the Villadge. They were quite prepared in case the army had been beat to have knock'd on the head all that would have Escaped from the Battle. Whenever any of the men Stragled or Stay'd behind they either murder'd them, or sent them to the Duke, and all the way from Carlisle to Darby all the men that were left sick † upon the road were either kill'd or after very much abused sent to jails off the great road.

* Mr Morgan was hanged in 1746 and Mr Vaughan is an officer in Spain.

† in towns

The 9 the army marched for Manchester. The quartermasters were sent on before with a party of horse to prepare quarters for the Army, but as the whole town was in an Uproar & show'd an inclination to attack them, they were oblidged to return to the army, and their was two Battalions and two Squadrons order'd in to Support them, upon which the mob dispersed and the whole army arrived at night. The town was taxed 2500 pd [1] which they paid next day. The Prince was for halting here, but upon its being represented to him that Wades army (which was reported not far off) might gett before to Rippel Bridge, and so Stop the army in front untill the Dukes came in the rear, he consented to move next day, and the Army march'd to Wigan. Roy Stuarts and Ogilvys regiments, who made the rear guard coming out of Manchester, were fir'd upon by the mob, who follow'd them, but whenever they faced about the mob always run away. They quarter'd that night at Leigh.

The Duke of Cumberland when he heard of the Princes retreat had put himself the 8, at the head of all his horse and Dragoons and 1000 foot

---

[1] The sum first demanded was £5000. This was reduced by Charles to £2500 (*M. R.* 203).

which he had mounted on horseback, to pursue
the Prince, with orders for Sir John Ligonier to
follow with the rest of the army. He marched by
Uttoxeter & Cheadle and came into Maclesfield
the 10th. Marechal Wades army was at Wakefield on the 10th in order to Gett into Lancashire
before the Princes; he detached Major General
Oglethorpe with Wades & Montagus horse, St
George's dragoons, & the Yorkshire rangers to
see & gett to Preston before the Prince, but he
only arrived at Wigan the 12th. The 11 the Prince
Marched into Preston, and the rear guard to
Charly, & next day they arrived at Preston.
The Dukes troops were at Manchester on the
11th. The Prince halted the 12 at Preston and
the Guards were order'd to guard Ripple Bridge.
He would absolutely remain here, and sent of the
Duke of Perth with the Hussars with orders to
bring up the army in Scotland. It was represented
here to him likewise that Wades Army might
gett to Lancaster, so putt him betwixt two fires.
Upon which he Agreed to Go to Lancaster, and
the Army march'd their the next day. An hour
after the rear of the army left the town General
Oglethorp took possession of it, and the Duke of
Cumberland came to Wigan. At Supper at

Lancaster the Prince talk'd much about retiring so fast, and said it was a Shame for to go so fast before the son of an *Usurper*, and that he Would stay at Lancaster. The principal Officers, who were not at all against fighting when it was reasonable, mett and Agreed, since Wades army could not now gett in betwixt them and Scotland that they would remain and fight the Duke at Lancaster, which at the Same time would Show them whither it was great Stoutness or Contradiction that made the Prince & his Irish favourites for Stoping in Every town. And Accordingly Lord George Murray went & ask'd the Princes leave to Go next morning and reconnoitre a field of Battle, which he consented to. Lord George went next morning with a party of the Guards to Chuse the Ground, and they made some of the Yorkshire rangers prisoners, who informed them that General Oglethorp was at Garstang. He sent them in with an escort to the Prince, who after he had examin'd them, order'd the Baggage to march, and the rest of the army to move early next morning towards Kendal, which they accordingly did. As soon as the rear left the town their was some Dragoons pursued them, but upon a disposition being made to receive them they retired. The army arrived that night at Kendall, where they learnt that the Duke of Perth had been oblidged to fight his way through the town and that two or three people had been kill'd on both sides. His Grace had pursued his journey on to Penrith, but finding the Country people all in arms to oppose his passage he was oblidged to return and join the army at Kendal. The 16 the prince marched to Shap and the villages about it, but Lord George Murray who commanded the rear guard, by reason of the badness of the weather and the roads that the country people had on purpose spoilt, could gett no further Than a place half way, and next day he arrived at Shap after having had much difficulty in getting all the Cannon and Waggons over the Steep hills in that country. The same day the Prince went on to Penrith and sent of the Guards and The Perthshire Squadron to Carlisle. Their had been a 100 Swiss and a great many militia in Penrith, but they left it upon the news of the Princes approach. The Country militia who were armed and on horseback had endeavour'd to harass Lord George Upon his March all the way from Kendal, and would sometimes draw up in Battle as if they intended to attack him, but

whenever he order'd any troops to march up
against them they always turned their backs &
made of. The 18 as Lord George was passing by
Lother hall the seat of the Viscount of Lonsdale
Lord Leiutenant of the County, he sent in some
men in order to Catch some of them, but in place
of Militia they found two footmen of the Duke
of Cumberlands, who informed them that the
Duke was very near with about 5000 horse. Lord
George had just time to march to a village call'd
Clifton (in a hollow) and dispose of his men in
the inclosures behind hedges, when the Duke
appeared and drew up his horse in battle on a
hill half Cannon shot above the village. Lord G^{rge}
sent of an aid de Camp to The Prince (who was
reviewing his men on a hill to the north of
Penrith) to inform him of what had happen'd and
to tell him that now was a good opportunity to
fight The Duke, for that numbers were pretty
near equal, and that the Ground was advantageous
for foot to fight in. As their was formerly a
Contradiction to make the army halt when
it was necessary to march, so now their was
one to march and shun fighting when their
Could never be a better opportunity gott for
it, so the Prince sent a detachment to Succour

Lord George (which arrived after the affair)[1] and march'd of the rest of the army to Carlisle and left orders for Lord George to follow. The Duke of Cumberland, after having reconoitred Ld Georges position, order'd some of his Dragoons to dismount and line the hedges opposite to the highlandmen, which they did about an hour after sun sett, and their was a very smart fire on both sides for more than half an hour, when Lord George order'd Clunie Macphersons battalion to draw their swords and follow him, which they did and drove the Dragoons first from the hedges and then to their main body on the hill after killing 40 or 50 of them, after which Lord George made his retreat first into Penrith and then to Carlisle without being molested. Lord George had twelve men kill'd, and Mr Hamilton Captain of Hussars was wounded & taken prisoner. The Duke did not come to Penrith that night. All the Princes army was in Carlisle early on the 19, and the Dukes advanced guard came that day to Heskett: he himself came only to Penrith, where he halted all the 20th. The Prince

---

[1] *i.e.* the Atholl brigade (*J. M.* 71).

Lord George says that at this time 'there was above eight miles from our van to our rear, and mostly an open country, full of commons' (*J. M.* 72).

march'd out of Carlisle the 20, but left M^r
Hamilton in the town with the Manchester
regiment and a Small detachment out of the
Lowland regiments. This was done against the
opinion almost of Everybody [1] but the Prince said
he would have a town in England and he was
sure the Duke could gett no Cannon to take it
with. The army cross'd the Esk near Longtown
without the Loss of a man, notwithstanding the
water was so high as to take the men up to their
breasts. All the Country people upon the borders
were in arms, for they had gott news from Edn^r
that the Duke of Cumberland had overtaken the
army near Lancaster and had given them a total
defeat, and that the Prince and the few that had
escaped were flying to Scotland, so they had gott
themselves prepared in Case it had been so, to
have knock'd all Stragglers on the head, and they
were only deceived when they saw the army ford
the water of Esk.[2] After the army had pass'd, the

[1] The resolution of Charles to leave a garrison at Carlisle was
generally condemned, and illustrates the autocratic authority which he
exercised. Lord George Murray and Maxwell agree that the town
was not tenable (*J. M.* 73; *M. K.* 88).

[2] 'We were a hundred men abreast, and it was a very fine show;
the water was big, and took most of the men breast high. When
I was near across the river I believe there were two thousand men
in the water at once. Some ladies had passed the water on horseback just before us; but had they looked back they could have seen

Prince divided it into three bodies. The first, which consisted of the Clans, Perths regiment, the Bagage and three piece of Cannon (for the other ten were left in the castle of Carlisle), he march'd himself to Annan ; Lord George Murray with the Athole Brigade, Ogilvys, Roy Steuarts, & Glenbucketts march'd to Ecclefichen, and next day to Moffat. Lord Elcho with all the horse march'd to Dumfries, with orders to disarm the town and to tax it in 2000^{pds} and 1000 pair of shoes. Upon his arrival the militia * quit the town, the tax was partly paid, and two hostages taken for the remainder untill it was also paid. The 21 the Prince arrived at Dumfries and halted their all the 22^d, as Lord George did at Moffat. The Princes army in their march into England lost very few men, and they brought just the same sum of money out of the country they had carried into it, so the Army just maintained itself. The Common Soldiers did little or no damage in going up to Darby, but in coming back they plunder'd a little, particularly at Penrith ; and the reason was that Mr Boyd and some gentlemen

* about 700 men.

nothing, the water was so big. The pipes began to play so soon as we passed, and the men all danced reels, which in a moment dried them. . . . I was this day in my philibeg ` (*J. M.* 75).

that had been left at Carlisle wanting to join the army had taken up their first nights quarters at Lowther hall. The Penrith people attacked them kill'd one or two, took some and sent them to Marèchal Wade ; the others that made their escape returned back to Carlisle. The principal people of the Princes army paid very minutely for everything they had in England. Upon the armies arriving in Scotland they gott certain intelligence of Lord John Drummonds[1] being landed at Montross with troops, arms, Cannon, and all sorts of military stores : the numbers were not known but it was given out all over this country that their was 4000 French. The 23 Lord George Murray march'd from Moffat to Douglass, and the Prince from Dumfries to Drumlanrig. The 24 Lord George pass'd the water of Douglass, which was very high, and march'd to Hamilton, and the Prince arrived that night at Douglass. The Duke of Douglass had refused Lord George admittance into the Castle, but as the Prince had Cannon with him his Grace was oblidged to open his Gates and receive him. Lord George gott

[1] Lord John Drummond landed Nov. 22nd : 'he brought about 800 men, composed of his own regiment of Royal Scots, and a piquet of 50 men from each of the six (French) Irish regiments under Brigadier Stapleton' (Blaikie, 27, citing Lord Macleod and *London Gazette*).

intelligence at Hamilton that the Earls of Hume
and Glencairn had march'd away from Glascow
to Edn[r] with the Glascow & west country militia,
and that Price & Ligoniers foot and Ligoniers
(late Gardners) and Hamiltons dragoons, had
likewise retired from Sterling to Edn[r]; Lord
George march'd to Glascow the 25 and the Prince
came to Hamilton. The highlanders of the princes
column plunder'd the town of Lesmahago because
they had taken prisoner and sent to Edn[r] M[r]
Macdonald of Kinlochmoidart,[1] who was going
from the north to join the army at Carlisle. The
Prince had sent him from Edn[r] to the Highlands
to see & persaude Sir Alex Macdonald and
Macleod to join him. The Prince halted all the
26, and went a shooting in Duke Hamiltons
Parcks, and the 27 he made his Entry into
Glascow at the head of a body of foot; the Streets
were crouded with people to see him, but they
were all much against his Cause. We shall now
leave the Prince at Glascow & return to Carlisle

---

[1] Donald Macdonald: he had been sent north at the end of
October; executed at Carlisle Oct. 18, 1746 (S. M. vii. 497). In
the letter found on him and signed 'C' there was the following:
'. . . desire you to give it out wherever you come that Sir Alexander
Macdonald and the Macleods are actually on their march, notwithstanding you may have received contrary information' (Ibid. vii.
540).

where The Duke of Cumberland arrived the 21 and took up his quarters at Blacklehall and invested the town on all sides. He was joined by 1000 foot of Mr Wades Army, who had marched from Rippon back to Newcastle, where he had arrived the 20th. The Duke sent for some battering Cannon from Whitehaven, and the 24th he gott 4 18 pounders & the 26th 6 more. From the Dukes first appearance near the town Mr Hamilton kept a close fire wherever he saw troops. The 28 the Besiegers raised a battery and Battered the walls of the town with six guns ; the 29th they did the same, the 30th the Besiegers had three more eighteen pounders mounted, but upon the first platoon of the Battery that morning Mr Hamilton hung out the white flag, and sent to the Duke to know what terms he would gett if he Surrender'd the town. The Duke returned for answere that the Garison should not be putt to the sword, but receved prisoners at discretion. Upon which Mr Hamilton surrender'd the town, and General Bligh that same day 30th of December took possession of it ; all the prisoners were confined in the Cathedral and were very ill Used. The Duke of Cumberland made his entry into Carlisle and sometime afterwards

returned to London.[1] Mrs Maxwell and Brown
made their escape out of Carlisle during the
time of the Capitulation and brought the news
of its surrender to the Prince at Kilsyth. Their
was a sort of a breach made in the wall
but not sufficient to enter by; the batterys
were raised opposite to the Irish and Scots
gate.

The Prince sometime after his arrival at
Glascow road through the town dress'd in the
French dress[2] attended by his Guards and made
a General review of all his army that had been
in England, and the loss the army had sustained
by its march into England was very inconsider-
able. As this town had been very active in raising
men and had made great rejoicings upon the
news of the pretended defeat at Lancaster the
Prince taxed it in 12000 Shirts, 6000 bonnets,
6000 p^r of Shoes, 6000 p^r of Stockings, & 6000
waistecoats amounting to near the value of 10'000
p^ds, and took hostages for the payment of it;
the Prince Supp'd every night in publick and

---

[1] The Duke was summoned south to command the forces
destined to oppose a French landing ; he left Carlisle Jan. 2nd, and
reached St. James's Jan. 4th (*M. R.* 257).

[2] 'The Prince dressed more elegantly when in Glasgow than
he did in any other place whatsomever' (James Gib, *L. M.* ii. 125).

their was always a great deal of Company came to See him. He received letters here from Ld John Drummond, wherin Lord John Acquainted him that he had sailed from Dunkirk and had arrived with six Ships in the harbours of Montross, Aberdeen, Stonehive, and Peterhead, that in these Ships was eleven companies of his own regiment about 550 men, a piquet of Dillons 50 men, one of Rooths 50, & one of Lallys 50, that he had 6000 Lewis d'ors in money, great plenty of small arms and military Stores, besides two brass Cannon of 18^{pd}, two of 12^{pd}, & two of 9^{pd} and some Voluntiers. That the Milford man of War [1] had oblidged a French frigate of 30 guns to run Ashoare, but that they had saved every thing that was aboard of her, that the Hazard Sloop of War [2] had enter'd the harbour of Montross, and that they had planted Batteries of Cannon upon the shoar and had taken her, that in Short what he brought with h^m was but the advanced gaurd of what was to follow. Lord John publish'd a declaration in French and in

---

[1] Commanded by Captain Hanway; the French frigate was named *Louis XV*. (*M. R.* 233).

[2] The *Hazard*, after doing valuable service for Charles, was eventually retaken at Tongue in Sutherland, March 25, 1746, by the *Sheerness*, Captain O'Brien (*S. M.* viii. 145).

English and sent a drum to the Commander
of the Dutch Troops with Marèchal Wade to
lett him know that their was French Coulours
in the Princes army, and required him to return
home, which they did soon after. The Declaration he published was, viz. :—

Nous Lord Jean Drummond commandant en
Chef des forces de S.M : T.C. en Ecosse de-
clarons par les presentes, que nous sommes venus
dans ce royaume avec des ordres par ecrit de
S.M.T.C. pour faire la guerre au Roy d'Angleterre Electeur D'Hannover et a tous ses adherens :
les ordres portent positivement d'attaquer tous
ses ennemis dans ce Royaume, et elle declare
qu'on doit regarder comme tells ceux qui ne se
rendront pas aussi tot qu'il leur sera possible
aupres du Prince de Galles Regent D'Ecosse
son Alliè que S.M.T.C. a resolu de concert avec
L'Espagne de maintenir et d'aider à prendre
possession des Royaumes D'Ecosse, D'Angleterre,
et D'Irlande, et d'employer en cas de besoin pour
cet effet, toutes les troupes et L'argent qui sont
en son pouvoir, les pretentions de la maison de
Stuart sur ces Royaumes etant justes et indisput-
ables. Les ordres positives de S.M.T.C. sont
aussi que ses ennemis seront traitès suivant le

tort qu'ils feront ou pretendront faire a la cause
de S.A.R.   Signè J. Drummond.

Fait à Montross
le 2 Dec: 1745.

Lord John sailed from Dunkirk in November
with 8 Ships, but two of them were taken by the
road with two Companies of his own regiment, a
piquet of Bulkelys, one of Clares and one of
Berwicks 250 men. Lord John likewise wrote
a letter to Monsr du Boyer and directed it, A
Son Excellence Monsieur le Marquis D'Equilles,
Ambassadeur de sa majestè tres Cretien aupres
son altesse Royal le Prince de Galles. Monsieur
D'Equilles ever after took upon him the title
of Ambassadeur de France, and every body
call'd him his excellency, he declared the
Prince, as well as Lord John had done, the King
his masters Ally, but Lord Johns declaration
and every puff Monsr D'Equille made was only
to encourage the people to join and to keep up
the Spirits of those that had joined, for they had
not the least authority for it from the Court of
France. Lord John brought letters from France
which give an account of what was doing their.
The Duke of York the Princes Brother had arrived

in that country in the month of August 1745, and
the first scheme the French had proposed was to
send over the Irish Brigade in fishing boats with
orders to join the Prince wherever they could in
England. This was laid aside, and a much grander
embarkation [1] formed which was to be Commanded
by The Duc de Richelieu and to Consist of the
Irish six regiments, two Battalions of the Royal
Grenadiers, two of Beauvosis, two of Biron, six
other Battalions, Fitzjames's Regiment of Horse
and Sept [*illegible in MS.*] Dragoons, in all 9000
foot and 1350 horse. The embarkation was first
to have been from Dunkirk, then from Boulogne
& Calais, and vast numbers of small vessels were
gott together in the harbours of Boulogne & Calais
for that purpose, but as the French took a great time
in Getting together a prodigious quantity of Stores
and Cannon to Carry with them, the Goverment
of England had notice of it, and sent Admiral
Vernon [2] with a Strong fleet into the Channel and

---

[1] 'L'embarquement devait être de onze mille hommes, un train
d'artillerie, quelques chevaux de trait . . . et des declarations dans
les deux langues toutes prêtes à publier' (D'Argenson, *Journal et
Mémoires*, vii. 318). The Declaration referred to was composed by
Voltaire (*Œuvres*, éd. Beuchot, xxxviii. 543).

[2] Edward Vernon (b. 1684, d. 1757), son of James Vernon,
principal Secretary of State (1698-1702); entered the Navy 1700;
Admiral 1745; later he attacked the Admiralty in anonymous
pamphlets, and was cashiered 1746. He sailed out of the Downs

order'd an army of 7000 foot & 2500 horse to the Coasts of Kent & Essex. Upon which the French gave it over the 6 of Jan^r 1746, and the Dukes of York & Richelieu returned back to Paris. The French proposed Landing in Dungeness. The Prince did not learn of That embarkations being given over untill he was at Inverness. The news the Prince gott at Glascow from the north was that their was a Spanish Ship Landed at Barra[1] with 2500 Stand of arms and 4000 ^pd in money; that Lord Loudoun, who Commanded for the Goverment in the north, had made two marches from Inverness, one to Supply the garison of fort Augustus with provisions, and another to Lord Lovats house of castle Dounie. He brought Lord Lovat to Inverness along with him as a sort of prisoner, but he sometime after-

on Dec. 21, 1745; the French expedition was appointed to start on Christmas Eve (D'Argenson, iv. 318). Vernon was recalled at the beginning of January and struck his flag on the 2nd (*S. M.* viii. 48).

[1] The Spanish officer in charge of the arms was a prisoner at Inverness in Feb. 1746. 'Ther was also a gentleman in the Spainish servise, one collenel Hendela, one of the best men I ever was acquaint with. It was he that cam to the Islland of Bara, in the North Hylands, and landed the arms that were found ther' (Letter of Mrs. Leith, *L. M.* ii. 286). In April 1746 there was still Spanish money lying at Barra, 'about £380 sterling,' and it was this sum that Æneas Macdonald went in search of and brought to Charles after Culloden (*L. M.* i. 160; Elcho, *Journal*).

wards made his escape. About the 10 of December Lord Loudoun sent the Laird of Macleod and Mr Monro of Culcairn to Aberdeenshire with 700 men to see and prevent the people of that country from taking arms for the Prince. The Laird of Grant joined them upon the road with 500 men, but Seperated from them at Strathbogie and return'd to his own country. Macleod and Culcairn arrived at Inverury the 20, and the 23 Lord Lewis Gordon march'd from Aberdeen with 700 men and attacked them at Inverury.[1] He beat and putt them to flight, took all their Baggage kill'd about 60 & took 100 prisoners ;* but as it was dark did not pursue them ; besides Macleods men never Stop'd untill they gott to Forress. Lord Lewis Lost 40 men in this action. The Prince Learned also at Glascow that General Campbell and his son were in Argyleshire and had raised 2000 men for the Goverment.

* MacLeod gave out he lost but 22.

Their was a great many people of the army were for marching from Glascow to take posses-

[1] Lovat was taken prisoner Dec. 11th ; on Dec. 20th he escaped, upon which the Clan Fraser marched to join Charles's army (*Lord Lovat's Trial*, 45 ; *L. M.* ii. 284). The troops accompanying Lord Lewis Gordon were Moir of Stoneywood's, Farquharson of Monaltrie's, Bannerman of Elsick's, two of Lord John Drummond's companies, a few men raised by Mr. Crichton, and Gordon of Avochy's men. 'The action lasted but a few minutes after the men were formed' (*L. M.* ii. 344).

sion a second time of Edn^r or else to go to East
Lothian to oblidge General Hawley[1] who was
marching the army Wade commanded down to
Scotland to Encamp every night and to keep in
a body ; which as the weather was very bad and
cold, could not miss to have done his army a
great deal of harm, but The Prince resolved to
Besiege Sterling Castle and sent an Express from
Glascow to Lord John Drummond with orders
for him to Assemble the troops under his command and to march and Assist at the Siege.
While the Prince was at Glascow he expected every
day to hear of his Brothers Landing in England,
and the Goverment expected it so much that all

---

[1] Henry Hawley (b. 1679(?), d. 1759), served with the present
4th Hussars 1706-1717 ; colonel of 33rd Foot 1717, of 13th
Dragoons 1730 ; Lieut.-General 1744 ; present at Dettingen and
Fontenoy ; appointed to the command in Scotland in succession to
Handasyde 1746 ; at Culloden he commanded the cavalry ; he was
a harsh disciplinarian, and known in the army as chief-justice or
'hangman.' Popular rumour alleged that he was a son of King
George, and that on this account his brutalities were condoned. He
left characteristic directions in his will: 'But, first I direct and
order, that, as there is now a peace, and I may die the common way,
my carcase may be put any where. . . . The priest, I conclude, will
have his fee: let the puppy have it. Pay the carpenter for the
carcase box.' He arrived in Edinburgh Jan. 6th ; twelve battalions
and four regiments of dragoons constituted his command (*H. B. A.*
ii. 138 ; *S. M.* viii. 34).

> To whom compared an Alva's name is sweet,
> Brave in the field tho' cruel in the State.

(*L. M.* i. 243.)

the troops the Duke of Cumberland Commanded at Carlisle were order'd to the South in order to oppose it. The town of Edn[r] upon hearing the Prince intended soon to leave Glascow was making great preparations for a defence and had gott a great many militia into town for that purpose, and upon the 2[d] of January 1746 the first division of General Hawleys army arrived at Edn[r], and he himself with the rest of the army some days afterwards. On the 3[d] of January the Princes army evacuated Glascow and formed the Blocade of Sterling. He himself marched the first day to Kilsyth and next day to Bannockburn,[1] where he establish'd his head quarters. The Athole brigade was cantooned at Bannockburn, and Ogilvys, Roy Steuarts, Glenbucketts, & Perths with the Baggage at S[t] Ninians. Lord George Murray march'd the first day to Cumbernald and next day took post at Falkirk with Lochyels, Appins, Clunies, Glengarys, Clanronalds, and Keppochs regiments.

[1] Sir Hugh Paterson's. 'The Prince who lived in the Castle of the Chevalier Paterson a league's distance from Stirling made the acquaintance of Miss Walkinshaw, who forthwith became his mistress' (Elcho, *Journal*). It was here that Sir John Douglas, M.P., visited Charles with a message from the English Jacobites to the effect that £10,000 had been collected for him in London. Sheridan's comment on this was 'Since they have collected Money, why the Devil did they not send it?' (*S. P. Dom., George II.,* Examination of John Murray of Broughton, Aug. 13, 1746).

Elcho's Troop of Guards was quarter'd at Elphingston, Lord Balmerino's at Glorat, Pitsligo's
Squadron at Airth, Kilmarnocks troop of Horse
grenadiers at Callendar, the Perthshire Squadron
at Leckie, and the Hussars at a Village near
Glorat. The Prince upon his arrival at Bannockburn sent to Summons the town of Sterling (in
which their was 400 militia) to surrender, which
they refused, but the 7 upon a batterys being
raised and firing some shot, they gave up the
town and the Athole Brigadge, Ogilvys, Roy
Steuarts, Glenbuckets, and Perths regiments took
possession of it; some of the militia dispersed
and went home; the rest with their officers retired
into the Castle. The Castle firr'd upon the
Princes troops as they were marching into town
but kill'd nobody; during the whole time of the
Siege they always firr'd wherever they saw any of
the Princes Troops and very often at single people.
Lochyels Regiment replaced the Athole brigadge
at Bannockburn.

Lord John Drummond according to the Princes
orders had putt all the troops under his command
in motion. Lord John arrived himself ye 8 with
four piece of Battering Cannon and a great deal
of amunition at Aloa, under the Escort of the

Earl of Cromarties regiment, in order to embark all aboard of a Ship at Aloa and send it up the river as far as it would go. All the rest of the troops and the lighter cannon march'd about by the frews,[1] the Cannon was escorted into Sterling by the three Irish piquets, and the rest of the troops that had pass'd the Frews, marched to Falkirk, where they were incorporated in The following manner, viz., Barisdale[1] with 200 men, young Glengary with 100, Raasa[y] with 100 into Glengarys regiment, 150 men into Clanronalds, Glenco with 100, & Glengyle with 50 into Keppocks, 150 into Ardsheils, 300 men with old Lochyel[2] into Lochyels, which made Lochyels regiment 800 men, Glengarys 800, Keppochs 600, Clanronalds 400, Appins or Ardshiels 300. The Master of Lovat with 300 Frazers was left at St Ninians, and The 400 Mackintoshes and Farquarsons were sent to quarter in the villages

---

[1] Lochgarry in his Narrative, addressed to young Glengarry, printed in Mr. Blaikie's *Itinerary*, p. 118, says: ' Your brother joined us here (Bannockburn) with a strong reinforcement to your regm^t: we then made two battalions your people of Urquhart and Glenmorison having likewise joined us. We muster'd then directly twixt nine hundred and a thousand men, which being devided, your brother commanded the first and I the second battalion. Barrisdale likewise join'd us on the battle-day with 300 clever fellows from the north, which made us compleat 1200 on the day of battle.'

[2] See *post*, p. 443 note.

in the Carse. Their was a great many Irish officers voluntiers came along with the piquets; they were all much caress'd by the Prince, were much about his person, and he gave them all much higher commissions than they had in France, which was of great service to them Upon their return to France as that Court confirm'd most of them in their service.

As the Battering cannon and most all the stores that was necessary for making the siege of Sterling castle was at Alloa and the scheme was to embark them aboard of a ship Laying there, & so send them up the river, the Prince had sent Colonel Grant the 9th with three 4 pounders in order to erect a battary to gaurd the passage of the river as well as possible, for the *Pearl* & *Vulture* sloops of war were laying in the river and had sent their boats the night before and had burnt two ships at Airth which they imagin'd the people at Alloa might have occasion for. Colonel Grant open'd a battery at Airth, and there was several Canon shot exchanged betwixt it & the Sloops, but Colonel Grant finding the river too broad at that place removed the battery to Elphingston pans where the Guards of 150 foot were quarter'd under the command of L[d] Elcho. That night the

Sloops boats well man'd sail'd up the river above
Aloa to a place call'd Keiny in order as it was supposed to seize Ld Elcho, who used to Lodge there
at nights. They search'd the house, but as he was
that night at the battery they miss'd their aim,
and as they return'd they were firr'd at from the
battery, and two of their men were kill'd. The
10th General Hawley sent a Battalion (under the
command of Coll: Leighton) in 9 arm'd sloops
up the river in order to attack Alloa & seize upon
the Cannon and amunition there ; he landed the
troops at Clackmanan * but upon hearing that
Lochyels regiment had pass'd the river, in order
to defend Alloa he reimbark'd them and the two
sloops of war, & the nine arm'd vessels came to
an anchor opposite to Airth in Kincardin road.
The 11th at the making of the tide they all weigh'd
anchor and stood for the battery at Elphingston
pans, and the two Sloops of war & another vessel
cast anchor very near it and the other eight stood
of and on & firr'd wherever they saw any troops.
Lord Elcho disposed of his men so as to support
the battery in case the troops aboard had landed
to attack it, and Colonel Grant kept a close fire
upon the ships, but as the Cannon were too small
it was impossible to do them much mischeif. Who-

* or Kincar-
dine.

ever he kill'd them about ten men, and Suppose they kept a close fire upon the battery during the whole time of the flowing of the tide they neither kill'd any body nor dismounted a gun ; when the tide began to Ebb Colonel Grant cutt the Sloops of war's Cables with his Shott, & the tide carried them down yᵉ river and all the rest of the vessels followed them. The very same tide the Ship with the Cannon & all the Stores aboard sail'd up the river from Alloa to Polmais; Lord Cromarties regiment went thither to gaurd it, the Cannon at Elphingston pans was removed to Bannockburn and the Guards were order'd to West quarter.

The 13 of Janʳ Lord George Murray having gott intelligence that the people of Linlithgow had gott orders from Ednʳ to prepare provisions and forage for the army, march'd from Falkirk in order to consume part of it & bring the rest away in carts which he carried with him for that purpose. He had along with him for this expedition, Glengarys, Clanronalds, Keppocks, Appins, and Clunies foot, and Elcho's & Pitsligo's horse ; he arrived at Lithgow early in the morning and order'd out parties to patroille upon the road to Ednʳ. About twelve o clock the officer that Commanded the patrouille sent word to Lord

George that he perceived a Small party of Dragoons advancing towards the town, upon which Ld George order'd the horse to mount and pursue them while he drew the foot up in Battle out of town. Ld Elcho pursued the dragoons untill they were joined by 60 more; he pursued them likewise untill they Gott to a Village where their was a great body of horse and foot. He sent to acquaint Ld George of what had happen'd, & Ld George order'd him to leave an officer with a party to watch their motions, and order'd all the rest of the horse & foot into town. About two hours after that, the officer that was left to watch their motions sent word into Ld George that their was a very large body of horse & foot advancing as fast as they could on the road to Falkirk, upon which Ld George call'd a councill of war, wherin it was determined to wait untill they arrived very near the town of Lithgow and then to retreat in Good order before them; for as their numbers were not know'n it was not thought proper to engage them, especially as a Generall battle was dayly expected. Whenever Ld George heard that the body of troops were very near Linlithgow, he order'd all his men to be ready to march, and when the regular troops began to form on the south side of the town, he orderd his men to pass the bridge and before his rear had pass'd the bridge the dragoons who was in the front of the regulars drew up close by the Bridge, and very abusive language pass'd betwixt both sides, but Ld George's rear made so Good an appearance & retreated in such order that the dragoons never offer'd to attack them, nor did any of them pass the bridge that night. Ld George halted that night at Falkirk, and next day he marched to the villages in the neighbourhood of Bannockburn, where he gott intelligence that the troops he had seen was Major General Huske[1] with half the army, and that Lt General Hawley had arrived at Linlithgow on the 14 with the other half. The 15 of Jan^r 1746 The Prince drew up all his army in battle upon a plain a mile to the East of Bannockburn, and sent of a large body of horse to reconnoitre Falkirk, who brought back intelligence that they had perceived a large body of horse near that town but no foot, upon which the Prince order'd his army back to their quarters and a body of horse to patrouille all that night as near Falkirk as they could with

[1] John Huske (b. 1692, d. 1761) ; Major-General for services at Dettingen 1743 ; led second line at Culloden ; Governor of Jersey 1760.

safety. Next day 16 that party sent word to the Prince that all the foot of Hawleys army were arrived at Falkirk, that they had been joined by 1000 Highlanders under the command of Colonel Campbell, and that they had pitch'd their Camp a little to the north of Falkirk & had the town on their left, and their horse advanced in their front at the brige of Carron. The Prince drew his army up in battle in ye same place as the day before and waited upon the field untill three o clock, but upon hearing that their was no appearance of their moving that day, he order'd his army to their quarters, which were so dispersed that if Gen: Hawley had marched his army that night forward to Bannockburn where the Prince lay, it would have been impossible to have Assembled 3000 men together in any one place all night. Lord Lewis Gordon this day joined the army with 800 men as did Sir James Kinloch with 600 and Lord John Drummonds regiment 350 men, So that at this period the Prince had an army of 8000 men and all in very good Spirits. This day also the Trenches were open'd before the Castle of Sterling under the Command of Le Comte Mirabel de Gourdon[1] knight of S^t

---

[1] M. Mirabelle de Gordon had arrived from France with Lord John Drummond. Johnstone says that 'he had not the shadow

Lewis, a French Engineer.   The Duke of Perth Commanded in the Town all the time of the battle and had 1300 men with him.   On the 17 the Prince drew up his army upon the same field he had done the day before, and sent of a body of horse to see if their was any motion in General Hawleys Camp at Falkirk, and upon report that their was none, he held a councill of war upon the field wherin it was determined to march forward and fight Hawley, and the march was so order'd that Lord John Drummond should go forward upon the Straight road to Falkirk as far as the Torwood with his own Regiment, the Irish Piquets, and all the horse, in order to Cover Lord George Murrays march, who with the rest of the army went about by the south side of Dunipace and was beginning to Gain the top of the hill to the South of Falkirk, where the Battle was fought, before General Hawley [1] knew any thing of his

of judgment, discernment, or good sense; his figure being as ridiculous as his spirits—the Highlanders changed his name of Mirabelle and called him always M. Admirable' (*M. J.* 70). 'He was so volatile, that he could not be depended upon' (Lord George Murray, *J. M.* 96).   Lord Macleod in his Narrative says that M. Mirabelle was always drunk (p. 384.).

[1] General Hawley had taken up his quarters at Callander House, the seat of Lord Kilmarnock, who was serving in the Highland army.   It was said that his delay in appearing on the field of battle was due 'to the influence of the wit and gaiety of his hostess' (*T. G.* ch. lxxxi.), suggesting a comparison with the deten-

Royal 500 Price 500 Ligonier 500 Howard 500

...nro 500 Fleming 500 Barrel 500 Batterall 500

Campbells 1000

300 Blocken

300 Scotts

300 Glenurchy &

1500 Glasgow militia

+ + +

450 Perth

450 Hamilton

450 Lygones

Like

200	200	300	400	500	600

Fergusson, Cromarty, Clune, Clanronald, Glengary, Keppoch

700
Ld Ogilvy

600
Athole Brig.

a boy

Hussars

Balmerino, Elcho,

300
the Piquets
regulars

k fought on
January 1746

march. The Appearance Lord John Drummonds Corps made upon the hill at Torwood made General Hawley & his army believe the Princes whole army was marching that way, and they were only undeceived when they saw The Highlanders upon the Hill by Falkirk, and Then General Hawley order'd his Dragoons to mount and endeavour to prevent Lord George from Gaining the top of the Hill until his foot Should Come up. At the same time Lord John Drummond march'd & form'd the Third line of the Princes army. The Clans made the first, & the Lowland foot the second, and the whole army Consisted of 6000 foot and 360 horse drawn up in the Following manner as in the plan of The Battle : Generall Hawleys army Consisted of twelve battalions of foot which made about 6000 men, three regiments or six Squadrons of Dragoons 900 men, 1500 hundred Glascow & Paisly militia,* and 1000 Highlanders with Colonell Campbell, in all about 9400 † men Commanded by Lt Generall Hawley, Major General Huske, and Brigadeer Generals Cholmondely & Mordaunt. They had ten piece of Brass Cannon from six to

* under the command of the Earls of Hume & Glencairne.

† & 600 voluntiers in all about 10000 men.

tion of James IV. at Ford Castle before the battle of Flodden. For General Hawley's orders preceding the battle of Falkirk, see Appendix F.

one pound & some Coehorns.   The Prince Commanded the Corps de reserve of his army, Lord George Murray the right wing, & Lord John Drummond the left; and the Princes army had no Cannon.   Lord George Murray notwithstanding of the Dragoons appearing marched up the hill with the front of the Colums to the East: mean while General Hawleys foot was marching up on the other side of the hill with Their front to the west, & the top of the hill prevented the two armies from seeing one another.   The Dragoons made several motions towards the front of Ld Georges Colum, and by coming very near often Endeavour'd to draw of the highlanders fire but to no purpose, for they marched on untill they came to a bog, and then the whole army wheel'd to the left, which made them front the north; in marching up, the second & third line march'd too fast which made them Cover only the right wing & not all the first line as was design'd.   As the Princes army in order to gain the top of the hill march'd East and General Hawleys for the same reason west, when the two armies came to be form'd, the Princes outflanked Gen: Hawleys on the right as much as his did the Princes left, so the Princes left was opposite to Hawleys centre. The Dragoons drew up in Battle opposite to the Princes right wing, and after having made several motions to intimidate the Highlanders, at last came down in a line at a full trott & attacked them sword in hand. The highlanders march'd up to them very Slowly, with their pieces presented, every man taking his aim, and when the dragoons came within half pistol Shot of them, gave them a full discharge, which kill'd a great many of them, & broke the rest, who in their flight run down all along the Princes first line and gott the fire of the whole line, by which means their was about 400 of them kill'd. Major M^cdonald of Keppock's having taken one of their horses & mounted him, the horse run away with him after his companions, and he was the only man of the Princes army taken prisoner. It was past four when the dragoons made their attack, & just as the attack began their came on a most violent Storm of wind & rain that blew directly in their faces which did them a great deal of mischief. Most part of the highlanders as usual Threw down their Guns and advanced very quick sword in hand ; some of the right wing fell in upon the Glascow militia and beat them, but most of the right wing finding no Enemy before them and it beginning to grow dark made a Stop and went into the greatest confusion. The left wing in advancing fell in with the centre & left wing of General Hawleys, attacked them sword in hand, & beat & putt them to flight, but as Hawleys right wing Stood firm, and had given them several flank fires they were oblidged to retire back again up the hill. Had the people upon the right been led down the hill at that juncture,[1] it is not to be doubted but most of Hawleys foot in the Confusion they were in would have been cutt to pieces, especially as the Highlanders would have gott in betwixt them and Falkirk, but the badness & darkness of the weather prevented the Princes right from seeing what had past on the left, and then all the Generals & their aid de Camps were on foot, whereas they ought to have been on horseback, for Generals business in a battle is more to command Than to fight as common Soldiers. Whoever it is certain the High-

[1] Lord George in his own account says he advanced with the Atholl men towards the foot of the hill, and that he there discovered three or four regiments of the enemy still in good order: not having a sufficient force with him, he refrained from an immediate attack (*J. M.* 86). He blames Sullivan for not having brought up men from the second line to extend the Highland left, and thus prevent the overlapping and outflanking by Hawley's right (*Ibid.* 91).

landers must have Example shown them and that was the reason for it. While Hawleys right had made the Princes left retire, The right remain'd upon the top of the hill, all the Corps mixed together in Great confusion and not knowing what was become of the left or Hawleys foot, who were all at that time marching to their Camp in Great Confusion, for his right finding themselves abandoned by their left as soon as they had made the Princes left retire, for fear of The Princes right coming down upon them went of very quickly & followed Their left. A little before They went away, a Squadron of Cobhams dragoons that had rallied by them, came in the rear of the Princes army as was Supposed to seek for himself, but upon the piquets marching up to them, they went of and followed the rest of their army, who went first to their Camp which they sett fire to, & then in great Confusion went to Linlithgow; whoever a great many of them left their corps & hid themselves in the farm houses in ye neighbourhood, where they were taken prisoners by The horse next day.

The Princes army, who remained upon the hill in great disorder, some in houses, and the rest That remained all mixed together (for some of

the left upon retiring had run away to Sterling),
observing the Camp sett fire to, & hearing no
noise about it, sent in some parties to Falkirk to
gett intelligence, who brought back word that
The rear of Hawleys army was marched out of
Falkirk and that their was nobody in the Camp,
upon which Lord George Murray with what men
he could gett together marched in at one end of
Falkirk & Lord John Drummond at The other.
Ld John received a wound in the arm from a
soldier who he was going to take prisoner as he
was going out of town ; Lord George immediately dispatched a party & took possession of their
Camp & all their Baggage, but as the troops had
greatly Suffer'd by the badness of the weather it
was not possible to pursue them to Lithgow ;
whoever a body of horse was order'd to go upon
the Lithgow road to pick up Stragglers. The
Compleatness of the victory was only known to
that half of the army that was at Falkirk that
night, for the other half that took up their
quarters in the villages betwixt the field of battle
& Sterling knew nothing of the matter untill
next morning. General Hawleys army had between 500 & 600 kill'd and 600 taken prisoners
few of them upon the field. Amongst the Slain

were 30 officers. Collonells Sir Robert Monro [1]
& Ligonier [2] Lt Coll: ^{s} Whitny, Biggar, & Powel
were of the number of the dead, & their was
8 or 9 officers taken prisoners. They lost seven
piece of Cannon which were never fired, and three
Standards and some Colours, all their Camp &
Baggage, for the fire had done it little damage.
The Princes army had about fifty kill'd & Sixty
wounded, five or six officers kill'd, but none above
the rank of a Captain ; Lochyel & his brother
were Slightly wounded. Had the Princes army
been able to have followed them the same night
to Linlithgow their is no doubt he would have
destroy'd them. They halted at Linlithgow all
the 17th, and next day they went into Edn^r, where
the people were very much astonish'd to see
them return beat, as General Hawley had made
so sure of the victory as to Erect Gibbets [3] in
Edn^r in order to hang his prisoners upon, and

---

[1] 27th Baron and 6th Baronet of Foulis ; M.P. for Wick 1710–
41 ; lieut.-colonel of the Black Watch, 43rd, 1739 (*B. H.* iv. 137).

[2] François Auguste Ligonier, brother of John Lord Ligonier ;
entered the army 1720 ; present at Dettingen ; colonel of the 48th
Foot April 25, 1745 ; at Falkirk also colonel of 13th Dragoons.
He died of pleurisy a few days after the battle. On April 6, 1746,
Conway was gazetted colonel of the 48th Foot.

[3] In the Grassmarket ; a gallows remained standing till Sept.
1746, when 'it was sawed through by some persons unknown'
(*S. M.* viii. 446).

some of the hangmen he had assembled for that
purpose were taken prisoners at Falkirk, and diss-
mis'd upon their parolles of honour as it was
Supposed they would keep them as well as the
officers did, for the Prince gott news that the
Officers taken at Preston pans had broke their
parolles, were return'd back to Edinburgh &
were preparing to serve against him, which many
of them did. The prisoners taken at Falkirk
were sent to Sterling, the officers were Confined
in the town house and the Soldiers in the Church ;
sometime afterwards they were sent to Down
Castle, any of them that had any liberty granted
them upon promise not to make a bad use of it
always broke it & went off, whenever they
Could. Their were Several prysbiterian ministers
taken at the Battle, who's brethren to a man were
all much against the Prince, and never would
preach in any place where he or his people were,
suppose they had liberty given them to pray for
whichever King they pleased. The Prince halted
all the day after the battle at Falkirk. There was
an Unlucky accident happen'd that day to a son
of Glengary's. One of Clanronalds men in working with his Gun, Carlesly, which the highlanders
are too apt to do, the piece went of & Shot M^r

M^cdonald [1] dead. The fellow was order'd immediately to be Shot in order to prevent mischeif happing between the two Clans. Several of the Officers were for marching and driving General Hawley out of Edn^r, but The Prince, who was determined to make the Siege of Sterling Castle, went back on the 19 to Bannockburn, and order'd all the troops into their former quarters, the Clans to remain at Falkirk with Ld George Murray, and a party of horse at Ld Napiers house on the road to Linlithgow. The Prince upon his arrival at Bannockburn order'd the Castle of Sterling to be Summon'd to surrender, but General Blakeny who Commanded it made answere that he would defend it to the last, Upon which the Trenches which were open'd on the 16 were Carried on with all diligence. Their was about 400 men mounted the trenches once in the four & twenty hours, General Blakeny firr'd upon them almost every day but not much, and their was a great many shells thrown from Coehorns on both sides, but as they were very bad they did little mischeif. The Prince came and visitted the trenches once; provisions were very scarce during the Siege at Sterling, for

1 See *ante*, p. 245.

General Blakeny had order'd an Arche of the
Bridge to be Broke down, which prevented the
Country people on that side of the river from
coming to town. On the 28 of Jan^r Monsr de
Mirabel had so far finished a battery (on the
Gowan hill very near the Castle) as to begin to
play upon it with three Battering Cannon, on the
29 in the morning ; and the Shot he firr'd did
the walls much damage, but Generall Blakeny
firr'd against it with a Battery of nine nine
pounders, and in a few hours time dismounted
the three Guns, and demolish'd the Battery ;
Monsr de Mirabell was much blamed for the
unsufficiency of his Battery and for Beginning
to play upon the castle with only three Cannon,
when if he had waited a day longer, he might
have had seven mounted, and people did not
hesitate to Say he had been bribed. The Princes
army at this siege had 30 men kill'd and 50
wounded, which loss fell upon the Lowland foot
and French piquetts, for the highlanders are not
fitt for Sieges. The news of The Duke of
Cumberlands arrival at Edn^r on the 29 and of
his intention to march to Sterling with Hawleys
army, reinforced by the Scots fusileers, & Sempills foot and Lord Mark Ker's dragoons, putt

a Stop to all further preparations about the Siege.

The 27 of this month the *Hazard* Sloop of war (taken by Ld John Drummonds men) Sailed from Montross with Capt Brown [1] an Irish officer aboard, who the Prince sent to Versailles to Carry the news of the Victory of Falkirk. It would have been better for his Cause he had sent some of the Scots gentlemen who had taken arms for him, for as a party concerned they would have lett the Court of France know the true State of his Affairs, and perhaps have procur'd him more Assistance, as it was not that Courts interest That the war in Scotland should soon end. But those Gentlemen that he Sent, as they were in the French service they just told ye French ministers what they thought would be most agreeable to them, in order to gett what they wanted, which was preferment and pensions. Sir Thomas Sheridan the Princes old Governor was an Irishman himself, and he had Succeeded very well in making the Prince partial in favours of that

---

[1] Brown on arrival at Versailles, Feb. 3rd, was made a colonel by Louis; he informed the French Court that Charles was at the head of 17,000 to 18,000 men, and that at Falkirk only 7000 of the Highlanders took part, defeating 15,000 of the Hanoverian troops; he also stated that 2400 of the Duke of Argyll's followers had deserted to Charles (*Mémoires du Duc de Luynes*, vii. 221).

nation, so in all these Comissions to the Court of France where their was something to be Gott, The Prince always made use of the Irish. Upon intelligence from Edinburgh That the Duke of Cumberland was to march west at the head of his army and be at Linlithgow on the 31, Lord George Murray & all the Chiefs of the Clans mett and held a Councill at Falkirk and drew up a paper which they all signed and sent to the Prince,[1] the purport of which was that vast numbers of their men was gone home, and that their numbers were greatly diminish'd since the late battle, and that they were no way in a Condition to face The Dukes army. They Concluded by advising the Prince to march his army north to Inverness, to destroy Lord Loudouns army and all his Enemies in that Country, to take and demolish all the forts in the north, by which means he would be intire master of that Country, and they Assured him all that Effected, they would by next Spring putt him at the head of Eight or ten Thousand highlandmen to follow

---

[1] 'When Charles read this paper he struck his head against the wall till he staggered, and exclaimed most violently against Lord George Murray. His words were Good God! have I lived to see this?' (John Hay's Account of the Retreat from Stirling, *H. H.* 355).

him wherever he pleased. The Prince at first was Against it, but afterwards Consented to it, and he and Lord George Murray concerted that on the first of Febrewary all the army should be order'd very early in the morning to cross the Forth at the Frews, that all the heavy Cannon Should be nail'd, and all the ammunition which could not be carried along should be destroy'd, and that Ld George Should have 1200 Chosen foot and Ld Elcho's troop, with which he undertook to wait a great while after the army and to make the arriere guard and prevent the Dukes horse from following. All this Schême was so far from being putt in Execution, that on the first of Febrewary, when the troops at Sterling who knew nothing of the Concert gott orders to march by the Frews to Dumblain, every body was Struck with amazement, for Every body that did not know of the Clans representation Expected a battle, and it appeared very Strange to run away from the very army that had been beat only a fortnight before. Never was their a retreat resembled so much a flight, for their was no where 1000 men together, and the whole army pass'd the river in Small bodies and in great Confusion, leaving Carts & Cannon upon the

road behind them. Their was no Arriere Guard,
& Ld Elcho's troop who was order'd to wait at
the Bridge of Carron untill further orders was
forgott, so that at two o clock when they
left it, they had near been intercepted by a
Sally from the town and Castle of Sterling. All
the battering Cannon at Sterling were naild, and
the Amunition at St Ninians was destroy'd. In
Blowing up the Gun powder, as it was near the
Church they by Accident blew up the Church.
Lord George blamed the Prince for this retreat,[1]
and he was so far blamable, that very often
orders that had been Agree'd upon betwixt him
& Ld George were changed afterwards by him
& his favourites, Sir Thomas, Mrs Murray &
Hay, for Since the resolution he took at Derby
to call no Councills he never advised with or
consulted any body but these Gentlemen, which
the people of fashion of his army took very
much Amiss, and undoubtedly in their Situation,

---

[1] Lord George says that it had been agreed overnight that
Stirling was to be evacuated the following morning, but after he
had retired to his quarters orders were issued that the army was
to march at break of day. 'I never got so much as a message nor
knew nothing of any change. . . . There was a council of war
called near Crieff next day. I complained much of the flight, and
entreated we should know who advised it. The Prince did not
incline to lay the blame on anybody, but said he took it on himself'
(*J. M.* 100).

fighting for their all without gain, they ought not to have been treated like mercinaries as the Prince affected to do, so that this flight over the Frews when without danger they might have gone Slowly and in order, or any other wrong Step that was taken could never be laid to the Charge of the principal officers of the Princes arms, as the orders always came from his quarters and he never Consulted any of them. He lay that night at Drummond Castle & next night at Fairnton: [1] his Army was the first night at Dumblain, & the environs, and next day half at Creif, & half at Perth. The Duke of Cumberlands advanced Guard came on the first to Sterling, where they made some prisoners, and gott all their sick & wounded taken at Falkirk. The Duke halted all that day at Falkirk & next day came to Sterling. Their was a resolution taken at Fairnton that the Prince with all the highlanders should march to Inverness by Wades road, and that all the French, the Lowlanders, and the horse Should march north by the Coast road under the command of Ld George Murray. The Prince march'd from Creif to Castle Menzies & then to Blair. Lord George Murray Assembled his Colum of the

[1] Now Fern Tower, seat of Lord Abercromby.

army the 3^d at Perth; he nail'd all the heavy Cannon that was at Perth, and sent the field pieces to the Prince at Blair. He order'd Lord Ogilvy with his regiment into the Braes of Angus to raise men & join the army by the hills in the north; he sent of Lord Pitsligo with his troop to Peterhead to Secure 4000^{pds} & 2500 stand of arms which a Spanish Ship had landed for the Princes use at that place; he dispatch'd Lord Elcho with the rest of the horse to nail up the Cannon & march of the Garison of Montross for Aberdeen, where he himself arrived with the rest of his Colum on the 8th. The Duke of Cumberland arrived at Perth the 6th, and sent of Sir Andrew Agnew[1] with 500 men & 120 Campbells to take possession of Blair Castle, & Lt Collonel Leighton with 500 men to Castle Menzies. Admiral Byng Landed some men from his fleet the 9th & took possession of Montross. All the Princes friends in the South were greatly dejected at this retreat, but he endeavour'd to keep up their Spirits by telling them he would be back amongst them in the Spring at the head of a much greater Army.

[1] Sir Andrew Agnew of Lochnaw, 5th bart. (b. 1687, d. 1771); lieut.-colonel Royal Scots Fusiliers (21st); fought in Flanders under Marlborough; distinguished at Dettingen; colonel of Marines 1746; Lieut.-General 1759.

On the 8 day of this month The Prince Frederic of Hesse Cassel arrived at Leith from Holland with 5000 foot and 60 Hussars; the Earl of Crawford[1] was along with them. They came to replace the Dutch who were sent home because they could not fight against the Prince as their were French Colours in his army. The Prince Landed that night and took up his Lodgings in Holyroodhouse, and in three or four days after the troops landed and were quarter'd at Edn^r & in the neighbourhood. The Duke of Cumberland came from Perth and Staid one night with the Prince his Brother in law. Much about the same time Kingstons horse, St Georges Dragoons, and Johnstons foot came to Scotland; Kingstons horse join'd the Duke, St Georges Dragoons remained with Prince Frederick, and Johnstons foot were order'd to Glascow. The Prince march'd from Blair to Dalnacardock and to Dalwhiny and so to Ruthven of Badenoch, where he took & demolish'd the Barracks. The Officer who commanded them had refused to Surrender to the Prince upon his first passing Ruthven because he

[1] John Lindsay, 20th Earl of Crawford (b. 1702, d. 1749); entered the army 1720; Scots representative peer 1733; served in the Russian army 1738; colonel of the 43rd (Black Watch) 1739; colonel Scots troop, Horse Guards, 1743; Adjutant-General at Dettingen; Brigadier-General at Fontenoy.

had no Cannon in his army, and at the taking of
them he obtain'd terms. From Ruthven the
Prince march'd to Moy Castle, the house of the
Laird of Mackintosh. The Laird was a Captain
in Lord Loudouns Regiment but his Lady was
at home, and so much attached to the Princes
Cause that she raised all her husbands Clan for
his service. The Prince Loged in the Castle
and about three hundred men with him, the rest
of his men were Scatterer'd about the Country
at one or two miles distance in order to gett
quarters. The Earl of Loudoun who Commanded about 2000 Highlanders for the Goverment was at Inverness, which place he had fortified
with a ditch and pallisadoes at all the avenues.
Hearing that The Prince was at Moy Castle
(which is only eight miles from Inverness) with
so few men with him, he form'd a Scheme to take
him prisoner, and on the 16 at night, he march'd
at the head of his men out of town for Moy
Castle. A blaksmith and a few men of Lady
Mackintoshes, patroilling upon the road to
Inverness, fell in with Lord Loudouns advanced
guard about three miles from The Castle, and
after Several shots had passed, the Blacksmith, in
order to make them believe The Princes whole

body of men was there, Cryed out to all The
Highland Chiefs by name to advance, for their
was their Enemy; the Blaksmiths invention had
the desired effect, for a Panick Struck Lord
Loudouns army and they return'd in Confusion to
Inverness. The Prince who had been alarm'd, Gott
up out of bed, and Assembled his men and pursued Lord Loudoun to Inverness, but Lord Loudoun abandoned the town, and Embarked all his
men on board of the Boats at the Ferry, and
pass'd into Rosshire ; as he Carried all the Boats
with him their was no following him that way, so
after Cannonading his rear as they pass'd, the
Prince order'd a detachment to go about by the
head of the Ferry Commanded by the Earl of
Cromarty. Lord Cromarty march'd after them
to Cromarty, and oblidged them to pass the Ferry
there, and sometime afterwards he pursued them
to Tain, where Lord Loudoun Cross'd the Great
Ferry into Sutherlandshire and Carried all the
boats with him.

The Prince the night of Lord Loudons retreat
lay at Culloden Castle, but his Army took possession of Inverness,[1] and that day the Fort St George

1 'He (Charles) had three things principally in view: to
reduce Fort Augustus and Fort William on one side; on the
other, to disperse Lord Loudon's army; and to keep possession, as

was besieged under the Direction of Mr Grant
Colonel of Artilery ; Fort St George was Commanded by Major Grant, and there was about 200
men in it and sixteen piece of Cannon.   Colonel
Grant, finding (after having erected his battery)
that his Cannon were two small to do the walls
of the fort any harm, begun a mine under one of
the Bastions with a designe to blow it up.   The
mine was not far advanced when Major Grant
desired to Capitolate, and the Capitulation was,
that he should surrender the Castle, the men and
Every thing in it, at discretion, which he agreed
to, on the 20 of febrewary ; and the Prince order'd
the works of The fort to be demolish'd and Came
himself and loged in town.   There was two or
three men kill'd on each side in this affair.   Lord
George Murray after Leaving 50 Hussars[1] at
Stonehive and 300 men with Mr More of Stoneywood at Aberdeen march'd from thence in a prodigious Storm of Snow, and Lay the 11 at Inverury,
with the foot ; the horse Commanded by The

much as possible, of the coast towards Aberdeen ' (*M. K.* 118),
and at the same time prevent a junction between Lord Loudon and
the Duke of Cumberland.

    [1] 'Under one Colonel Baggot, a French officer, and a very
rough sort of man and so exceeding well fitted to command the
Banditti of which that Corps was composed ' (MS. in the possession
of Mr. Blaikie).

Viscount of Strathallan lay at old Meldrum. Upon Lord Georges Leaving Aberdeen the Duke of Cumberland sent three regiments of foot and one of Dragoons into Angus. Lord George march'd from Inverury to Strathbogie and Keith, and Lord Strathallan to Bamff and Cullen, and both Corps join'd the 17 at Gordon Castle. Lord Strathallan was order'd with his Squadron to remain at Cullen, and Ld George with the rest of the army pass'd the Spey and march'd to Elgin. Next Day Lord Ogilvy join'd the army with 600 men, Gordon of Abuchie with 300, and Sir Alexander Bannerman with 150; at the end of this Long march Lord Kilmarnock, Lord Pitsligo, and Lord Balmerino's Troops went to nothing, the length of The march had destroyed all Their horses. The Prince made Lord Pitsligo Governor of Elgin, and he gave the Earl of Kilmarnock a Comission to raise a Regiment of foot Guards out of the dismounted horsemen. The 19 Lord George march'd from Elgin with the Athole Brigade and Lord Elcho's troop to Forress; Lord Elcho's troop remain'd about Forress, and Lord George march'd to Nairn.[1] The Prince after the taking of Fort George re-

[1] Lord George rejoined Charles at Culloden the same day (*J. M.* 103).

main'd at Inverness with only the Duke of Perths
Regiment. For the Earl of Cromarty had with
him at Tain, his own Regiment, Glengary's, Clanronalds, Appins, Barrasdales, and the Macgregors ;
The Mackintoshses, and the Macphersons were
left in their own Country to recruit, and Lochyel
and Keppoch had march'd away to Blocade Fort
William. The Frazers were likewise at home,
and Brigadeer Stapleton[1] had march'd with Lord
John Drummonds regiment and the Irish Piquets,
to besiege Fort Augustus, which he took about
the 1 of March. Major Wentworth who Commanded with three Companies of Guises, were
made prisoners at Discretion ; the Princes Cannon
did not do much mischief as they were small, but
by means of Coehorns, Mr Grant blew up the
magazin and destroy'd all the roofs of the
quarters. The Prince intended to Send over all
his prisoners to France by way of hostages for
his people, but before the Battle of Colloden,
They all Except the Master of Ross made their
Escape from Nairne and went to the Dukes Army.
The Prince lost about three men kill'd at the

---

[1] Walter Stapleton, lieut.-colonel in the French regiment of
Berwick ; died of wounds received at Culloden. Maxwell says
Fort Augustus fell March 5th (*M. K.* 119), but cf. *S. M.* viii. 139,
which agrees with Elcho.

Siege of Fort Augustus and they as many.
From fort Augustus he order'd Brigadeer
Stapleton to march and invest Fort William,
which place General Campbell (who Commanded a body of Highlanders in Argylshire)
had taken care to provide with every thing
necessary for a Siege, and besides the regular
troops that were in it, he had order'd in some
Companies of Campbles, so that the garison
consisted of 600 men under the Command of
Cap[t] Campbell.

On the 23 of Febrewary the Prince, who was
at Inverness, received a letter from Captain
Shee[1] of the Duke of Fitzjames's[2] regiment
of horse, wherin he told him, that he had
Sail'd from Ostend with an Embarkation of
troops Commanded by the Marquis de Fimarcon,
that the Embarkation consisted of four Squadrons
of Fitzjames's horse 600 men, one of which
he had landed at Aberdeen with all their arms
and horse furniture ; that the Comte de Fitzjames, the Comte de Tyrconnel, Messieurs
Rooth, Cook, & Nugent, all General officers,

---

[1] Captain Robert Shee of Fitzjames's Horse, stated to have been
taken prisoner at Culloden (*S. M.* viii. 189); but see *ante*, p. 205.

[2] Charles, Duke of Fitzjames (b. 1712, d. 1787), son of Marshal
Berwick, the natural son of James II.

were along with the other three Squadrons ; that
The Duke of Fitzjames, and Lord Durkell,
were with Mons[r] de Fimarcon, and that he
had with him Lord Clares regiment, and five
piquets out of the other five Irish regiments,
in all about 800 foot ; and that in all the Ships
their was money. At the Same time a Ship
came of Peterhead and landed 2000 Lewis d'ors,
but refused to Land her men without an order
from Le Marquis D'Equilles ; upon which the
Prince Sent of the Marquis with Lord John
Drummond ; whom he order'd to Assemble all
the troops that were quarter'd to the East of
Inverness, and march to Aberdeen, in order to
facilitate the landing of the French. But upon
Lord Johns arriving at Fochabers, he mett Cap[t]
Shee and Stoneywood, who had been obliged to
quite Aberdeen ; for the Duke of Cumberland,
upon the news of The french landing, had putt
his army in motion from Perth, and they all
arrived at Aberdeen about the 27 of Febrewary.
The Marquis D'Equilles dispatched of Boats with
instructions for the French Ships they mett with,
to Sail up the Moray Firth, and Land at Findorn,
but many of the Boats were taken by the men of
war on the Coast, and the rest mett with none of

them, for of this Embarkation[1] their never landed but Capt Shee's Squadron, and one piquet of Berwicks regiment Commanded by Capt de la Hyde at Portsoy. The other three Squadrons of Fitzjames's horse were taken by Comodore Knowles and Carried to the river Thames, and the Marquis de Fimarçon, who Came so near the Coast of Scotland as to send a boat ashoar, imagining by some false intelligence he gott that the Duke of Cumberland was in possession of all the towns on the Coast, he held a Councill of War aboard, wherin it was determined to Sail back to France, which they accordingly did.

Lord John Drummond drew up all the troops under his command at Fochabers and order'd Elcho's & Fitzjames's horse to Elgin, along-with Kilmarnocks, Glenbucketts, and Bannermans foot. Lord Ogilvy's foot and Lord Strathallans horse were sent to Cullen, Roy Stuarts and Abuchies foot to Keith, and the Hussars to Strathbogie. The Athole Brigade under Lord Nairne

---

[1] The total number of French troops in Scotland at this time was 780, made up as follows:—

> Royal Scots, 350.
> Berwick's Regiment, 42.
> Fitzjames's Horse, 131.
> Irish Picquets, 260.
> (*Correspondance du Marquis d'Eguilles*, 36.)

was sent to Strathspey to prevent the Grants from taking arms for the Goverment; Lord John himself remain'd at Fochabers with Berwicks piquet, Stoneywoods, and 100 Chisholms of Strathglass who had lately joined the Princes Standard. On the 4 of March the Prince left Inverness and lay at Forress, and next day he Came to Elgin, where he fell ill of a fever and was Sick ten days. All the Irish officers lately Landed gott Superior Commissions from him, and he mounted 70 of Fitz-James' on horseback. He gave out at Elgin that he had received letters from France that the French were Equiping a Squadron of men of war at Brest & Rochefort in order to Send over his Brother the Duke of Yorck. It was necessary to give out such pieces of news in order to keep up his mens Spirits, for as he had but little money he now had begun to pay them in meal, which displeas'd them so much that they sometimes threatned to leave him and often disobey'd orders. He order'd impositions to be Lay'd on upon all the Parishes in the Counties he was master of, by which means great quantities of all kind of Victual was gott together & Lay'd up in magazins at Nairne, Inverness, & Fort Augustus. The Prince went from Elgin to Gordon Castle, where he dispatched

Colonel Roy Stuart with 500 foot, 30 of Ld Elcho's troop, and 20 Hussars to take possession of Strathbogie ; part of the Dukes army was at Old Meldrum and Inverury. He order'd Colonel Stuart to remain at Strathbogie untill he Should be forced away ; he order'd likewise barracks to be built upon the north side of the Spey with an intention to defend the river in Case the Duke should attempt to pass it before he took Fort William, destroyed Lord Loudoun, and assembled his army, which at this time extended from the East sea to the West, and from Dalnacardoch to Tain, but as the River was not deep it would not have been easily defended, except by an Equal force. From Elgin the Prince return'd to Inverness, where he gott the news of a Spanish Ships being landed at the Isle of Barra with 4000^{pds} and 2500 Stand of arms, for his use. He sent of Mr Æneas Macdonald of Kinlock Moidart to take care of it. The Duke of Cumberland, who had his head quarters at Aberdeen since the end of Febreary, had sent out several parties to ye braes of Mar and Angus to Search for arms and threaten the inhabitants if they were not quiet. About The first of March he sent orders to Prince Frederick of Hesse Cassel to march the Hessians

by Sterling to Perth and Creif, and the Earl of
Crawford, who Commanded S[t] George's, Naizons,[1]
& Hamiltons Dragoons, march'd along with them.
The Prince of Hesse had his head quarters at
Perth. By the 10th of March, a body of Hesseians
were at Creif & the Dragoons were quarter'd
about the Bridge of Erne. On the 12 of march
the Duke had order'd Major General Bland[2] to
take possession of Old Meldrum & Inverury
with six Battalions, two Squadrons of Horse, and
two of Dragoons, and six Hundred Campbells.
Before this march there was only small parties in
these places. On the 17th General Bland and the
Earl of Albemarle[3] received orders to march and
endeavour to Surprise Colonel John Roy Steuart
at Strathbogie, and Brigadeer Mordaunt march'd

---

[1] Philip Naison succeeded Ligonier as colonel of the 13th
Dragoons.

[2] Humphrey Bland (b. 1686 (?), d. 1763), entered the army
1704 ; served under Marlborough ; Quartermaster-General at headquarters 1742 ; Governor of Gibraltar 1749 ; Commander of the
Forces in Scotland 1753.

[3] William Anne Keppel, 2nd Earl of Albemarle (b. 1702,
d. 1754), gazetted to the Coldstream Guards 1717 ; present at
Dettingen and Fontenoy; in 1746 summoned from Flanders to join
Cumberland in Scotland ; commanded the first line at Culloden;
succeeded Cumberland as Commander-in-chief in Scotland Aug. 23,
1746; sailed for Flanders March 1747; Minister Plenipotentiary
in Paris 1748, and again in 1754. 'Milord Albemarle, lieutenant-
général a tout l'extérieure d'un François et me parait d'avoir
tout l'intérieur d'un Anglais' (*Correspondance du Marquis d'Eguilles*,
61).

from Aberdeen to Old Meldrum to Sustain them. Colonel Steuart had news of their march, drew up his men and waited their arrival, and when they were close by the town, he begun his retreat, the foot in the front and the few horse in the rear. Major General Bland dispatch'd the horse and Dragoons after him, but the retreat was made in such good order, that The Dragoons durst not attack him, and only fired their Carabines at a distance ; he arrived that night at Keith and next day pass'd the Spey without the loss of a man. The 19 Lord John Drummond order'd all the troops to pass the Spey, and they were quarter'd mostly in hutts built on purpose, from Rothes quite to the mouth of the river, on the north side, and guards placed all along it.

On the 20th in the Evening their came a reconnoitring party of 70 foot and 30 horse to the top of the hill above Gordon Castle, and after having taken a view of the river they return'd to Keith and placed their Guard in the Church and barricaded the Churchyard ; Lord John having notice of it order'd Major Glascow[1] with 150 of L[d]

[1] Major Nicolas Glascoe ; taken prisoner at Culloden ; at his trial at Southwark Hill it was proved that he was a native of France and a lieutenant in Dillon's regiment ; he was detained as a prisoner of war. He had raised the battery at Montrose and captured the *Hazard* sloop, Nov. 1745 (*S. M.* viii. 527-529).

Ogilvys men, 20 of Ld Elcho's troop, & 30 hussars to march and attack them. The Detachment arrived at Keith at one o clock of the morning, and after taking possession of all the avenues leading to the town, they attacked the Churchyard, and the Campbells defended it for about half an hour, in which time their was six or seven men kill'd * on both Sides. After making everybody prisoners in the Church, all those that were in town were taken except one or two who Escaped to Strathbogie, where ever after this Surprise they were very alert and very often kept the troops under arms all night. Major Glascow return'd next day to Spey side with his prisoners;[1] they were putt in prison at Forress and very ill used as They had plunder'd several gentlemens houses in Bamff and Aberdeenshire who were in the Princes army. They were afterwards putt aboard of a Ship at Findorn and sent to France, where they were Confined at Lisle, but this Schême of sending hostages to France was begun too late. After the Surprise at Keith their never was any troops of either side pass'd the night there,

* Capt Campbell of the Dukes army was kill'd at Keith.

[1] 'In this action there were 9 of Cumberland's men killed, a good number wounded, about 80 taken prisoners and betuixt 20 or 30 horses, which Major Glasgow with his partie delivered at Spey a little before Sun rising ' (L. M. ii. 217).

but every day their was parties of horse from
Strathbogie & Speyside sent to Keith, and they
Generaly mett on different sides of the river at
Keith, & fired Guns and pistols across the river
at one another, but neither party ever Cross'd the
river. About this time a party was sent to
plunder the Earl of Findlaters at Cullen because
he refused to pay Contribution to the Prince.
About the 14 of March Lord George Murray
went into Strathspey where the Athole Brigade
was quarter'd and putt himself at their head,
and march'd away to Athole. In his road he was
joined by some Macphersons and Mackintoshes,
so that he had along with him about 800 men.
Sir Andrew Agnew commanded in Blair castle
where he had 500 men ; besides there were 200
Argylshire men quarter'd at Blairfitty, Kinachin,
Lude, and a place or two more near Blair. On the
morning early of the 17th, Lord George so Contrived it that just as he himself appeared near
Blair all those parties were attacked and Surprised
at the same time ; their were about ten or twelve
kill'd and all the rest taken prisoners. Lord
George seized several Copies of their orders from
the Duke of Cumberland and signed by their
Colonel Campbell, in which they were order'd

to attack the rebells and disarm them wherever they mett them, and in Case they made any resistance, it was his Royal Highness the Dukes orders they should gett no quarter.[1] On the 18 Lord George begun to fire against the Castell with two four pounders, and as he had a furnace along with him, finding his Bulletts were too small to damage the walls, he endeavour'd by firing red hott balls to sett the house on fire, and severall times sett the roof on fire, but by the care of the Besieged it was always Extinguished. Their was a Constant fire of small arms kept against the windows, and the besieged kept a Close fire from the Castell with their Small arms. As the Castell is Situated upon a rocky ground their was no blowing it up, so the only chance Ld George had to gett possession of it was to Starve it, which he had some hopes of, as their was so many mouths in it; but on the 24 of March the Hessians from Perth and Creif moved to its relief. They encamped the first night at Nairn house, and next day at Dunkeld, and their was some firing betwixt them and a party

[1] On this raid Lord George captured 300 prisoners without the loss of a man on his own side (*J. M.* 107). He makes no mention of any orders of Cumberland's refusing quarter. At Wemyss Castle, however, there is such a document, dated Nairn House, Feb. 20th, signed F. C.

of Ld Georges at Dunkeld across the river.
Those that marched from Crief encamp'd at Tay
Bridge on the 27. Upon this motion of the
Hessians Ld George sent an express to the Prince
to tell him that if he would send him 1200 men
he would pitch upon an advantageous ground and
fight them ; the Prince sent him word he Could
not send him them in the way his army was then
situated. On the 31 The Earl of Crawford
marched with St Georges Dragoons, 500 Hessians
and 60 Hussars and encamped at Dowallie four
miles north of Dunkeld, and next day they
advanced to Pitlochrie. Both these days Lord
George had several schirmishes with the Hussars,
but Suppose he laid several snares for them he
never could catch but one of them, who was an
officer and a Swede, who had had his horse Shott
under him. Ld George used him very civilly, and
sent him back with a letter of Compliment he
wrote to The Prince of Hesse. On the 1 of april
Lord George Murray drew his men up in Battle
opposite to Lord Crawford at Pitlochrie, and
then retreated before him, in order to draw him
into the Pass of Killicrankie, but Ld Crawford
never moved, but sent for reinforcements to
The Prince of Hesse. Lord George upon

hearing of the march of that reinforcement, to sustain Lord Crawford, and that The body of Hessians from Tay Bridge were marching to Blair by Kinachin, he quite the Country and marched his men into Strathspey and from thence to Spey side. He himself went to Inverness, where he found his Enemies had persuaded the Prince that he might have taken Blair Castell, if he had had a mind, but that he had spared it because it was his brothers house, and in Short they made the Prince Believe that in the letter [1] he had wrote to the Prince of Hesse he had engaged to betray him the first opportunity, and that by the Prince of Hesse and his brothers means he was intirely reconciled with the goverment. What Mr Murray had insinuated to the Prince against Lord George at his first Coming to Perth had made such an impression that the Prince always believed it, notswithstanding that Lord Georges behaviour was such (Especialy in action) as to Convince the whole army of the falsity of such accusations. Whoever the Prince open'd his mind upon the matter to the Irish French [2] Officers, so far as to

[1] The enemies of Lord George insinuated to Charles that this letter was written with a treasonable design. See *ante*, p. 91 ; also Appendix A.

[2] Writing from Inverness before Lord George's return, D'Éguilles tells D'Argenson that he fears it is Lord George's intention to betray

make some of them promise to watch Lord George's motions particularly in case of a Battle, and they promised the Prince to Shoot him,[1] if they could find he intended to Betray him. Upon Lord Georges leaving Athole, Prince Frederick of Hesse marched to Blair Castell with a large body of troops, where he remain'd a few days, and then march'd back the Hessians to Perth. Much about this time Lees regiment came to Edinburgh; five Battalions more were order'd to Scotland, viz. Houghtons, Handasydes, Richbells, Skeltons, & Mordaunts, but they did not arrive untill after the battle of Culloden. The Earl of Loudoun since his retreat from Tain across the muckle Ferry had remain'd in Sutherlandshire and had thrown up entrenchments at the head of the Ferry to prevent the Princes troops from going about that way, & as he had carried all the boats along with him, he thought himself pretty safe from an attack. But The Duke of Perth, who commanded a body of 1500 men at Tain, in a thick fog had gott to-

Charles. 'The Prince shares my fears on this point,' he adds, 'and will take precautions' (*Correspondance*, 27); see *ante*, p. 90. D'Éguilles continued to harbour his unjust suspicions, for in December 1749 D'Argenson notes that D'Eguilles had told him that Charles had been betrayed by Lord George at Derby (D'Argenson, *Journal et Mémoires*, vi. 112).

[1] See *ante*, p. 90.

gether a quantity of Boats from the Murray and
Nairne Coast, and on the 20th of March in the
morning in two Embarkations he pass'd the ferry,
and upon his passing, seeing a body of men with
drums and Colours retreat from the ferry to
Dornock, he thinking it was Lord Loudoun
pursued them and came up with them near
Dornock, and made them prisoners. It happen'd
to be Major Mackenzie, Capt Sutherland of Fors,
and the Laird of Mackintosh with only 100 men ;
Lord Loudoun who was quarter'd with the rest
of his army a little above where the Duke Landed,
and who might Likewise have been Surprised with
The President Duncan Forbes, and the Laird of
Macleod, profited of the Dukes mistake, and
marched away up the Ferry, towards Lochbryn.
The Duke sent to pursue him, but he afterwards
gott safe to the Isle of Sky with about 900 men.
The Duke of Perth seized two Ships at Dornock
Loaded with things belonging to the Earl of
Loudouns army, but they had found means to
send the military Chest aboard of a man of war in
the road. The Earl of Sutherland saild from the
Country at this time to Aberdeen and carried with
him all the publick money of the County ; these
disappointments of money was a great loss at this

time to the Prince, as his army Stood greatly in
need of it. The Duke of Perth march'd back to
Inverness with Glengarry's, Clanronalds, and Ardsheils regiments, and the Earl of Cromartie
remain'd at Dunrobin Castle with his own regiment, Barasdales, & the Macgregors ; he sent his
son Lord Macleod into Caithness, and parties into
the Orkneys, to raise the publick money, and
it was supposed a great many of the Caithness
gentlemen would join the Prince, as Several of
them had held a Correspondence with his Secretary. Clanronalds & Ardsheils regiments upon
their arrival at Inverness were order'd to Speyside.
The Prince Upon this Success sent one Mr Warren [1]
to France with the news of it ; this Gentleman had
so much witt upon his arrival at Versailles as to
make so much of this Affair, and to give the
Ministers so favorable accounts of the Princes
situation as to gett a pension of 1200 Livres a
year, and from a Leuitenant in the Irish Brigade
to be made a Colonel. About the 25 of March
the *Hazard* Sloop of war, now Call'd the *Prince*

---

[1] Captain in the regiment of Clare ; on his arrival in France,
Louis bestowed on him the rank of colonel and the order of St.
Louis (*Stuart Papers: B. H.* iii. 459). In Sept. 1746 he returned
to the west coast of Scotland with two French ships, on one of
which, *L'Heureux,* Charles escaped to France.

Charles, was after a long running fight drove ashoar in Tongue bay by the *Sheerness*[1] man of war. The people on board of her, which consisted of some Spanish and French officers, fifty soldiers and the rest Sailors, in all about 120, with 13000 Lewis d'ors, landed, and intended to Endeavour to gett to Inverness, but they were attacked by Lord Rea's men, and after an engagement, where they had six or seven men kill'd and as many wounded, they surrender'd themselves prisoners, and were carried first to Tongue, Lord Reas house, and then putt aboard of the *Sheerness* and carried to Berwick. This was a great loss to the Prince as he was in Great distress for want of money ;[2] he order'd Lord Cromarty to march and destroy Lord Reas Country, but future incidents hinder'd that Schême from being undertaken. About the end of Febrewary Lochyel and Keppoch with their regiments invested Fort William, but as the *Serpent* and *Baltimore* Sloops of war were at that place they

---

[1] The *Sheerness* 'fired between 8 and 900 shot, beside double shot and cartridge' during the engagement (*S. M.* viii. 183). The names of the prisoners and the details of the capture are given *S. M.* viii. 139.

[2] It was at this time that Sir Robert Strange was commissioned to design and issue Jacobite bank notes (Denistoun, *Memoirs of Sir Robert Strange*, i. 51).

never could cutt of the comunication by sea; they had several skirmishes with the Sloops crews and took one of the *Baltimores* boats. On the 20th of March Brigadeer Stapleton open'd the Siege by discharging 18 small mortars, but as the battery was 800 yards off they fell Short of the fort. The 21 their was a new battery erected about 400 yards nearer at the foot of the Cow hill, and a great many Shells thrown from it, which did some damage to the roofs of the Buildings. On the 22 the Battery of small mortars was advanced 100 yards nearer the fort, and the same day Colonel Grant Erected a battery on Sugar loaf hill for three pieces of Cannon betwixt four and Six pounders. The 23 their was another battery of Cannon erected at the foot of the Cow hill; all the 24, 25, 26 their was a continual fire both from and Against the fort. The greatest damage done to the fort was by the Shells and red hott balls and pieces of Iron which Stuck in the roofs of the houses with a designe to Sett them on fire; the Besieged damaged a good deal the batteries. The 27 a new battery of four six pounders was erected on a high Ground 200 yards from the fort and a Continual fire

kept all day on both sides both of Cannon &
mortars, and the besiegers had one Cannon
dismounted. The 28 Colonel Grant, finding
his Cannon could make no breach in the walls,
Erected a new battery of three four pounders on
a very high ground Call'd the Craigs at 100
yards distance from the fort. As this Battery
swept the whole parade, Brigadeer Stapletons
Schême was, by firing partridge shott, to destroy
their men and make them Surrender that way.
All the 29 and 30th the firing continued very
briskly on both sides. On the 31 Captain Caroline Scott, at the head of 150 men, Sallied out
from the fort and attacked the works at the
craigs, beat the men of from it with the loss
of two or three men on both sides and took the
three Cannon and Carried them with him after
demolishing the Battery; their was another attack
made at the same time upon another of the Bat-
tarys by the same number of men as Capt Scott
had with him, but they were repulsed with the
loss of five kill'd. All the 1 & 2 of April the
firing Continued as usuall, but the 3d Brigadeer
Staplleton finding he Could not take it with the
Cannon he had, and likewise that all provisions
and amunition was most done, he Spiked up 5

Cannon and 9 Coehorns, raised the Siege,[1] and marched to Inverness. The Besieged had about thirty men killed and wounded, and the Besiegers about as many ; the Sloops of War Landed their men and burnt all the houses and villages about the Country. Much about the same time that The Prince received the news of the raising of the siege of Fort William, Two Gentlemen, M[rs] Haliburton and O Neal,[2] arrived from France ; they Brought news that The French had laid aside all thoughts of Sending any men over either to England or Scotland, and that the Duke of Yorck was at Paris. The Prince used always before this to talk of his landing daily in England, and after this he gave out that the Squadrons the French were fitting out at Brest and Rochfort was for England, but they sometime after the battle of Culloden Sailed for Cape Breton. M[r] Haliburton told him that Brigadeer Lesly was at Gottenburgh in Sweden, with 300

---

[1] The military situation immediately before the raising of the siege of Fort William is thus summarised by Maxwell : 'Brigadier Stapleton was carrying on the siege of Fort William, Lord George Murray that of Blair Castle, Lord John Drummond was making head against Major-General Bland, the Duke of Perth was in pursuit of Lord Loudon, and the Prince, as it were, in the centre, whence he directed all these operations' (*M. K.* 130).

[2] An Irish officer in French service ; he attended Charles in his wanderings after Culloden, and left a narrative.

Swedish Officers, that the French had given Commissions to, that each of them had a Servant, and
that by an Agreement betwixt the French and
Swedish Ministers they were to Sail for Scotland
and join the Princes Army, but the Battle of
Culloden prevented that Scheme from taking
Effect. The Prince Since his return from Elgin
had remain'd close at Inverness, Except one day
that he went to Braan Castle to pay a visitt to
Lady Seaforth; he very often went a Shooting,
and sometimes gave bals at night where he danced[1]
himself, and Endeavour'd to keep up the peoples
Spirits that aproach'd him by despising his
Enemy, and Assuring that the Duke of Cumberlands soldiers would be so conscious of the
highness of the crime of fighting against their
true & Lawfull Prince, that whenever he appear'd
they would certainly run away. Suppose he
himself believed this firmly, he had difficulty in
persauding other people of these notions who were
any ways acquainted with the English Soldiers.
Their was great discontent in his Army at this
time both amongst the Officers and Soldiers. As

---

[1] 'He (Charles) appeared gayer even than usual; he gave
frequent balls to the ladies of Inverness, and danced himself, which
he had declined doing at Edinburgh in the midst of his grandeur
and prosperity' (M. K. 136).

money was very Scarce with him, he paid his
troops mostly in meal, which they did not like
and very often mutiny'd, refused to obey
orders, and Sometimes threw down their
arms and went home; and it would have
been impossible for him ever to have march'd
the face of an Army over Spey without money,
for people that would willingly have given a days
fighting near Inverness, would never have march'd
out of the Country with him without pay. What
displeased the people of fashion was that he did
not Seem to have the least Sense of what they
had done for him, but on the contrary would
often Say that they had done nothing but their
duty as his fathers Subjects were bound to do ;
then as he had his head full of the notions of
Commanding his army as if they had been mercinaries and had their fortunes depending upon
his will and pleasure, he never Consulted with
any of them or lett them know in the least any
of his Schêmes, but managed all his Affairs in
a hidden way with his favourites Sir Thomas
Sheridan, M^rs OSullivan, Murray, and Hay, but
particularly Mr Hay, who governed him entirely ;
and it was so far a great loss to him, that Suppose
every body looked upon Mr Hay as a very honest

man, yett he was Generally Esteem'd a man
of neither parts nor Capacity, and as men of
that kind are apt to Change their Behaviour
with their fortune, he was reckoned to Carry it
too high to his Superiors, which created him
a great many Enemies. M[r] Murray, who knew
very well that the Prince was always to be in
the hands of Somebody, and who had govern'd
him a long time himself, introduced M[r] Hay
about the Prince in order to keep out other
people who he was more Afraid of, so that
the Prince had either the one or the other constantly with him, but M[r] Murray [1] happening to
fall Sick, M[r] Hay Gott the Prince intirely to
himself, which M[r] Murray Complained much of
Afterwards.   Another thing the Officers took
much amiss was the preference the Prince gave
the Irish to the Scots, which he did upon all
occasions; his reasons for that were they were
of his own religion, and paid always more Court
to him in their discourse.   As they had nothing
at Stake and were only there to Gain his favour
and protection, whatever he proposed they were
for ; whereas as many of his Schêmes were very

---

[1] John Murray became ill during Charles's residence at Elgin,
March 11-20, and was succeeded in the secretaryship by Hay.
Murray never saw Charles again.

ill formed & as the Scots had their lives &
fortunes depending, they Somtimes took the
liberty of representing against them, which the
Prince took highneously amiss. And then their
was people about him that profited of his dis-
pleasure, to represent The Scots to him as a
mutinous people, and that it was not so much
for him they were fighting as for themselves, and
repeated to him all their bad Behaviour to King
Charles the first, and Second, and putt it into
the worst lights to him, which wrought upon
him So far, that at the Battle of Culloden he
thought all the Scots in generall were a parcell
of Traitors, and he would always have Continued
in the Same way of thinking if he had immediately gott out of the Country, but the care they
took of his person while he was hiding made him
Change his mind and fix treason only to particulars. His having sent three Irish Gentlemen
to France to Carry the news of His Success
against Generals Cope and Hawley and Lord
Loudoun was likewise taken much Amiss ; for
these Gentlemen, as all they wanted was to gett
Something, told the Ministers just what they
thought would please them, by which means the
true State of his Affairs and Situation was never

known at Versailles. All these prejudices in favours of Passive obedience, Absolute monarchy, the Roman Catholick Religion, and Consequently the Irish who professed it, had been Strongly inculkated into the Princes head by Sir Thomas Sheridan, who was infinitely fitter to bring up Jesuitts than Princes who Pretend to the British Crown ; for Sir Thomas in Company always used to Argue that the Nation had Usurped every priviledge they possess from their Kings, for that all the Subjects of Great Britain are the Kings property, and in Consequence a parcel of Slaves. As most all the Gentlemen of the best fashion who had join'd the Prince had very different principles, it is Easy to Imagine what Uneasiness it gave them to be Governed by people who's heads were fill'd with these Idea's. But as the French Says Le Vin etoit Versé il falloit le Boire, and as the Prince in his Conversation used always to Swear he would never lay down his arms, as long as too men would Stick by him, nobody ever thought of asking terms from the Government, but on the Contrary to Stand by the Cause whither good or bad as long as it would last. Private Gentlemen who had no Command in this Affair were very much to be pitied, and some

such their were of very good Estates who never
either Spoke to the Prince or Eat with him ; and
as he knew nothing of the familys of the Country,
he used to look upon them in the light of Common Dragoons. About the 4th of April the
Prince talked of marching to Attack the Duke
of Cumberland at Aberdeen, but it would have
been impossible, and if money had not Arrived
the army would have gone to nothing even in
the North, so a great many people thought the
Best thing that could happen to the Prince was
that The Duke Should march north, and Soon,
as provisions were becoming very Scarce, and
if he Should chance to be beat in the north he
had a long retreat to make throw a Country full
of his Enemies. The Prince as he gave out he
would march towards Aberdeen had order'd all
his army to Assemble as fast as possible, but All
Schemes of marching to Aberdeen were laid aside
when news of the Dukes marching Forward
came to Lord John Drummond at Spey side.
The Duke of Cumberland left Aberdeen the 8 of
April, and was at Bamff on the 10 ; the Body
of the army that was at Strathbogie advanced and
Encamp'd that day at Keith, and the 11 both
Colums join'd, and the whole army encamp'd at

Cullen. The 12 by Six o clock in the morning their advanced Guard appeared at Gordon Castle, and in half an hour after the whole army and a fleet of eight and twenty sail cast anchor at the mouth of the river. This fleet which Carried their baggage and provisions, always Sail'd when the Army march'd, and cast anchor at night opposite to where the army encamp'd. Upon The Dukes armys appearing, the Duke of Perth and Lord John Drummond assembled all the troops they had with them upon the side of the Spey, and as it was not possible to prevent The passage of the river, as it was Fordable every where, they retreated to Elgin in good order, where they arrived about twelve o clock. Lord John Drummond Sent out Mr Hunter of Burnside with a party of Lord Elcho's troop to Gett intelligence. Mr Hunter went so near their advanced guards, as to gett his horse Shott under him, and if Mr Vaughan to the great risk of his life had not taken him on behind him, Mr Hunter would have been taken prisoner. Mr Hunter inform'd Lord John that the Dukes army had pitch'd their Camp on the north side of the Spey; at ten o clock at night the Duke of Perth march'd all the troops out of Elgin to Forress, and than to

Nairn. The 13 The Duke of Cumberlands army encamp'd near the kirk of Alves, betwixt Elgin and Forres, and his fleet cast anchor off Findorn. The 14 the advanced guard of his army appear'd near Nairn. Very Early in the morning, the Duke of Perth, who Commanded the Colum that had retreated from Spey Side, in order to gain time sent out Clanronalds and Ardshiels foot and 70 of Fitzjames's horse to Attack them, but they finding that their advanced guard Consisted of all their Cavalry, they were oblidged to retreat before them to Nairn. The Dukes horse follow'd the Duke of Perths Colum two miles out of town, but as the rear kept in good order they never attempted to make an attack, but only firr'd a few Shot which did no harm. The Duke of Cumberlands whole army Encamp'd that day at Nairn, and his fleet cast anchor opposite to it; the Duke of Perth received orders from the Prince upon the march to halt at Culloden, where the Prince Came himself at Night with all the men he Could gett together, for as the Duke of Cumberland had made quick marches from Aberdeen a great many of the Princes troops did not Gett time to join the Army. Their was 800 men belonging to the different highland regiments that were at home in the highlands and were not at the Battle ; the Macgregors 300, and Barasdales 400, only Came to the Ferry opposite to Inverness two hours after the Battle, and Clunie Macpherson with 300 men was upon his march during the Action : Lord Cromartys regiment 300 men were attackt'd on the 15 at Golspie in Sutherlandshire by the Earl of Sutherlands men, a great many of them were kill'd and the rest taken prisoners ; the Earl of Cromartie and Lord Macleod, who had Staid behind their men at Dunrobin Castle, were both taken and putt aboard the *Hound* Sloop of War. All these men made 2100 that were not with the army. The Prince made all his men lay out upon their arms the night of the 14, and Suppose their was plenty of meal at Inverness, by the mismanagement of the people that were Charged with it there was none of it Baked, by which means the army had no provisions but what they Could pick up in the Environs of Colloden ; and in case the Prince had retreated on the 16 and not fought the Duke, This neglect of provisions would have made it impossible to have kept the army together in a body, but the Prince was so far from thinking of retreating that he would have taken it much Amiss if any body had doubted so far of a Victory as to have ask'd him where the army Should rendezvous in Case of a defeat, and for the only reason of their not daring to face their righteous Prince. On the 15 by Break of day he drew his army up in order of Battle upon a Spacious moor to the South of Culloden with some park walls to their right, and their left towards the descent That goes down to Culloden. Their front was Straight East. His first line Consisted of the following regiments viz. the Athole Brigade 600, which was Lord George Murrays, Lord Nairns & Shian Menzies's, Lochyells 700, Ardshiels 150, Roy Stuarts 200, Lovats 800, Mackintoshes's 500, Farqursons 150, Macleans 150, Macklachlins 100, Glenbucketts 200, Perths 300, Chisholms 100, Keppochs 200, Clanronalds 200, & Glengarys 300, which made in all 4650 foot. The Second line was divided into three Bodies, one on the right, another on the left, and one in the Center. The right division was Composed of Elcho's and Fitzjames's horse 110, Lord Strathallans 70, Abuchies foot 300, Lord Ogilvys 500; the Centre division was formed of the Irish piquets 300, Lord John Drummonds regiment 300, and the

Earl of Kilmarnocks 300; in the left division was
the Hussars 60, Sir Alexander Bannermans foot
150, Stoneywoods 200, which made the second
line in all 2050 foot, and 240 horse, So that the
whole army made 6940. The right Wing was
Commanded by Lord George Murray, and the
left by the Duke of Perth, the Centre of the first
line by Lord John Drummond, and the Centre
of the Second by Brigadeer Stapleton. Their was
five Cannon on the right and four on the left of
the Army.[1] The Duke of Cumberlands Army
Consisted of fifteen battalions of foot, viz. Pul-
tenys 500, the Royal 500, Cholmondeleys 500,
Price's 500, Scots Fusileers, 500, Dejeans 500,
Barrels 500, Battereaus 500, Blakenys 500,

[1] Finlayson's map of Culloden, which Mr. Blaikie (*Itinerary*,
p. 97) cites 'as the most detailed and probably the most accurate
plan of the battle,' places the Macleods in the first line, but Elcho's
omission to do so is accounted for by the fact that he has already
stated that the Macleods were brigaded with the Glengarry Macdonalds (see *ante*, p. 365). Finlayson also places Glenbucket in the
second line, but it appears that during the course of the battle
Glenbucket's men were advanced from the second to the first line
(*L. M.* ii. 279 ; *J. M.* 124)—to the position, in fact, which they
appear to have occupied on the 15th. With this exception Elcho
and Finlayson agree as to the arrangement of the second line, but it
will be found that Elcho gives greater detail. With regard to
Cumberland's army Elcho substitutes Sackville's for Bligh's (as a
matter of fact Sackville had taken over the command on April 9th)
and omits Lord Loudon's regiment: he also gives the strength of
each battalion as 500; but see *S. M.* viii. 216.
The following are the regiments engaged, with their regimental
numbers and their strength on the field of battle, taken from the

Howards 500, Flemings 500, Sackvilles 500, Sempills 500, Conways 500, Wolfes 500, and six hundred Campbells, which with Lord Mark Kers Dragoons 300, Cobhams 300, and Kingstons horse 300, made 8100 foot, and 900 horse. The day of the Battle they were drawn up in two lines, seven Battalions in the first and Eight in the second line, Supported by the two Squadrons of Horse on the right and four Squadrons of Dragoons on the left.* Their was two pieces of Cannon betwixt Every Battalion in the first line, and three on the right, & three on the left of the Second. The Army was Commanded in Cheif by The Duke of Cumberland, and under him by Lt Generals Earl of Arbemarle, Hawly, and Bland, Major General Husk, Brigadeers L^d

* the Campbells were on the left with the dragoons.

official return in the Cumberland Papers. The same report gives the strength of the Highland army as 8880 men :—

Pulteney's (13th), 474.
Royal Scots (1st), 481.
Cholmondeley's (34th), 459.
Price's (14th), 359.
Scots Fusiliers Campbell's (21st), 412.
Dejean's late Munro's (37th), 491.
Barrel's (4th), 373.
Battereau's (disbanded), 418.
Blakeney's (27th), 361.
Howard's (3rd), 464.
Fleming's (36th), 415.

Sackville's, late Bligh's (20th), 467.
Sempill's (25th), 475.
Conway's, late Ligonier's (48th), 386.
Wolfe's (8th), 374.
Cobham's Dragoons (10th Hussars), 276.
Lord Mark Kerr's Dragoons (11th Hussars), 300.
Kingston's Horse (disbanded), 211.

Total, 7197.

Sempill, Chomly, and Mordaunt. If the Prince
had had all his men together both armies would
have been equal in numbers, just 9000 men Each,
but as it was the Dukes was Superior by two
thousand, and the day ot the battle for reasons
which follows by four. The 15 early in the
morning the Prince (after he had drawn his
army up in battle) sent of Lord Elcho with a
party of horse to Gett intelligence of the Dukes
army. Lord Elcho went and Staid within veiw
of them untill twelve o clock, and then he went
Back and lett the Prince know. They were quiet
in their Camp at Nairn, and by all appearance
they did not intend to move that day. Upon
which the Prince Assembled all the Principal
officers and Asked them for the first time since
Derby what was best to be done. Lord George
Murray made a Speech, wherin he enlarged upon
the advantages Highlanders have by Surprising
their Enemy, and rather Attacking in the night
time than in day Light, for as regular troops
depend intirely upon their discipline, and on the
Contrary the Highlanders having none, the Night
was the time to putt them most upon an Equality,
and he Concluded that his Opinion was that they
Should march at dusk of ye Evening, So as that

the Duke should not be aprised of it, that he Should march about the town of Nairn and attack them in their rear, with the right wing of the first line, while the Duke of Perth with ye left Should attack them in front, and the Prince Should Support the Duke of Perths attack with the Second line. Every body Agreed to Lord Georges opinion ; it was only objected to him, that as he did not propose to march from Culloden, untill the dusk of the Evening, and as Culloden was Eight miles from Nairn, it was to be fear'd the Army would not Accomplish that march before day light. Lord George Said he would Answere for it, So the march was resolved upon. The Army lay upon their arms all day without any provision for either Officer or Soldier. About six at night all the Ships that Sail'd along the Coast with the Dukes army Came and Cast anchor off Inverness, and at nine o clock at night the Prince caused sett fire to the heather to make believe he was Still at Culloden, and march'd off his Army ; [1] but instead of marching

[1] 'But before the time the army was to march, a vast number of the men went off on all hands to get and make ready provisions ; and it was not possible to stop them. Then, indeed, almost everybody gave it up as a thing not to be ventured. His Royal Highness was extremely bent upon it, and said that, whenever we began the march, the men would be all hearty, and those that had gone off would return and follow' (*J. M.* 122).

in three Colums, it marched only in one, and in Consequence marched very Slow. By the time the front of the Colum gott within three miles of Nairn, it began to grow day light, So the front where Lord George was, halted, and Lochyell came from the front to the Prince, who was between the Center and the rear, and told him that now as it was day light the project of Surprising the Duke had fail'd, and that it was better to march back Than Go & attack the Duke who would be prepared; and insisted Strongly upon going back, and Said all the Officers in the front were for going Back. The Prince was not for going back, and said it was much better to march forward and attack, than march back and be attack'd afterwards, when the men would be all fatigued with their nights march. During the time of this Conversation the army, by what means I know not, began to move back ;[1] and in much Shorter time than they had march'd return'd to the parks of Culloden, where Every body seemed to think of nothing

[1] Accounts of the night march are to be found in most contemporary narratives: they agree substantially with Elcho's statements. Lord George Murray's own version of what occurred is contained in a letter to William Hamilton of Bangour printed *H. H.* 359 *et seq.* ; see also *H. H.* 371-372 for the account given by Hay and Charles. See also Appendix B.

but Sleep. The men were prodigiously tired with hunger and fatigue, and vast numbers of them went into Inverness, and the Villages about, both to Sleep and to pick up what little nourishment they Could gett. The principal officers went all to the house of Culloden and were so much tired that they never thought of Calling a Councill what was to be done, but Every one lay'd himself down where he Could, some on beds, others on tables, Chairs, & on the floors, for the fatigue and the hunger had been felt as much amongst the officers as Soldiers. About two hours after the Princes Arrival at Culloden a party of horse that had been left to Observe the Duke of Cumberlands motions, brought word that their was a party of his horse within two miles, and that his whole army was not above four miles off. Upon which the Prince and the Duke of Perth, Lord George Murray, and Lord John Drummond mounted their horses, ordered the drums to beat & the pipes to play, which Alarm Caused great hurry & Confusion amongst people half dead with fatigue. They Endeavoured to gett the men together as fast as possible, but as they were dispersed all over the Country as far as Inverness, their was near two thousand of

them that was not at the Battle, so all The Prince
Assembled was about five thousand men,[1] which
he march'd up the hill from Culloden, & drew
them up in the same place they were drawn up
in the day before with their right to Some park
walls. It was a dark, misty, rainy day, & the wind
blew in the face of the Princes army. Their was
no manner of Councill held upon the Field, and
indeed their was but one party to take, which was
to have cross'd the water of Nairn which was
upon the right and march'd up a hill where the
Dukes army could not have follow'd, and have
waited there untill night, and then attack'd him.
But this Scheme was never Spoke off ; for retreating into the highlands, it was not possible, as the
army for want of provisions must have dispersed.
Besides, what putt a Stop to all Councills was that
the Prince always believed firmly that the Dukes
army would be Struck with a panick ; so with
these notions, it was Equal to him to have nine
or only five thousand men. In the plan of the
Battle all the Corps are Supposed to be as they

---

[1] ' Of towards 6000 men, which the Prince's army at this period
consisted of, about 1000 were asleep in Culloden parks, who knew
nothing of the action till awaked by the noise of the cannon '
(*Memoirs of Sir Robert Strange*, i. 65).
Elcho's estimate agrees with Patullo's (*H. H.* 332).

were on the 15, but as was said before their was two thousand absent on the 16, some asleep & others gone too far of in Search of provisions. On Wednesday, the 16 of April 1746, about half an hour after Eleven, the Duke of Cumberlands army appeared two miles off, Straight in front of the Princes, form'd in two lines with most all their horse upon their left wing. They march'd down the two miles form'd in the Same way. When they Came within a mile they detach'd a Small party of horse to reconnoitre the left of the Princes army ; when they Came within Cannon Shot their was a great many huzzas pass'd on both Sides. The Princes Cannon began to fire first, and presently after they fir'd theirs, which when they Came pretty near they charged with grape shott, and as they were well pointed they did great execution. The highlanders had orders not to move untill the word of Command to advance was given them, and then they were to give their fire very near, draw their Swords and rush in ; they suffer'd the Cannonade very impatiently, a great many of them threw themselves down flatt upon the Ground, and some of them, but few, gave way and run off. When the Dukes army came within muskett Shott, they detach'd

600 Campbells and a Squadron of Dragoons, to See and flank the Princes right wing, but Lord George Murray order'd Abuchies regiment and Elcho's & Fitzjames horse to face them, which prevented them from passing a ditch which Cover'd the right wing. As most of their horse was upon their left, the Duke of Perth made a motion as if he would attack their right, which made them draw of some of their horse from the left to the right. When both armies were very near one another the Dukes outflanked the Princes both on the right and left, and the Dukes Second line was longer than his first, whereas the Prince had no Continued second line, but only three bodies to cover the right, left, and centre of the first line. The Dukes army Continued always advancing and keeping a Continued fire both of Cannon and muskettery, which kill'd a vast number of the Princes people. At last when they were very near, the word of Command to Advance was given, and all the line moved forward,[1] but in the advancing the

[1] The Macintoshes were the first to advance ; inclining to the right, they were joined by the right wing of Charles's army, and moving forward in a body they succeeded in breaking through Barrel's and Dejean's, but a devastating fire from Wolfe's on their flank and from Sempill's on their front rendered further advance impossible ; it was then that 'they threw stones for at least a minute

Campbells

Fraziers Glide

150   150   Abhams   500   Dejeans   500   Fusiliers   500   Price

500   Wolfe   500   Conway   500   Sempill   500   Sackville

The Battle of
Wednesday .

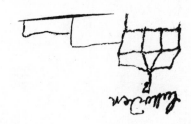

Culloden

500 500 500 150 150

Regal Pulteny Kingston

500 500 500

Howard Blakeny Batterau

...loden fought on
+ April 1746

whole left wing of the Princes army gave way, and run away without firing their musketts ; the Centre join'd the right, and in a Sort of a mob, without any order or distinction of Corps, mixt together, rush'd in and attack'd the Dukes left wing, and broke the regiments opposite to them in the first line, but the Second line marching up beat them off, and oblidged them to turn their backs, and run away ; and as the Campbells had taken possession of the park walls on the Right, they received several flank fires which kill'd and destroy'd great numbers of them. The Body of the Second line behind the right wing after this attack went of in Good order ; the rest of the Second line, Except the Irish piquets & Royal Scots, had run away with the left wing. The Irish piquetts & Royal Scots, after the right wing was repulsed, march'd up in order to Sustain it, and gave & received Several fires, and then retreated towards Inverness, and on the road Surrender'd themselves prisoners of war. In the attack upon the right many of the Highlanders were kill'd with bayonetts, and it was the more easy as they had no targetts, for they would not be at the

or two, before their total rout began ' (Cumberland to Newcastle, *H. O. Scot.* xxxi., April 18, 1746) ; see also Lord George Murray's letter (*H. H.* 231).

pains upon a march to carry them. The Prince
who at the beginning of the Action was behind the
Irish piquetts guarded by Sixteen of Fitzjames's
horse, turn'd about his horse and went off as soon
as the left wing gave way, and never offer'd
to rally any of the broken Corps ; but indeed it
would have been to no purpose, for none of the
highlanders who Escaped ever Stop'd untill they
gott home to their own houses.[1] As the Dukes
army after the deroute Continued to pursue in
order of Battle, always firing their Cannon and
platoons in Advancing, their was not so many
people kill'd or taken as their would have been
had they detach'd Corps to pursue, but Every
body that fell into their hands gott no quarters,[2]
except a few who they reserv'd for publick
punishment ; the Earl of Kilmarnock and Colonel
Farquharson were taken on the field. The
Princes army had about a Thousand men kill'd,

[1] See *ante*, p. 92 *et seq.* 'He was at the head of the Second Line
at the beginning of the Action, but went off at the first appearance of
Disorder among the clans' (Letter from Sir Edward Fawkner,
Hist. MSS. Commission, x. i., p. 445).

[2] Cumberland in his despatch writes : 'Major-General Bland
had also made a great slaughter, and gave quarter to none but about
fifty French officers and soldiers he picked up in his pursuit' (*Hist.
MSS. Commission*, x. 443 ; *H. O. Scot.* xxxi.). It has constantly been
asserted that orders were issued to the Highland army to give no
quarter, but the original order is to be found among the Cumberland
MSS. at Windsor, and a copy of it will be found in Appendix G.

among whom were Colonels Mercer of Aldie, Menzies of Shian, Frazer[1] of Inveralachie, Macgilvray of Drumaglash, Maclachlin of that ilk, Chisholm, Macdonald of Keppoch, Brigadeer Stapelton and the Viscount of Strathallan, and a great many officers of lesser note. The Dukes army lost Lord Robert Ker[2] and about 250 men some officers included. In the Flight of the Princes army most of the left wing took the road to Inverness, the right wing Cross'd the Water of Nairn and went to Ruthven of Badenoch, the rest to the number of 500 mostly Officers follow'd the Prince into Stratharick, where he had Stop'd about four miles from the field of Battle. As he had taken it into his head he had been betray'd and particularly by Lord George Murray, he Seemed very diffident of Every body Except the Irish officers, and he appeared very anxious to know whither he had given them all higher Comissions then they had at their Arrival, on purpose that they might gett them Confirm'd to them Upon their return to

[1] Colonel Charles Frazer, younger of Inveralochy; he was wounded at the battle and murdered the following day (*L. M.* i. 190).

[2] 2nd son of the Marquis of Lothian; captain in Barrel's, 'a handsome young gentleman, who was cut to pieces with above thirty wounds' (Walpole, *Letters*, April 25, 1746).

France. He neither Spoke to any of the Scots officers present, or inquired after any of the Absent,[1] (nor at any of the preceding battles he never had inquired after any of the Wounded Officers). He appeared very Uneasy as long as the Scots were about him, and in a Short time order'd them all to go to Ruthven of Badenoch, where he would Send them orders, but before they had rode a mile, he Sent Mr. Sheridan[2] after them, to tell them that they might disperse and every body Shift for himself the best way he Could. Lord George Murray and Lord John Drummond repeated the Same orders to All the body of the army that had assembled at Ruthven. The Prince kept with him some of Fitzjames's horse, and went that night to a house[3] in the head of Strathyrick, where he mett Lord Lovatt, and a great many other Scots Gentlemen, who advised him not to quit the Country, but Stay and gather

[1] Colonel Ker of Graden states that Charles inquired particularly about Lord George Murray (L. M. i. 264); but if true, some other motive than solicitude may have been at work.

[2] Cf. Maxwell's account: 'Sheridan at first pretended to conduct them to the place where the Prince was to assemble his army again, but having conducted them about half a mile on the road to Ruthven, he dismissed them all in the Prince's name, letting them know it was the Prince's pleasure they should shift for themselves' (M. K. 158).

[3] Gortleg or Gorthlic.

together again his Scatter'd forces. But he was
so prepossess'd against the Scots, that he was
Affraid they would give him up to make their
peace with the Government ; for some of the
Irish were at pains to relate to him in very Strong
terms, whow the Scots had already Sold his Great
Grand Father to the English ; and as he was
naturaly of a Suspicious temper it was no difficult
matter to persaude him of it ; and he always
believed it, Untill the fidelity the Highlanders
Show'd him during the long time he was hid
in their Country Convinced him and every body
else of the Contrary. The 17 early in the morning he Sent away all Fitzjames people from him
(who went and Surrendred themselves to the
Duke at Inverness), and he himself disguised[1] like
a Servant, and mounted before a portmanteau,
and only attended by M^r OSullivan and a guide,
went and lay that night in Lochargey, and next
day in Glenbuisdale in Arasey,[2] where he sent
for one Mr Macleod[3] a famous pilot, who he sent
off to the Western Isles to See and hire him a

[1] Charles exchanged clothes with the guide, Edward Burke
(*L. M.* i. 191). Alexander Macleod, one of Charles's aide-de-camps,
and Allan Macdonald, a priest, also accompanied him (*L. M.* i. 321).
[2] Glenbeasdale in Arisaig.
[3] Donald Macleod of Gualtergill ; his narrative is given *L. M.*
i. 155.

Ship for France. Mr Macleod went, and hired a
Small Vessel at Stornway in the Lewis, and Came
back and Acquainted the Prince of it. The
Prince the day before he left the main land wrote
several letters[1] to Some of his principal Officers,
desiring them to meet him such a day in
Locharkey, where he intended to Assemble the
remains of the army and defend the Country as
long as possible, untill Succours came to him
from France. This he was advised to do in order
to prevent the Duke of Cumberland from fixing
his intention intirely upon pursuing him. The
25 of April, the day after he had wrote these
letters, he went to Borodale, the very place he
had first Landed at, and there embark'd on board
an open boat, for the isle of Ouist, only attended
by M^rs OSullivan, ONeal, and Macleod the
Pilott. They Landed in Ouist, and travell'd from
thence through the Lewis to Stronway; but the

---

[1] O'Neil says Charles wrote 'circular letters to all the chiftains,'
from Knoidart, calling on them to join him immediately' (*L. M.*
i. 103). In the *Journal*, Elcho says he received one of these letters, and
that Loch Arkaig was to be the place of meeting. See *ante*, p. 100.
The only letter of this kind hitherto published is one written from
Gortleg, 9 P.M. April 16th, by Macleod (aide-de-camp to Charles) to
Cluny, naming Fort Augustus as a rendezvous for the clans on the
following day (*A. C.* 220). Maxwell mentions no letter, but says
that Charles entertained the idea of assembling his scattered forces
(*M. K.* 160).

people of the town having heard of the battle of
Culloden, and Suspecting that the Ship was hired
for the Prince, had oblidged the Captain to putt
to Sea. This was a great disappointment, and
was the reason why The Prince was Oblidged to
Wander in disguise, Sometimes in these Islands,
and Sometimes on the Continent, every day in
danger of being taken, Untill the end of Sept^r,
that the French Court sent two frigates to the
bay of Loch Noua where he imbark'd on board
of them, about the beginning of October, landed
at St Malo's, and about the twelfth of the same
month, Arrived at Paris. On the 28 of April
three days after the Prince had left the Country,
their Came into the Bay of Loch Noua, and Cast
anchor opposite to Borodale, two French frigates
the one The *Bellona* of 34 and the other the
Mars of 32 Guns, both from Nantz. The Coming
of these Ships brought a vast number of people
to Borodale who were all Astonish'd to hear of
the Princes departure. The principal people were
Surprised he had not Acquainted any of them of
it, or so much as ever wrote to thank them, for
any of the services they had render'd him ; and
the Commonalty were enraged because he Used
always to tell them he would never Abandon

them while two of them would Stand by him.
His friends Mr Murray and Sir Thomas Sheridan
to appease these murmures forged a letter[1] wherin
they made the Prince Say that he Was Gone to
France to Ask money and men and that he Would
be back Again to Scotland with Every thing
necessary to Carry on the War, but all that was
only to Endeavour to Apease the clamours of
the people, who were very much Exasperated
against him for Abandoning them. Two Ships
brought 36000 Lewis d'ors with them besides
arms and Amunition of All Kinds, but the people
who were intrusted with the money hearing y^e
Prince was not in the Country refused to Land
the money. Upon the Arrival of the two French
Ships a vast Number of people Assembled at
Borodale, who were all Astonish'd to hear of the

[1] A copy of this letter is printed *B. H.* iii. 263 ; in a footnote
it is stated that it is taken from a copy of the original among the
Stuart Papers at Windsor endorsed in Charles's own hand 'The
Prince's Letter to ye Chiefs in parting from Scotland 1746.' It is
also stated that the letter to the Chiefs is dated April 28th, and is
enclosed in a letter dated April 23rd from Charles to Sheridan, a
copy of which is said to be given in the Appendix ; but no such
letter is to be found in the Appendix, nor so far as I have been able
to discover is the copy of the letter to the chiefs to be found among
the Stuart Papers.   There is nothing, therefore, to show that Elcho's
statement is inaccurate.   The style of the letter to the chiefs does not
suggest that it was composed by Charles himself, while the endorse-
ment must have been made long after the letter was written, and
affords no clue as to the real author of the original.

Princes having Abandoned the Country in the
Scandalous Way he did. The people who Were
intrusted with the money made Difficulty about
Landing it as the Prince was gone and as it was
Sent for his Use, but Upon the Highlandmen
threating to keep them Ashoar and Use them ill
they Landed Every thing they had. The French
Captains of the Ships had given out that the
French fleet which was ready to Sail from Brest
was destined For Scotland, and as Mr Murray in
his forged letter had made the Prince say that he
was Gone to France to solicite Succours in person,
and would immediately be back with them, the
Highlanders Gave out that they would Assemble
& defend their own Country and never lay down
arms Untill he did Come back or they gett terms
from the Goverment, but they never did Assemble.
On the 3^d of May about 2 o clock in the morning
three English Frigates, viz. the *Greyhound* of 20
Guns Capt Noel, the *Baltimore* 12 guns Capt
Fergusson, and the *Teror* 8 guns Capt Duff, Came
into ye bay. As Soon as day broke they immediately Stood into ye Bay, where the French Ships
were Laying att Anchor, made Up to the *Comodore*, hoisted British colours, and fired their Broad
Sides at him before he Cutt his Cable, which

disabled him very much. The Other French Ship
Cutt her Cable & Stood to them and their was
a very Brisk Engagement for three hours, but as
the English had the Wind the French never
Could gett nearer them then they chose, & at
Last the two French Ships were drove by the
Wind quite into the Bottom of the Bay, where
they cast anchor. The English Stood off & on and
Canonaded them for Several hours, and at Last
the *Greyhound* took out a great many men out
of the other two Ships and sent them out of the
Bay and Stood down Upon the French to Board
them, but she was so Briskly received that she
tack'd about & Stood out of the Bay after the
others about 4 o clock in the Affternoon. The
French had a good many men kill'd* Especialy
aboard of the *Comodore*, who did not fight so
well as his Companion, for if he had Cutt his
Cable & Stood towards them immediately Upon
his Seeing them they Would not have gott off so
Easily. That night the French refitted their Ships
and putt to Sea having taken on board the Duke
of Perth,[1] Ld John Drummond, Lord Elcho, Old

* 95
70 in one &
25 in ye other

[1] 'In the ship I was in there raged a contagious distemper which
carried off 67 in 25 days: and about the 10th day of our voyage I
saw the body of my friend the Duke of Perth thrown overboard:
which afflicting sight, joined with my violent sickness, I expected
would put an end to my life' (Daniel's Progress).

Lochyell,[1] Sir Thomas Sheridan, and his nephew,[2] M[r] Hay, M[r] Maxwell of Kirkconel, M[r] Lockart of Carnwath, who all Arrived Safe at Nantz the 6 of June following.[3] Four[4] English Ships Came into Loch Noua the day after the French had Saild. The French Captains Would have Gone to Search for the Prince if any Body Could have told them where he Was. They Steerd their Course[5] by the north & West of Ireland. Lord Ogilvys Landing at Bergen in Norway with Eleven Gentlemen

---

[1] John Cameron, 18th chief of Lochiel, son of Sir Ewen Cameron (b. 1629, d. 1719). Sir Ewen made over his estates to him in 1696, and he did the same to his son Donald (the Lochiel of the '45) in 1706. John was 'out' in 1715, and attainted. Retired to France (returning for a short time in 1719 for the Glenshiel affair) ; remained in France until 1745, when he came over to Scotland ; joined the army at Perth in December, and received a temporary command, which was merely nominal owing to his advanced age. Died at Nieuport, Flanders, 1747. ' C'est un vieillard qui n'a jamais eu grande considération, il ne va chez le Prince que très rarement' (F. F. O., vol. 79, fol. 235).

[2] Mr. Sheridan : 'Il a le même titre, les mêmes appointements et la même médiocrité de Mr. Stafford ' (F. F. O., vol. 79, fol. 235).

[3] ' As we were very badly dressed, having only the clothes we had worn at the battle of Culloden, and having had no change of linen for six months, the people commenced to insult us, but when they knew we were officers of Prince Edward's, they loaded us with attentions ' (Elcho, Journal).

[4] The Greyhound, Baltimore, and Terror had been joined by the Raven. The French appear to have owed their victory to the superior accuracy of their fire (see captains' logs, Baltimore and Greyhound, Record Office ; also Daniel's Progress).

[5] ' We were pursued one day by an English vessel of three decks, which gained rapidly upon us, but we had the good luck to lose it during the night ' (Elcho, Journal).

where they were putt prisoners into the Castle
and these Gentlemens landing in France was the
first Sure proofs the people on the Continent
had of the Affairs being intirely over.   All the
Gentlemen that Landed at Nantz Came to Paris
as did sometime after the Gentlemen From Norway with the King of Denmarks order ; the King
of France gave them all pensions Equivalent to
the Comissions they bore in the Princes Army,
and they were very well receiv'd.   Everyday that
winter almost their were people arriving at Paris
who had made their Escape, and they Gott all
Something from the Court.   The King of France
Sent Two frigates to Loch Noua in the month
of September to Search for the Prince ; Colonel
Waren went with them.   They found him and
Brought him either to Morlaix or St Malos, and
on ye 12 of October[1] 1746 he Came to Paris and
with him Young Lochyell and his Brother, Lochgary, and Colonel Roy Stuart.   Mr Murray his
Secretary would not leave Scotland, and people
imagined his reason for Staying was to See &
gett a Large Share of the money that was landed
in the highlands, which Money was Afterwards

[1] Charles was conveyed to France on a vessel called *L'Heureux*,
and landed at Roscoff Oct. 10th.   Barrisdale was at once put in
prison at Morlaix (Luynes, vii. 459).

Given to Cluny Macpherson to take Care off for
the Princes Use, but he Gott little of it. The
Prince when he Gott himself Equip'd in Cloaths
went to the Court at Fontainbleau,[1] where he was
Very well receiv'd,[2] and it is not doubted but at
that time had he behaved right, he Would have
Gott anything done for His Followers he pleased;
but instead of that, he behaved so as to make all
the French ministers his Enemys, and never
Ask'd any thing for any of his people but Young
Lochyell, who he Gott named to a Regiment. His
reason for behaving so ill to the people that
followèd him was, Some of his Irish Favourites
had putt it into his head that if he Gott the Scotts
Employments they would not be so dependant
Upon him as if he kept them poor, but the Irish
principal reason Was they were jealous of the
Scots & did not want they Should gett a footing
in France. The Duke of Yorck who was Likewise at Paris ask'd a regiment for Lord Ogilvy
and Gott it. The Court of France of themselves

[1] Oct. 19th (Luynes, vii. 453).

[2] Luynes thus records his impression of Charles and Henry at
Fontainebleau: 'Le prince est assez sérieux : son frère le duc d'York
est d'un caractère différent: il parle davantage, il rit volontiers, il
paroît vif et aimer la musique passionément : il est beaucoup plus
petit que son frère, et sa figure est moins bien ; ils ont toujours
porté ici le ruban bleu de la Jarretière par-dessus leur habit'
(vii. 462).

settled 40'000 livres a Year to be distributed in
pensions amongst those that were not placed in
these Regiments. The Prince talk'd very ill of
Lord George Murray, Lord John Drummond, and
M^r AEneas Macdonald; Suppose their was nobody
in his Army had Served him With more zeal
Activity and Fidelity than these three Gentlemen
did on all Occasions. He made Mr Kelly his
minister Upon his Arrival at Paris, and behaved
very uncivily to the Scots in General and did not
Seem in the least Concerned for any misfortunes
that he had brought upon them. It is Said the
Court of France Offer'd to Send him Back to
Scotland with 6000 men but that he refused to
Go. In the winter 1748 after the Peace of Aix
la Chapelle the French Court Sent to tell him that
they were going to make a peace with England,
and that if he would leave the Kingom quietly,
they Would Assure him a retreat in Switzerland
at Fribourg, where he Should have a Company of
Guards, and be treated as Prince of Wales, have
a Large Pension, and that they Would do for all
his Followers whatever he Should demand. All
Which he Absolutely refused, and Said he would
not quite the Kingdom. Upon which one night
as he was Going into the Opera he was seized
by the Guards & Bound hand and foot and putt

into a Coach and putt into prison at Vincennes, and from thence in a post Chaise Accompanied by an Officer of the Musquatiers he was Carried to Avignon ; All his people that lived in the house with him were putt into the Bastille, but were soon lett out again with orders to quite Paris. His Brother had gone to Rome[1] in ye year 1747, where the Pope afterwards made him a Cardinal ; it is Said the Prince Undertook the mad project of Staying in France (Against the Kings will) because he thought it would please the English. From Avignon he went to Venise attended only by Colonel Goring, but the Senate as soon as they knew of his being their order'd him Away, So he return'd to Flanders, where in ye Year 1751 miss Walkinshaw[2] came to him From Scotland with whom he has lived ingognito ever Since, Sometimes in Switzerland & sometimes in Flanders, and now and then making trips to Paris where no Soul of Fashion ever Saw him. Mr Goring left him in the Year 1754 & my Lord Marechal procured him a Comission of Major

[1] So secret had the Duke of York kept the news of his intended departure that he invited Charles to supper with him at Clichy on the day of his flight (April 29, 1747). The supper was duly prepared, but the host was absent, nor did Charles learn till the following day that his brother had left for Rome. D'Argenson accuses the Duke of York of 'insigne fourberie.' He was created Cardinal by Benedict XIV. on July 3, 1747.

[2] See *ante*, p. 138.

in the Prussian Service. Mr Goring gave out
Publickly that he found him so Unworthy of
being a Prince of Wales and so Void of all the
Qualitys that people of Birth ought to be Endued
with, that he Would have nothing more to do
With him, and that he had remained so long with
him more for the sake of the Party than for any
regard he had for him.

There was a Stupid plott[1] form'd for him in the
Year 1752 by Mr Alexander Murray, Brother to
Lord Elibank. Mr Murray had made the Prince
Believe that he had Gott 60 men together in
London who had swore to Attack St James's and
Assasinate all the Royal Family at a time. When
the Assasination was to be Comitted the Prince
was immediately to come from the Coast of
Flanders and offer himself to the English Nation ;
at the Same time Mr Macdonald of Lochgary and
Mr Cameron were to raise a Comotion in the
Highlands. Lochgary & Mr Cameron went to
Scotland, & Mr Cameron was taken & hanged.
Mr Murray went to London, but upon finding that
his Assasins Courage had fail'd them, he Came
back to France. And so Ended so Wise a project,
Which Shows the Princess Good Understanding
for having Approved of it and Come into it.

[1] For an account of the Elibank Plot, see *ante*, p. 139.

APPENDIX

APPENDIX A

From the Cumberland Papers.

SIR,—As our men have taken one of your Serene Highness' people prisoner, I return him to your Serene Highness.

I shall be very glad to know upon what footing Your Highness proposes making war in these kingdoms and wither you would incline (as we do) to have a Cartel setled.

As many of the officers of the Elector of Hanover's Armie whom we took Prisoners and us'd with the greatest tenderness have broke their words of Honour, given in the most Solemn Manner and the Common Soldiers who were liberet upon Condition not to serve any more against us, have again enter'd into the Elector's pay, His Royal Highness the Prince Regent is much difficulted, how to use the other Prisoners who have lately been taken, for tho' He desires to show the greatest lenity to His Father's subjects, that even opposed him upon his first coming to these kingdoms and Setting up the Royal Standard, yet those who have the Honour to serve Him, cannot but resent the unpresidented behaviour of their Ennemies, who I have some reason to believe have orders to give no Quarters.

As I have the most profound respect for the Illustrious House of Hess Cassel and in particular for Your Serene Highness I have the Honour to subscribe myself.—May

it please Your Serene Highness, Your Highness Most
Devoted and most Humble Servant,

GEORGE MURRAY.

30 *March* 1746.

Copy of George Murray's Letter to the Prince of
Hesse, dated 30th of March 1746.

APPENDIX B

Letter of Charles Edward from the Stuart Papers.

Ye 1st March 1759. Instruction for Baret. You
are to assure with my moste humble Respect and duty
Mr. Orry [James] that he has been many years deceived
by-people either approching him or in correspondance
I shall only enter in ye moste essentiall points Ld G. M.
has bein in his time ye ruin of ye affaire.

It is certain, and many were witnesses, he refused a
certain person's orders to besiege Carlisle, that Carlisle
was taken after which he made his submission, and his
master was so good as to forguive him, hoping he woud
not strangness any more. All and many knows after
that ye Bolde Marche to Darby by ye assurances of
France also ye P never assured his contry ye Fr were
sincere but trusted only in them that he was shure coud
have accomplished ye hole glorios event had there not
been tretors or such which comes to the same case
disobé orders in ye moste critcall instant; who is to
answer if a Lefftenant (only by comparison) revolts to
ye orders of his Captain, what is ye Law? Death, who
only is answerable but the Captain iff he be obeid but
not otherwise. In ye affaire of ye Athol Castell he
took a Hessian Officer and sent him back to his core
without giving notice or asking concent of his Chife

Commander in fine he afterwards disobede in ye moste
criticall guncture desided by a Councill of war he proposing ye night attack and ye Commander as all ye rest
approving it.

According to all military rules and even to ye little
armi composed of 8000 men a march by surprise shoud
have bein maide by three divisions but this Ld G M
droped notwithstanding all remonstrances ye moste con-
victive however tho one was obliged to march in one
colone by his opposition wee were in time even to have
destroyied ye Enemy the proof was when he put panick
in Locquell [Lochiel] and made him take a side Rode to
return after ye was sent back to ye Cheif Commander,
and that he orderd him on his perrill to advance, according to ye Councill of War agreed by all ye Chiftins he
turned a crose Rode to retret back, so that Clenronald's
Regiment not knowing ye trick advanced ye write rode
and came to spake to ye senteris whom he found quite
surprised, so that all would have been over after all this
Ld G M. who took a slip.   Instructions in short to
Baret ye 1st March 1759.   Ld G's vilany proved out of
all dispute : Eneas Macdonald a worthless felow.

APPENDIX C

*Extract translated from The Expedition of Charles
Edward Stuart in 1743-44-45-46 : done in
Latin in 1751 by the Jesuit Giulio Cordara,
and translated into Italian by Antonio Gussalli
1845.*

Finally there were Elcho, Lochiel, MacDonald,
Lovat, mentioned above, and other Scots, most illustrious not less for their military glory than for their

lineage. Superior to them all in power and military skill was the commander Elcho, and he would have surpassed all the others in authority if he had been less impetuous and headstrong. Their opinions were asked. Elcho was of opinion that they might be quite confident if only things were properly directed; he maintained that the remnants of the army should be got together and formed into a body; that they should send out into the mountains for help, appoint a place where each of their friends could assemble with his followers: renew the war and sustain it until fortune or time should improve their position. He maintained that this was not only possible, but easy and without any great risk, if they were only ready and willing. They should not believe that the defeated troops would be willing to expose themselves to fresh risks unless the chieftains led them, and above all unless they saw their Prince present. If only he would show himself to the Highlanders not only would the fugitives return to his standard but many, many others would take up arms and go with him. Should he go into hiding, or, worse still, leave the island, every man would think of himself and provide for his own safety by passing over to the enemy. And having made a long speech on this he turned to the Prince :—

'If only your Highness will listen to me, no one to-day shall persuade you either to fly or conceal yourself. Do not act in such a way that so many valiant men ready to lay down their lives for you should look in vain for their beloved Prince and Captain. Betake yourself at once to the mountains of Lachaber and Badenoch. There I hope we shall soon be able to collect a sufficient force, which we shall be ready to lead wherever you may order.'

He was speaking in this fine way when Sheridan, either from some secret grudge or from his natural sourness, or—and I think this is nearer the truth—from weariness at all they had endured, burst forth and reproached Elcho with his poor defence of the Spey :—

'Captain Elcho, it is useless now to play the undaunted hero : you ought to have done so elsewhere. Now we have been ruined by you, we must bear patiently that which cannot be remedied and adapt ourselves to what needs must be. You must think the enemy a fool to be willing to leave us time to get the army together again : on the contrary, from every side he is pursuing us with his victorious troops ; he is closing the passes ; victory flows unrestrainedly, and possibly while we are deliberating about the remedy, the enemy will surprise us and finish it. And suppose—though I have no hope of it—that he is slack and gives us time, shall we, who, with eight thousand brave and well-trained soldiers, suffered defeat like ours, with much less people and more timid recruits, without money, or arms, or food, face the conqueror ? Unless I am entirely mistaken, I can see no help for it except that the Prince should get off to the Continent and reserve himself for better times, if only they will come.'

This bitter speech exasperated Elcho beyond all measure, as he saw that the unhappy issue of the war was imputed to him. Flushed with anger and indignation, he declared that he had been insulted by this impudent villain and would have his revenge.

The Prince intervened, and by praying them not to ruin the common cause by a private quarrel, put a stop to the nascent discord and gave orders for others to speak freely their opinion.

During Sheridan's speech Sullivan appeared : he added his reasons for hastening the departure for the Continent. Lovat at first seemed to hold with Elcho ; then, after a better consideration of the circumstances, was undecided and said nothing. The others, because in evil fortune no advice is safe, thought it better to listen than give counsel which might turn out ill, but not one of them declined, to do whatever he could, for the safety of the Prince. In this alone all agreed that it seemed dangerous to stay in Aird : they should quit forthwith a place so near and so suspected by the enemy : the King's men were moving here, there, and everywhere : there were bound to be spies and informers everywhere. It was by general agreement resolved that the Prince should leave Aird that night.

The one thing to do was to determine where and how to go, for there were no slight difficulties in either case. As for the place, Edward himself chose Fort Augustus, the fort which only the day before, as I have said, had been set on fire by his orders. And this place pleased him above all others : many soldiers agreed in thinking it a refuge : he might from there make himself acquainted more conveniently with the state of affairs, and when that was known (as it is wise to adapt one's plans to circumstances) he might take a final resolve. As to the means of getting to Fort Augustus, Elcho, always firm on going back to arms, maintained that they should set out with all the fugitive troops in Aird. For two reasons : the one, that if the Prince fell in with enemies in ambush, he would have defenders ; the other, that the noise of such a departure would inform the stragglers of the place where they should join the Prince, whom they were going about anxiously seeking. But others thought very differently, possibly, no doubt, the Prince was sought for by his friends : on the other hand, the enemy were most certainly hunting him : a single troop of a hundred and twenty could suffice to arouse the enemy in their rear with their din, but were not enough for the purposes of defence. In the present circumstances there seemed no reason to expose the Prince to a very serious and certain risk for a light and doubtful hope. Edward embraced this view, saying that when the enemy were so near, he would much rather have no soldiers at all than have so few.

The conference broke up: no decision had been come to upon Captain Elcho's proposal. Orders were given to the soldiers to make their way to Lochaber assemble at a place stipulated, and be ready to answer to the first call. Edward, at midnight, with a very few companions, started on his journey. Elcho and Lochiel, on horseback, went before him; about a mile behind came the Prince himself, likewise on horseback; by his side Sheridan and Sullivan: at the same distance followed MacDonald with seven retainers, and all went with their arms in their hands ready for any issue. It seemed to many that they should not have disregarded that which Elcho had proposed in council: if his opinion had prevailed, hostilities might easily have been renewed or protracted: since the soldiers had only been dispersed, not estranged or driven over as yet to the conqueror. They wanted a head, not courage or fidelity. Meanwhile, how much might not happen to change things? Often in a day happens that which no one expected or foresaw. Thus many spoke: how prudently, I am not going to say. Edward reached Fort Augustus at three o'clock in the morning and remained astonished at finding the place deserted. Keeping to his own quarters he only saw Lochiel, who, as I have said, had gone on before with Elcho, but they had taken different ways, not from any change in their fidelity, but through the reproaches of Sheridan that they thought so much of their pride; and moreover Elcho took it ill that in the discussion other people's opinions had been preferred to his. And, before setting out, he himself said this to Lochiel, enjoining him to convey it to Edward; protesting that it broke his heart to abandon in so sad a moment his most beloved Prince, but that regard for his honour, which ought to be most precious to all, constrained him. Edward hearing this was in great distress at the loss of such a man, who had for so long proved willing and faithful; and he grieved the more for it because he could not call him to blame for his action; on the contrary, saying that any one wounded in his honour had good reason for getting angry. But very soon a more bitter grief than this came on the top of this sorrow.

APPENDIX D

Sir James Gray to the Duke of Newcastle.

VENICE, *January* 6, 1746 *N.S.*

MY LORD,—A few days ago Ld Marshall arrived here from Moscovy. He calls himself Baron Keith, has laid aside his green Ribbon and taken a house in a remote part of the town, where he says, he hopes to be allowed to pass the remainder of his days in quiet, being tired of the world, and resolved on his part to give disturbance to nobody. This is the language that he holds; and I have good reason to believe that he intended these declarations should be told again to me. Ld Elcho and one Hunter are also arrived here, he affirms that he did not see the Pretender's Son while he was in France; that he heartily repents of the rash scheme he engaged in, and has hopes of obtaining his Majesty's Pardon. I cannot yet learn whether he proposes to settle here, but am told that he is firmly resolved not to go to Rome. I shall carefully watch their conduct till such time as I may receive any further orders from Your Grace.—I am with great respect, Your Grace's Most faithfull and Most obedient servant,

J. GRAY.

State Papers, Venice.

APPENDIX E

The following is the reply (printed from Elcho's *Journal*) of the Queen of England to Prince Charles of Mecklenburg, and shows the vindictive attitude of the English Ministry towards the Jacobites.

1774.

MY VERY DEAR BROTHER,—I crave your pardon that I have so long delayed to answer you with regard to the request of the Margravine of Baden Dourlach. Seeing that the Princess takes a deep interest in her friend, I have taken some time to acquaint myself thoroughly with the affair, and I find, as I knew before, that one must not think of doing a favour to any one that was engaged in the late rebellion. The case mentioned in the *Gazette* with regard to General Frazer is a case altogether extraordinary in character, and too long for me to give you a detailed account of. Have the goodness to convey this answer to the Margravine, with sincere compliments to her from me, and with assurances of friendship to all her household.

(Signed) THE QUEEN OF ENGLAND.

APPENDIX F

From a Manuscript Book of the Orders issued by General Hawley to the English Army 1745-46, belonging to Mr. W. B. Blaikie.

EDINBURGH, 12 *Jany*. 1745/6 *Sunday*.

Parole/Derby.

Field Officer for the day tomorrow Major Willson.

The Manner of the Highlanders way of fighting which there is nothing so easy to resist. If Officers and

Men are not preposess'd with the Lyes and Accounts which are told of them   They Commonly form their Front rank of what they call their best men, or True Highlanders the number of which being allways but few, when they form in Battallions they Commonly form four deep, and these Highlanders form the front of the four, the rest being lowlanders and arrant scum, when these Battallions come within a large Musket shott, or three score yards this front Rank gives their fire and Immediately thro' down their fire-locks and Come down in a Cluster with their Swords and Targets making a Noise and Endeavouring to pearce the Body, or Battallions before them becoming 12 or 14 deep by the time they come up to the people they attack.

The sure way to demolish them is at 3 deep to fire by ranks diagonaly to the Centre where they come, the rear rank first, and even that rank not to fire till they are within 10 or 12 paces but If the fire is given at a distance you probably will be broke for you never get time to load a second Cartridge, and if you give way you may give your foot for dead, for they being without a firelock or any load, no man with his Arms, Accoutre-ments &c. can escape them, and they give no Quarters, but if you will but observe the above directions, they are the most despicable Enimy that are.   The Cannon of the Field Train, and such Tumbrills and Waggons as are already loaded to come from the Castle to the Abby tomorrow morning at Ten. . . .

APPENDIX G

Endorsed Original 'Orders' under Lord George Murray's own Hand; from April 14 to 15 1746. (From the Cumberland MSS. at Windsor.)

Orders from the 14*th* to the 15*th April* 1746.
Rie James (in Inglish King James).

It is His Royall Highness posetive Orders that evry person atatch themselves to some Corps of the Armie and to remain with that Corps night and day till the Batle persute be finally over; this regards the Foot as well as the Horse.

The Order of Batle is to be given to evry Ginerall Officer and evry Commander of Regiments or Squadrons.

It is requierd and expected that each indevidual in the Armie as well officer as souldier keeps their posts that shall be alotted to them, and if any man turn his back to run away the next behind such man is to shoot him. No body on Pain of Death to Strip the Slain or Plunder till the Battle be over.

The Highlanders all to be in kilts, and no body to throw away their Guns; by H.R.H. command,

GEORGE MURRAY.

[On the day succeeding the battle the following order was issued by the Duke of Cumberland :—

'INVERNESS, *April* 17*th*.

' A Capt & 50 men to march imediatly to the feild of Battle & search all cottages in the neighbourhood for Rebels. The officer & men will take notice that the publick orders of the Rebels yesterday were to give us no quarter.'

To justify the barbarous usage here suggested, reliance has been placed by the apologists for Cumberland on a mutilated version of Lord George's order which runs as follows :—

'It is his Royal Higheness' positive orders, that every person attach himself to some corps of the army, and remain with that corps night and day, until the battle and pursuit be finally over : *and to give no quarter to the Elector's troops on any account whatsoever.*' See *William Augustus, Duke of Cumberland*, by Archibald Campbell Maclachlan, p. 293.

There is no positive evidence to show when or by whom the words printed in italics were interpolated, all that can be stated with certainty is that they were not contained in the original order issued to the Highland Army.]

INDEX

ABERDEEN, 79, 356, 388, 392, 395, 396, 399, 408, 419.
Abuchy (Avochy). *See* Gordon.
Agnew, sir Andrew, 388, 403.
Aiguilles, marquis d'. *See* De Boyer.
Aiguillon, duc d', 183.
—— duchess of, 128.
Airth, 364, 366.
Aix-la-Chapelle, 124, 134, 135.
Albany, Charlotte, duchess of, 138, 211.
Albemarle, 2nd earl of, 235 *n*, 400, 425.
Algarotti, count, 156.
Alloa, 365, 366.
Altringham, 333, 334.
Alves, kirk of, 421.
Amelot de Chaillon, 41, 42, 43, 48.
Anderson, Mr., 269.
Angers, 16, 17, 18.
Angoulême, 131, 132, 133.
Annan, 351.
Antibes, 229.
Antin, duke d', 231.
Appin. *See* Stewart.
Aquaviva, cardinal, 49.
Ardshiel. *See* Stewart.
Arisaig, 240.
Ashburn, 336, 341, 343.
Ashbury, 334.
Assemblies, the Edinburgh, 65, 66.
Athole, William, Jacobite duke of, 236, 243, 248, 308.
—— brigade, 308, 325, 326, 334, 349 *n*, 363, 364, 393, 397, 423.

Aubeterre, marquis d', 206.
Auchenleck of Kunucky, Andrew, 287.
Avignon, 126, 233, 447.
Avuchie (Avochy). *See* Gordon.

BAGGOT, colonel, 288, 392 *n*.
Bakaldie (Bohaldie, Balhaldies). *See* Macgregor.
Balcarres, lord, 67.
Balmerino, Arthur Elphinstone, 6th lord, 83, 91, 92, 259, 288, 393.
Baltimore sloop-of-war, 410, 439, 443 *n*.
Banff, 419.
Bannerman, sir Alexander, of Elsick, 283, 393.
Bannockburn, 138, 363, 364, 368, 381.
Barailh, marquis de, 175, 231.
Barefoot (Bearford's) parks, Edinburgh, 245.
Barisdale, 365.
—— *See* Macdonald.
Barra, 239, 360, 399.
Barrowbridge, 325.
Barrymore, lord, 129.
Battoni, Pompeio (painter), 206.
Bedford, 4th duke of, 23.
Bellisle, 238, 239.
—— Marshal, 173.
Bellona, ship, 101, 103, 107, 439.
Bergen, 443.
Berwick, 273, 410.
Berwick's regiment (French), 397-8.

Blacklehall, 354.

Blaikie, Mr. W. B., 96 *n*, 279 *n*, 336 *n*.

Blair castle, 91, 246, 248, 387, 388, 389, 403, 404, 407.

Blairfitty, 403.

Blakeney, general William lord, 253, 381, 382.

Bland, major-general, 400, 401, 425.

Bligh, general, 354.

Bohaldie. *See* Macgregor.

Bôle, 216.

Bologna, 30.

Borghese, cardinal, 203.

Borrodale, 97, 101, 240, 241, 438, 439, 440.

Bouillon, duc de, 236, 247.

—— castle of, 182.

Boulogne, 44, 54, 129, 136.

Bounty offered to Government recruits, 299 *n*.

Boyd, Mr., 351.

Brahan Castle, 414.

Brampton, 311, 312.

Brest, 239.

Brett, captain, 239.

Bridge of Earn, 400.

Brown, ——, 103, 104.

—— captain, 294, 383.

Brugh, 309.

Brussels, 57.

Bryce (Bruce) of Kennet, 252.

Buchanan (Jacobite messenger), 48, 50, 228, 229, 237.

Buck Club, 62; memorial of the, 63, 64, 68, 69.

Burke, Edward, 97, 437 *n*.

Burt, Edmund, 66.

Burton, 325.

—— (head-master of Winchester), 11.

Butler (French agent), 43.

Byng, rear-admiral John, 296, 388.

Byrom, John, 333 *n*.

CALLANDER HOUSE, 372 *n*.

Callendar, 364.

Cameron of Lochiel, John, 63, 443.

—— —— Donald, 78, 243, 256, 257, 394, 410, 428, 444, 445, 457.

—— —— clan regiment, 269, 271, 363, 365, 410, 423.

—— Dr. Archibald, 130, 131, 139, 140, 448.

—— of Torcastle, Ludovick, 321.

Campbell, captain, 395.

—— of Inverawe, 242.

—— of Mamore, general John, afterwards 4th duke of Argyll, 318, 319, 361, 395.

—— —— colonel John (his son), 371.

—— lieut.-general Sir James, 56.

Campo Florido, Prince, 247, 248.

Canale, Mademoiselle, 115, 116.

Canonisation, ceremony of, 206, 207.

Carberry hill, 266.

Carlisle, 310, 311, 312-24, 347, 349, 350.

Carlyle, Dr. Alexander (of Inveresk), 80, 264 *n*.

Carnegie, 63 *n*.

Carnival at Venice, 208, 210.

Carron, bridge of, 371, 386.

Caryll, John Baptist, 3rd Baron Caryll, 230.

Castle Menzies, 387, 388.

Chantilly, 137.

Charenton, 166.

Charles Edward, Prince, early life in Rome, 24-26; leaves Rome, 49, 50; French expedition abandoned, 51-53; his landing, 70, 239, 240; his suspicions of Lord George Murray, 75, 76, 90, 91, 117, 118,

119, 182, 316, 406, 407, 435; conduct at Prestonpans, 81 ; proposes to invade England, 301-4 ; his conduct on the way to Derby, 329 ; wonders in what manner he should enter London, 332 ; the retreat from Derby, 341 ; attempt to kidnap, at Moy, 390, 391 ; sanguine before Culloden, 89, 414, 423 ; conduct at Culloden, 93-95, 434 ; partiality to the Irish, 94, 289, 290, 295, 340, 341, 366, 383, 384, 416, 417, 418, 435, 437, 445; after Culloden, 435-440, 445-6; Elcho's unfavourable estimate, 98-100 ; at Fontainebleau, 109 ; contemplates another expedition, 121 ; projects of marriage, 121 ; difference with his father, 122 ; expelled from Paris, 125-126 ; and Princesse de Talmond, 126, 127 ; his visit to London, 128 ; and Miss Walkinshaw, 138, 146, 147, 153 ; his ingratitude, 148, 149, 182, 415; joins the Anglican communion, 153, 154 ; negotiates for French invasion, 182, 183 ; in Rome, 195-197, 200, 201 ; his love of money, 205; his sanguine nature, 301, 302, 331-333, 340, 341; other references, 30, 79, 98-100, 147, 205, 303, 317, 453-8.

Charly, 345.

Charteris, colonel, of Amisfield, 1, 2.

—— Francis (afterwards earl of Wemyss), 37, 67, 74, 140, 163, 190, 193, 255 *n*, 265 *n*.

Chartres, 165.

Chaudefontaine, 134.

Chevalier de St. George, 19, 20, 23, 24, 25, 30, 45, 49, 117, 118, 122, 129, 195.

Choiseul, duc de, 166, 184, 211.

Cholmondely, brigadier, 373, 426.

Clackmanan, 367.

Clancarty, lord, 129.

Clanranald. See Macdonald.

Cluny. See Macpherson.

Clement XIII., pope, 197, 203, 204.

Cleves, 123.

Clifton, skirmish of, 348.

Cochran of Ferguslie, William, 286.

Cockeny (Cockenzie), 270.

Cocoa-Tree club, 39.

Colbert, abbé, 164.

Colombier, 177, 187.

Coltbridge, 254.

Coltness, 62.

Comodore, ship, 441, 442.

Congleton, 333 *n*, 334.

Cope, sir John, 71, 76, 79, 242, 245, 263, 264-276.

Corierg (Corrieyairack), 245.

Corstorphine, 254.

Cotton, 'Chevalier' (sir John Hynde Cotton), at Angers, 17.

Council, the Prince's, 288.

Councils of war, 289, 290, 301, 312, 323, 332, 337, 341 *n* ; abandoned, 341, 386 ; 384, 426.

Coutts, John (ex-provost of Edinburgh), 76, 77, 256.

Craigie of Glendoick, Robert (lord advocate), 264 *n*.

Cranston, lord, 67.

Craon, Prince, 19.

Crawford, John Lindsay, 20th earl of, 389, 400, 405.

Crefeld, 174.

Crieff, 245, 387.

Cromarty, earl of, 391, 394, 409, 410, 422.

Cromarty's regiment, 365, 368, 394.

Cullen, 393, 403, 420.

Culloden, battle of, 91, 423-436.

—— castle, 391.

Cumberland, duke of, 90, 91, 97, 173, 324, 333 *n*, 336, 341, 344, 345, 354, 355 *n*, 382, 387, 388, 396, 399, 419, 421.

Cumbernauld, 363.

Cumming of Pitully, William, 123, 286.

Cunninghame, Robert, 265 *n*.

DALKEITH, 304, 307.

Dalnacardoch, 245, 246, 389.

Dalwhinny, 245, 246, 389.

Damiens, 167, 170, 171.

D'Argenson, 150, 151, 154, 169.

Dawkins, Mr., 148.

De Boyer (Marquis d'Aiguilles), 294, 296, 323, 328, 358, 396, 406.

Dediston. *See* Duddingston.

Derby, 86, 336.

Desertions on the march to Derby, 310.

Devonshire, William Cavendish, 3rd duke of, 336.

D'O, captain, 238.

Doncaster, 301, 328, 342.

Dornoch, 408.

Douglas, 282, 352.

—— duke of, 352.

—— sir John, M.P., 67, 363 *n*.

Doune, castle of, 284 *n*, 322.

Dounie castle, 360.

Dowallie, 404.

Drink money, 325 *n*.

Drumlanrig, 352.

Drummond castle, 387.

—— lord John, lands at Montrose, 103, 352, 356-358 ; at siege of Stirling, 364 ; at Falkirk, 374, 378 ; at Culloden, 424, 429 ; after the battle, 436 ; his escape, 101, 105, 442 ; other references, 46, 109, 322, 371, 396, 397, 401, 420, 446.

Drummond, lord Louis, 51.

—— of Bakaldie. *See* Macgregor.

—— George, 252.

Drummore, lord, sir Hew Dalrymple, 263.

Duddingston (Dediston), 82, 258, 262, 265, 266, 277, 278, 301.

Dumfries, 88, 308, 351.

Dunbar, 79, 263.

—— Jacobite earl of, 20.

—— of Durn, sir William, 285.

Dunblane (Dumblain), 253, 385, 387.

Dundas of Arniston, Robert, 264.

Dundee, 251, 306.

—— James (titular viscount), 287, 290.

Dundonald, William Cochrane, 7th earl of, 293.

Dungeness bay, 232.

Dunkeld, 248, 404.

Dunkirk, 50, 52, 102, 175, 230, 232, 233, 358.

Dunrobin castle, 409, 422.

Durand, lieutenant-colonel, 312, 315.

Durkell, lord, 396.

Dutch auxiliaries, arrival of, 279, 280.

Dutillet, ship, 239 *n*.

D'Uxhull, baron, 215.

ECCLEFECHIN, 308, 351.

Edgar (secretary to the Chevalier), 19.

Edinburgh, 64, 77, 78, 79, 252, 256-306, 308, 353, 362, 363.

Éguilles, marquis d'. *See* De Boyer.

Elchies (lord of justiciary), Patrick Grant, 263 *n*.

Elcho, David lord, birth and ancestry, 1-6 ; at Winchester, 8-10 ; in London, 13, 14 ; on the Continent, 14-34 ; interviews with the Chevalier, 22, 23, 30 ; returns to England, 34-36 ; visits Scotland, 37 ; in London, 38 ; in France, 44-54; returns to Scotland, 54 ; the Buck Club, 62, 63 ; last visit to London, 67 ; and lord president Forbes, 71; joins the Prince, 73, 74 ; gives the Prince 1500 guineas, 77, 255 ; his efforts to recover the money, 110, 129, 197, 198, 202-204 ; the entry into Edinburgh, 78, 258-261 ; his narrative of the campaign, 227-448 ; after Culloden, 96-107, 453-8 ; in Paris, 107; solicits pardon, 107, 109, 129, 174, 194, 219 ; charges against, 107-8 ; resentment against the Prince, 111 ; his relations with Earl Marischal, 111-117, 152, 155, 162, 163, 176, 185-188 ; meets Lord George Murray, 117-119 ; requests French commission, 123; receives pension from French King, 132 ; his appeal to the Chevalier, 135 ; appointed to French service, 135, 136 ; as marriage negotiator, 66, 136, 137, 180, 194, 214 ; in Paris, 141-153, 163-172, 210, 216 ; at Neufchâtel, 162, 163, 193 ; at Padua, 155-157 ; in Venice, 159-161, 208, 209 ; colonel of Royal Scots, 174 ; offers services to Pitt, 174; at Rome, 198-207 ; audience of the Pope, 203, 204 ; at a consistory, 207; at Naples, 207-208 ; Order of Military Merit conferred on, 210; visits Miss Walkinshaw, 211; at festivities at Louisberg, 212-214; marriage, 215; death of Lady Elcho, 215; death of Lord Elcho, 216 ; characteristics, 85,

108, 109, 216-219 ; his bitterness against England, 219-21.

Elcho, lady, 215, 216.

Elgin, 393, 397, 398, 420.

Elibank plot, 131, 138-140, 448.

Elizabeth, ship, 238, 239.

Elphingston, 364.

—— pans, 366.

English hatred of the Scots, 11, 12.

Eriskay, isle of, 240 n.

Esk river, 309, 350.

Espionage in Rome, 28, 29.

FAIRNTON (Ferntower), 387.

Falkirk, 89, 254, 363, 365, 370, 371-380, 381-387.

Family Compact, the, 179.

Farquharson of Balmurle (Balmoral), 320.

—— of Monaltrie, Francis, 319.

Ferrybridge, 336 n.

Fimarçon, marquis de, 395, 396, 397.

Finchley common, troops on, 338 n.

Findhorn, 402, 421.

Fitzjames, Charles, duke of, 395, 396.

Fitzjames's horse, 91, 92, 359, 395, 397, 398, 432, 434, 436.

Fitzwilliam, 3rd earl, at Angers, 17.

Fletcher, Andrew. *See* Milton, lord.

—— of Benchy, Robert, 286.

Fleury, cardinal, 24, 40, 41, 42.

—— duc de, 164.

Florence, 18, 19.

Florentun, 124, 129.

Fochabers, 396, 397, 398.

Fontenoy, 59.

Forbes of Culloden, Duncan (lord president), 71, 300, 408.

Forres, 361, 393, 398, 420.

Fort Augustus, 97, 360, 394, 395, 398, 456, 457.

Fort George, 391, 392.

Fort William, 394, 395, 410.

Fotheringham, David (Jacobite governor of Dundee), 284, 306.

—— of Bandaine, Thomas, 287.

Fowkes, general, 255, 263, 271.

Fox man-of-war, 292, 296.

Fraser, Charles, younger of Inverlochie, 435.

Frederick the Great, subsidies to, 174.

French invasion projected, 48, 49, 102, 229-231, 296, 359, 360.

—— troops destined for England, 230.

—— declare war, 233.

—— troops in Scotland, 397 *n.*

Frews, the (Ford of Frew), 253, 365, 385.

Fribourg, 446.

Fuessen, 162.

GALLOWS raised in Grassmarket, 379.

Gambling in Paris, 210.

Garden, Francis (afterwards Lord Gardenstone), 265 *n.*

Gardiner, colonel James, 254, 274.

Garrick as Macbeth, 11.

Garstang, 326, 346.

Genoa, 229.

Geoghegan, sir Francis, 327.

Georgites and Jacobites at Winchester, 9, 10.

Gladsmuir, 277.

Glascoe, major Nicolas, 401, 402.

Glasgow, 281, 353, 355.

Glenbeasdale, 100, 437.

Glenbucket. *See* Gordon.

Glencairn, William Cunningham, earl of, 318, 353, 373.

Glencoe. *See* Macdonald.

Glenfinan, 241, 243.

Glengarry. *See* Macdonald.

Glenorchy, lord, 206.

Glocester, ship, 296.

Glorat, 364.

Golf played in Rome, 25.

Golspie, 422.

Goodtrees, 54, 55.

Gordon castle, 393, 398, 420.

—— lord Lewis, 129, 283 *n*, 319, 361, 371.

—— of Avochy (or Abuchie), John, 91, 319, 393.

—— of Carnoussie, Arthur, 285.

—— of Cobardie (or Cowbairdie), 123, 129, 285.

—— of Drumlethie (or Dorlathers), 285.

—— of Glenbucket, 110, 129, 243, 246.

—— of Glenbucket's regiment, 308, 351, 363, 364, 423.

—— of Halhead, George, 129, 285.

—— of Park, sir William, 285, 291, 339.

—— M. Mirabelle de, 371, 382.

—— lady Frances, 74, 265 *n.*

Goring, colonel, 147, 148, 447, 448.

Gortleg or Gorthlic, 436 *n.*

Graham, sir John, 50.

—— James, younger of Airth, 260.

—— Miss, of Airth, 66.

Grant, laird of, 301, 361.

—— of Glenmorisden, 284.

—— colonel, 295, 366, 367, 368, 392, 394, 411, 412.

—— major, 392.

—— the Abbé, 29.

Gravelines, 51, 174, 230, 232.

Gray, sir James, 114.

Gray's mill, 74, 255.

Greyhound frigate, 441, 442, 443 *n.*

Groeme, general, 192.

Guadalaxara, 121.

Guards, Elcho's, 287, 307, 308, 325, 326, 333, 334, 347, 351, 364, 368, 393.

Guest, general Joshua, 252 *n*.

HALDEN (Haldane) OF LANRICK, JOHN, 286, 291.

Halket, lieut.-colonel, 273.

Halkston of Rathilet, Heleneas, 287.

Hamilton, 282, 352, 353.

—— 6th duke of, 61, 62, 63 *n*.

—— of Bangour, William, 83, 260.

—— of Redhouse, George, 265 *n*, 287.

—— John (afterwards governor of Carlisle), 286 *n*, 324, 350, 354.

—— Robert, younger of Kilbrachmont, 260 *n*.

—— William (British envoy at Naples), 201.

Handasyde, lieut.-general, 318.

Hanway, captain, 356 *n*.

Happy Janet, ship, 296.

Hastenbeck, 173.

Hawick, 309.

Hawke, Lord, victory of, 184.

Hawley, general Henry, 362, 363, 367, 370, 372 *n*, 425, 459.

Hay, Andrew, younger of Raness, 285.

—— John (chamberlain to the Chevalier), 19, 21, 22.

—— John, of Restalrig, 101, 105 *n*, 200, 286 *n*, 341, 386, 415, 416, 443.

Hazard sloop-of-war, 296, 356, 383, 409.

Henderson's *History of the Rebellion*, 78, 258 *n*.

Hepburn of Keith, 63 *n*, 129, 140, 260 *n*.

Hesket, 349.

Hesse Cassel, Prince Frederic of, 389, 407.

Hessian troops, 389, 400, 405, 407.

Hexham, 318.

Hochkirchen, battle of, 177.

Holyhaugh, 309.

Holyrood, 78, 81, 82, 259, 261, 262, 389.

Home, William, 8th earl of, 67, 263, 273, 318, 353, 373.

Hope, hon. Charles, 264 *n*.

Hornby castle, 326.

Hound sloop-of-war, 422.

Hunter, David, of Burnside, 109, 122, 129, 286, 291, 420.

Huske, major-general John, 370, 373, 425.

Hussars, the Prince's, 308, 345, 364, 397.

Hyde, captain de la, 397.

INCH, the, 297.

Inveraray, 318.

Invergarry, 244.

Inverness, 301, 319, 390, 391, 394, 398, 399, 406, 409, 414 *n*.

Inversnaid, 284 *n*.

Inverury, 361, 392, 399.

Irish brigade, invasion by, projected, 359.

—— piquets, 397, 433, 434.

Irvine of Drum, 285.

Irwin (physician to the Chevalier), 19.

JEDBURGH, 309.

Justice-clerk, lord. *See* Milton.

KEINY, 367.

Keith, 393, 401, 402, 419.

—— Marshal, 122, 177, 178, 458.

Kellie, Alexander, 5th earl of, 259, 284.

Kelly, Rev. George, 110, 123, 237, 295, 446.

Kelso, 309.

Kendal, 325, 347.
Kenmure, viscount, 63, 287, 288.
Ker of Graden, colonel, 436 *n.*
Kerr, lord Robert, 435.
Kilmarnock, William Boyd, 6th earl of, 83, 283, 334, 393.
Kilmarnock's Horse, 308, 324, 334, 364.
Kilsyth, 355, 363.
Kinachin, 403.
King, Dr., 128, 205.
King's park, Edinburgh, 258.
Kingston, Evelyn Pierrepont, 2nd duke of, 334.
Kinloch, sir James, 320, 371.
Kinlochiel, 244.
Kinlochmoidart, 97, 101, 241.
Kirkliston, 254.
Knowles, comodore, 397.

LA PRISE, 176, 184, 214.
La Vraix Croix, 238.
Lancaster, 325, 326, 345, 346.
Lang, Andrew, 25, 128 *n*, 183.
Lauder, 309.
Lauderdale, lord, 67.
Leckie, 364.
Leek, 336, 343.
Leigh, 330, 344.
Leighton, lieut.-colonel, 367, 388.
Leith, 245, 282, 389.
Lennox, lord George, 166.
Leslie, Charles (brother of earl of Rothes), 165.
—— of Milndeans, James, 264.
Lesly, brigadier, 413.
Lesmahago, 353.
Leyden, 60.
L'Heureux, ship, 109, 444 *n.*
Liége, 124, 138.
Ligonier, lieut.-colonel François Auguste, 379.

Ligonier, sir John (afterwards lord), 328, 345.
Lille, 56.
Lincoln, lord (afterwards 2nd duke of Newcastle), 31, 107.
Linlithgow, 254, 368, 369, 384.
Lion, man-of-war, 239.
Lisle, 124.
Litchfield, 336.
Loch Arkaig (Lochargey, Locharkey), 97, 437, 438.
Lochgarry. *See* Macdonald.
Lochnanuagh, 97, 101, 240, 439, 443, 444.
Lochyell. *See* Cameron.
Lockhart, George, younger of Carnwath, 101, 105 *n*, 260, 443.
Longtown, 309, 350.
Loudoun, John Campbell, 4th earl of, 245, 273, 301, 319, 360, 390, 391, 407.
Louisberg, 212.
Lovat, Simon Fraser, 12th lord, 298, 361 *n*, 436.
—— (Simon), master of, 320, 365.
Lowther hall, 324, 348, 352.
Lubersac, comte de, 164.
Lude, 403.
Ludlow Castle, ship, 296.
Lumisden, Andrew, 196, 200.

MACCLESFIELD, 333, 343, 345.
MacDonald or MacDonell of Barrisdale, Coll, 235 *n*, 320, 365, 444 *n.*
—— Archibald (3rd son of Coll), 274 *n.*
—— of Boisdale, Alexander, 239 *n.*
—— of Clanranald, Ranald (chief), 63 *n.*
—— Ranald (younger of Clanranald), 241 *n*, 243.

MacDonald of Clanranald clan regiment, 269, 363, 365, 368, 409, 423.

—— of Glencoe, Alexander, 63 *n*, 244, 321.

—— or MacDonell of Glengarry, John (chief), 63 *n*.

—— —— Alastair Ruadh (eldest son: *Pickle the Spy*), 51, 70, 130, 131, 235 *n*.

—— —— Angus (or Æneas), 245 *n*, 380.

—— —— clan regiment, 269, 363, 365, 368, 409, 423.

—— or MacDonell of Keppoch, Alexander, 63 *n*, 242, 244, 375, 394, 410.

—— —— clan regiment, 269, 363, 365, 368, 410.

—— of Kinloch-Moidart, Donald, 353.

—— Æneas, banker, 34, 48, 100, 111, 135, 136, 237, 239, 399, 446.

—— or MacDonell of Lochgarry, 130, 139, 288 *n*, 365 *n*, 444, 448.

—— of Lorn, 63 *n*.

—— of Sleat, sir Alexander (7th bart.), 240, 300, 353.

—— Allan (priest), 97, 437 *n*.

—— sir John, 73, 236.

Macgillivray of Dunmaglass, Alexander, 320.

Macgregor (or Drummond), of Bohaldie (or Balhaldie), William, 40, 42, 43, 46, 48, 50, 51, 53, 227, 228, 230.

—— of Glengyle, 284 *n*, 322.

—— (or Drummond), Malcolm, 274 *n*.

Mackenzie, major, 408.

Mackinnon of Mackinnon, 284.

Mackintosh, laird of, 390.

Mackintosh, lady, 390.

Mackintoshes at Culloden, 432 *n*.

Maclachlan, laird of, 262, 322, 323.

Maclean of Duart, sir Hector, 69, 130, 235.

Macleod, lord, 322 *n*, 409, 422.

—— of Macleod, Norman, 63, 240, 300, 353, 361, 408.

—— of Gualtergill, 437, 438.

—— of Rasay, Malcolm, 321.

—— Alexander, 437 *n*.

Macnamara, Daniel, 148 *n*.

Macpherson, Cluny (Evan, younger of Cluny), 104, 130, 307, 445.

—— clan regiment, 308, 363, 368.

Macvicar, rev. Neil, 280 *n*.

Maillebois, marquis de, 237 *n*.

Manchester, 330, 331, 333, 344, 345.

—— regiment, 331.

Mandrin (smuggler), 151, 152.

Mann, sir Horace, 19.

Marischal, earl, 44, 51, 53, 111, 113, 120, 122, 139, 140, 141, 148, 149, 151, 153, 162, 176, 178, 179, 180, 185, 229, 232, 447.

Mars, ship, 101, 103, 107, 439.

Matthews, admiral, 67, 229.

Maupertuis, 150.

Maurepas, comte de, 127.

Maurice of Nassau, prince, 279.

Maxwell of Kirkconnel, James, 83, 96, 101, 105 *n*, 287, 443.

May, Madame de, 180, 181.

Meaux, 210.

Menzies of Shian, colonel, 270, 279.

Mercer of Aldie (hon. Robert Nairn), 248.

Meriden common, 341.

Milan, 18.

Milford man-of-war, 356.

Milton, lord justice-clerk (Andrew Fletcher), 54, 107, 263 *n*, 318.

Minorca, capture of, 173.
Mirabel, M. (Mirabelle de Gordon), 371, 382.
Moffat, 308, 309, 351.
Moir of Stonywood, James, 319, 392, 396.
Monaco, Prince of, 231.
Monro, sir Robert, of Fowlis, 301, 379.
Montrose, 294, 295, 352, 356, 383, 388.
Mordaunt, brigadier, 373, 400, 426.
Morgan, David, 85, 86, 327, 342.
Moy castle, 390.
Munro, captain George, of Culcairn, 246 *n*, 361.
Murray, hon. Alexander, 137, 139, 140, 164-167, 182, 183, 193, 448.
—— sir David, 4th bart. of Stanhope, 260.
—— lord George, joins the Prince, 249; at Prestonpans, 268, 269, 273; proposes the march through Cumberland, 304, 305; counsels retreat at Derby, 337-340; at Clifton, 348, 349; at Falkirk, 374, 376 *n*, 378; at siege of Blair, 403-406; at Culloden, 424, 426, 429, 432; and Lord Echo, 117-119; the Prince's suspicions of, 75, 76, 91, 111, 117, 118, 119, 182, 315, 316, 406, 407, 435; death, 123 *n*; other references, 77, 84, 250 *n*, 254, 258, 309, 324, 325, 326, 334, 351, 352, 363, 368, 384, 386 *n*, 387, 392, 393, 436, 446, 451-2.
—— John, of Broughton, appointed secretary, 250; his influence with the Prince, 75, 250, 315, 341, 386, 406; other references, 38, 41, 43, 55-59, 61, 62, 69, 70, 73, 101, 104, 108, 118, 233-236, 241,

243, 281, 288, 323, 340 *n*, 415, 416 *n*, 440, 444.
Murray, John (British resident at Venice), 157, 159.
—— hon. William, of Taymount, 247.
Musselburgh, 265, 277, 297.
Mutinous spirit in Prince's troops before Culloden, 415.
Mynshull, Miss, 136, 137.
Myrton, sir Robert, of Gogar, 293.

NAIRN, 90, 393, 398, 421, 426.
—— house of, 248, 404.
Nairne, lord, 63 *n*, 130, 248, 262, 265.
Nairne's regiment, 270.
Naison, colonel Philip, 400.
Nantes, 238, 443.
Napier, Francis Scott, 6th lord of Merchiston, 263.
Naples, 207.
Navarre, 236, 238.
Negroni, cardinal, 203.
Netherbow, Edinburgh, 257.
Neufchâtel, 151, 152, 155, 188, 189.
Newbattle, 307.
Newcastle, 307, 336, 354.
Nithsdale, earl of, 63 *n*, 283.
Noailles, duc de, 102.
Norris, sir John (admiral), 231, 232.
North, lord, 219.

O'DUN, Mr., 183.
Ogilvy, David lord, 110, 174, 191, 249 *n*, 282, 388, 393, 443, 445.
Ogilvy's regiment, 308, 344, 351, 363, 364, 388.
Oglethorpe, major-general, 345, 346.
Old Meldrum, 393, 399, 400.
Oliphant of Gask, Laurence, 63, 247, 278, 306.

O'Neal, captain, 413, 438.

Opera at Rome, 24, 25.

Order of Military Merit bestowed on Elcho, 210.

Ormond, James Butler, 2nd duke of, 232, 233.

Ostend, 55.

O'Sullivan, col. (quartermaster-gen.), 73, 97, 100, 237, 376 *n*, 415, 437-8.

PADUA, 119, 122, 155, 156 ; social life in, 158.

Paris, 33, 130, 141-146, 163, 195, 210, 216, 233, 234, 439, 444.

Parliament house, Edinburgh, 257.

Paroles broken by Government officers, 360.

Paterson, sir Hugh, 138, 363 *n*.

Pattinson, Thomas (deputy-mayor of Carlisle), 311 *n*.

Pearl sloop-of-war, 366.

Peebles, 308.

Peglioni, 164.

Penrith, 324, 325, 347, 349.

Perdigou, abbé, 164.

Perth, 73, 248, 253, 306, 387, 388, 389, 400

—— James Drummond, duke of, joins the Prince, 248; at Prestonpans, 269; at siege of Carlisle, 312-316; at siege of Stirling, 372; at Culloden, 424, 429, 432; escape and death, 101, 105, 442; other references, 63 *n*, 69, 78, 234, 258, 308, 339, 345, 407, 409, 420, 421.

Perth's regiment, 269, 324, 325, 351, 363, 364, 394, 423.

Perthshire squadron, 253, 334, 347, 364.

Peterhead, 356, 388, 396.

Petitpierre, pastor, 184.

Petre, Father, 317.

Pickle the Spy. See MacDonald.

Pinkie house, 266, 277, 307.

Pitlochry, 404.

Pitsligo, 4th lord Forbes of, 63, 83, 282, 388, 393.

Pitt, Elcho's appeal to, 174.

Place de la Grève, 169, 170.

Playhouse, the, in Edinburgh, 65.

Plundering in England, 351, 352.

Polmaise, 368.

Pompadour, Madame de, 109, 125, 141, 142, 144, 168, 169, 173, 182.

Portsoy, 397.

Preston, 9, 85, 327, 328, 329, 345.

—— hall, 74.

—— lieut.-general George, 6, 253, 291, 292.

Prestonpans, 79 ; battle of, 270-277.

Priuli, signor, 156, 159, 209.

QUARTER or no quarter, 404, 461, 462.

Queensberry house, Edinburgh, 278 *n*.

RAMSAY OF OCHTERTYRE on Scottish customs, 13.

Rank, distinctions of, at Winchester, 10.

Raven, ship, 443 *n*.

Reay, George Mackay, lord, 300.

Redens (Reddings), 309.

Regiments, Government—

CAVALRY.

Bland's dragoons (3rd H.), 335.

Cobham's dragoons (10th H.), 335.

Gardiner's dragoons (afterwards Francis Ligonier's, afterwards Naison's) (13th H.), 243, 245, 253, 254, 271, 275, 318, 335, 353, 400.

Regiments, Government, *cont.*—
  Hamilton's dragoons (14th H.),
    243, 245, 254, 271, 275, 318,
    353, 400.
  Kerr's, lord Mark, dragoons (11th
    H.), 382, 425.
  Kingston's dragoons, 335, 425.
  Ligonier's dragoons. *See* Gardiner's.
  Montagu's horse (2nd D.G.),
    335, 345.
  Naison's dragoons. *See* Gardiner's.
  St. George's dragoons (8th H.),
    345, 400, 405.
  Wade's horse (3rd D.G.), 345.

INFANTRY.

  Barrel's (4th), 425.
  Battereau's, 425.
  Blakeney's (27th), 425.
  Bligh's (afterwards Sackville's)
    (20th), 335, 425.
  Campbell's (Scots Fusiliers) (21st),
    382, 425.
  Cholmondeley's (34th), 335, 425.
  Conway's. *See* Ligonier's.
  Dejean's. *See* Munro's.
  Douglas's (32nd), 335.
  Fleming's (36th), 425.
  Gower's, 335.
  Granby's, 335.
  Guise's (6th), 246, 271, 275.
  Halifax's, 335.
  Handasyde's (31st), 407.
  Highland regiment, Lord John
    Murray's (42nd), 243, 275.
  Houghton's (24th), 407.
  Howard's (the Buffs), 335, 425.
  Johnson's (33rd), 335.
  Lascelles's (47th), 242, 243, 271,
    275.
  Lee's (44th), 243, 271, 275, 407.

Regiments, Government, *cont.*—
  Ligonier's (afterwards Conway's)
    (48th), 318, 353, 425.
  Loudoun's highlanders, 246, 275.
  Montagu's, 335.
  Mordaunt's (18th), 407.
  Munro's, (afterwards Dejean's)
    (37th), 425.
  Murray's (46th), 243, 271, 275.
  Price's (14th), 318, 353, 425.
  Pulteney's (13th), 425.
  Richbell's (39th), 407.
  Royal Scots (1st), 425.
  Sempill's (25th), 335, 382, 425.
  Skelton's (12th), 335, 407.
  Sowles's (11th), 335.
  Wolfe's (8th), 425.

MILITIA, VOLUNTEERS, ETC.

  Argyleshire militia, 319.
  Cumberland and Westmoreland
    militia, 312, 313 *n*.
  Edinburgh volunteers, 252.
  Edinburgh train-bands, 252.
  Glasgow militia, 318.
  Yorkshire hunters, 299 *n*.
  Yorkshire rangers, 345.

Religious zeal in Scotland, 15.
Rendezvous after Culloden, 100,
  101, 438.
Rheims, 15.
Richelieu, duc de, 102, 154, 173.
Riddle of Lathrick (probably Riddle
  of Grange), 287.
Ripon, 354.
Rippel bridge, 326, 345.
Robertson of Strowan, Alexander,
  249 *n*.
Rollo of Powhouse, 260, 286.
Roman Catholics, the Prince's par-
  tiality for, 316, 317, 328.
Rome, 18, 199, 229.

Roquefeuille, de, admiral, 231 *n*, 232.
Roscoff, 109, 144.
Ross, master of, 301, 394.
Rossbach, 173.
Roth, colonel de, 175.
Rothes, 401.
Rotterdam, 57, 58, 61.
Rousseau and the Earl Marischal, 186, 188.
Rowcliff, 310.
Royal Scots (French), 46, 174, 191, 397, 433.
—— —— (British), 242, 425.
Ruthven of Badenoch, 389, 435, 436.
Rutledge, Walter, 239.

SABBATH gloom in Scotland, 64.
St. Aignan, duc de, 25.
St. Ann's Yards, Edinburgh, 245, 259.
St. Germaine, comte de, 60, 61.
St. Malo's, 439.
St. Ninian's, 365, 386.
Saunderson, Mr., 325.
Saxe, Maurice, comte de, 50, 230, 247, 248.
Scott, captain (afterwards general Scott of Balcomie), 242 *n*.
—— captain Caroline, 412.
Scott's *Journal*, 92, 93.
Seaforth, Kenneth Mackenzie, lord, 300.
Seceder volunteers of Edinburgh, 252.
Sempil, Francis lord, 42, 46, 50, 227, 228, 229, 232, 237 *n*.
—— brigadier lord, 426.
Serpent sloop-of-war, 410.
Seven Years' War, 190, 191.
Shee, captain Robert, 205, 395, 396.
Sheerness man-of-war, 410.

Sheridan, sir Thomas, 20, 101, 105 *n*, 236, 240, 289, 317, 383, 386, 415, 418, 436 *n*, 440, 443, 454, 455.
Sinclair, lord, 37.
Slachmuick (Sloghd Mor), pass of, 246.
Social life in Rome, 25-27.
Spa, 135.
Stafford, 336.
Stapleton, brigadier Walter, 394, 395, 411.
Steuart, sir James, of Goodtrees and Coltness, bart., 38 *n*, 54, 55, 62, 83, 132, 307.
—— captain, Elcho's nephew, 167, 194.
Stewart, John Roy, 247, 265 *n*, 284, 401, 444.
Stewart's (John Roy) regiment, 284, 342, 351, 363, 364, 399, 423.
Stewart of Invernahyle, Alexander, 321.
—— Charles, 5th of Ardshiel, 63 *n*, 244.
—— Archibald, provost of Edinburgh, 67, 252 *n*, 262.
—— of Appin's, captain, 274.
—— of Appin's (or Ardshiel's) battalion, 269, 282, 363, 365, 368, 409, 423.
—— 'Chevalier de,' 67.
Stirling, 88, 243, 245, 253, 363, 364, 381, 386, 387.
—— of Craigbarnet, James, 260.
—— of Keir, James, 286.
Stockport, 343.
Stone, 333 *n*, 336.
Stonehive (Stonehaven), 295, 356, 392.
Stornoway, 438.
Strafford, William Wentworth, 2nd earl of, 36.

Strangarside, 309.

Strange, sir Robert, 410 *n*.

Strathallan, William, 4th viscount, 63 *n*, 80, 129, 247 *n*, 258, 278, 393.

—— master of, 294.

Stratharick (Stratherrick), 435, 436.

Strathbogie, 393, 399, 419.

Strathspey, 398, 403.

Strickland, Francis, 20, 237.

Sullivan. *See* O'Sullivan.

Superstitions of highlanders, 268, 327.

Sutherland, William, 18th earl of, 300, 408.

—— of Fors, captain, 408.

TAIN, 391, 394, 407.

Tales of a Grandfather, 96.

Talmond, Princesse de, 126, 127, 128.

Tay bridge, 245, 405.

Taylor's hall, Edinburgh, 65.

Tencin, cardinal, 102, 132, 238.

Terror brig, 441, 443 *n*.

Tew (informer), 85.

Thicknesse, Philip, 172.

Thomson, Alexander, of Feichfield, 286.

Threipland, sir Stuart, 3rd bart. of Fingask, 254 *n*.

—— David, 276.

Tiddeman (Elcho's servant), 74 *n*.

Tiepolo (Venetian ambassador at Paris), 192.

Tippermuir, 3.

Tongue, 410.

Torrigiani, cardinal, 202.

Torwood, 371, 372.

Touch, 253.

Townley, Francis, 86, 331.

Train-bands, Edinburgh, 232.

Tranent, 266, 267.

Traquair, earl of, 38, 63, 67, 68, 69.

Treviso, 114, 116, 120.

Truité, Mademoiselle, 194, 195.

Tyrconnel, comte de, 395.

UIST, South, 239, 240, 438.

Union, hostility to, in Scotland, 8.

University education in Scotland, 15.

Urquhart, Mr., 200, 201.

VAUGHAN, WILLIAM, 86, 327, 343, 420.

Venice, 31, 111, 114, 117, 119, 127, 159-161, 208, 209, 447.

Venetian nobility, exclusiveness of, 31, 32.

Vernon, Edward, admiral, 359.

Versailles, the Prince at, 109, 110.

Vigano, Madamoiselle, 119, 122, 129, 130, 140.

Vincennes, 126, 447.

Vulture sloop-of-war, 366.

WADE, GEORGE, marshal, 301, 318, 324, 328, 336, 342.

Wakefield, 345.

Walkinshaw, Clementina, 138, 147, 148, 153, 182, 210, 211, 363 *n*, 447.

Walpole, Horace, 16, 17, 18, 30, 107, 108.

—— sir Robert, 24, 39.

Walsh, Antony, 183, 238, 241.

Walton, John, 28, 29, 49.

Warren, captain, 409, 444.

Weigh-house (or Tron), Edinburgh, 257, 292.

Weir (spy), 334, 335.

Wemyss castle, 1, 2, 5, 6, 7, 8 *n*, 37, 70.

—— John (1st earl), 2, 3.

—— David (2nd earl), 3, 4.

Wemyss, David, (3rd earl), 4, 5.
—— James (4th earl), 1, 5, 44, 45, 61, 162.
—— countess of, 1, 82, 123, 163, 164-167, 193.
—— a Venetian earl of, 33.
—— John, (admiral - depute of Firth of Forth), 7.
—— hon. James, 162, 190.
Wentworth, major, 394.
West kirk, Edinburgh, 292.
West port, Edinburgh, 256.
Westquarter, 368.
Wetherby, 336 n, 342.

Wigan, 330, 344, 345.
Willes, lord chief-justice, 338 n.
Winchester (school), 8, 9, 10, 11.
Winton, lord, 20.
Women in Paris, their callousness at executions, 172.
Wooler, 309.
Würtemberg, Charles Eugène, duke of, 212, 213.

York, duke of, Henry Stuart (cardinal), 24, 25, 30, 49, 121, 122, 202, 295, 358, 413, 445, 447 n.

Printed by T. and A. Constable, Printers to His Majesty
at the Edinburgh University Press